Preludes

Preludes

An Autobiography in Verse

JEFFREY JAY NIEHAUS

RESOURCE *Publications* · Eugene, Oregon

PRELUDES
An Autobiography in Verse

Copyright © 2013 Jeffrey Jay Niehaus. All rights reserved. Except for brief quotations in critical publications or reviews, no part of this book may be reproduced in any manner without prior written permission from the publisher. Write: Permissions, Wipf and Stock Publishers, 199 W. 8th Ave., Suite 3, Eugene, OR 97401.

Resourse Publication
An Imprint of Wipf and Stock Publishers
199 W. 8th Ave., Suite 3
Eugene, OR 97401

www.wipfandstock.com

ISBN 13: 978-1-62032-883-5

Manufactured in the U.S.A.

Δοῦλοι ἀχρεῖοί ἐσμεν

"Hallowe'en Night

    The witch rides on her broom tonight,
    While everything is still,
    And everyone cries out in fright,
    Down by the old stone mill!
    Hallowe'en is a scary time,
    The moon is very bright,
    With skeletons all the color of lime,
    On scary Hallowe'en night!

    Jeff Niehaus, aged 9,
    Martins Ferry"

—Martins Ferry *Times Leader*
    Friday, November 4, 1955

Contents

Book I *Borealis* | 1
Book II *Solitude, Art and A Night to Remember* | 19
Book III *Australis* | 41
Book IV *Lake Worth and Junior High School* | 65
Book V *A Florida Boyhood* | 87
Book VI *Paradise and Old Masters* | 105
Book VII *Farewell to Florida* | 123
Book VIII *Atlanta and Cross Keys* | 141
Book IX *Cross Keys and a New Road* | 159
Book X *Yale, New Haven and New York* | 175
Book XI *Yale and Art* | 197
Book XII *Junior Year and a Titan* | 213
Book XIII *Bavaria and the Alps* | 229
Book XIV *Final Year at Yale* | 251
Book XV *Australis Redux* | 265
Book XVI *Portals of Dawn* | 297

Book I

Borealis

Born of April, among showers
And a sun that encourages flowers
I came,
I saw, I was.

In Ohio's industrial valley,
In Martins Ferry,
I saw the day.

Across the brown Ohio,
In Wheeling,
I found a way   10
Out of my crib,
Down long stairs,
And out the door.
A highway lay before.
At age two
I wanted to explore
What lay beyond
Grandma's door.

On a green Ohio slope,
In Martins Ferry, on North Seventh Street,   20
My parents bought a bungalow—

Book I

A house of modest age
And made of common wood
For ordinary folk—
A bargain basement house
In need of work.
How busy now
My father's hands:
He handled a hammer and saw
Floor and board, roof and wall,   30
Bath, porch, attic and hall
Assume a durable form.
A blowtorch played upon our walls
And pillars of our porch—
Cosmetic work, that day.
Her old face peeled away
And showed available wood.
Then able manly strokes
Painted a bold facade—
Casa nova, come today,   40
Casanova, come to stay.

Our porch on a July day
Oversaw a town
Full of tall trees,
A valley
Full of folks and trade.
On Ohio's bank
A blast furnace roared
And shook our town.
Slopes across the water   50
Full of sunny joy
Sang a song of trees,
Sang a song to me.
Clouds afloat above
Gloriously sailed,
And on our porch
An artist sat,
A young Gauguin,
And sought to make

Borealis

Another valley　　　　　　　　　　　　　　　60
On a Magic Pad.

On darkling Halloween
A young skull and bones
Romped across our yard
And down North Seventh Street.
Spooks and hobgoblins,
Draculas and ghouls
Witches and warlocks
Buccaneers at large
And random royalty　　　　　　　　　　　　70
Dukes and dunces
Scholars and nobles
A poet, a sage,
A soldier
A space man
A sailor
And more
A panoply of characters galore
Laughed from door to door
And made our road a stage.　　　　　　　　80

Sun cascaded in
And I awoke to Easter
And an Easter egg hunt
In our living room.
I sought and found
A chocolate Easter bunny
Under a sofa,
Chocolate crème–filled eggs
Under a cushion
And jelly beans　　　　　　　　　　　　　　90
Wrapped in plastic grass
Behind a radio.
Before that joy could fade
We played
A game with colored eggs
Mom had made.

Book I

We cracked
End against end:
Slim versus slim,
Fat versus fat, 100
And now,
Once all were cracked,
We ate them,
And that was that.

On a summer's eve
On a squeaky glider
Back and forth
Back and forth
We sat,
Mom, Dad and I, 110
And looked across
A dark valley.
A sudden meteor
Like a sack of flame
Cut a path across the sky.
It sizzled on its way
But so far away
It made no sound.
On our porch step
We watched it fall toward 120
Slopes above Wheeling
But no—it passed
Beyond those slopes
And out of sight.
I had hoped it was
A flying saucer
But it was only
A young astronomer's delight
One summer night.

On a snowy day 130
We drove to a farm
In Dad's Studebaker.
We found a young pig

Borealis

Doomed.
A farmer and his hand
Caught and bound
Porky's snout.
I saw no blade,
But blood suddenly spurted
And stained the snow beneath					140
Amid squeals and thrashings
That stopped soon.
Then we drove to Grandma's house
With porky in our trunk, and then
Our afternoon's work
Lay on Granddad's cellar table.
Our family was able,
Almost as in a fable
Of old days,
A fable of old European ways,					150
In harmony to butcher
And turn that carcass into family fare.
Granddad, who had learned
So much in Europe as a boy,
Showed the way, and made a smart incision.
Father helped him as a young apprentice,
And soon our afternoon of blood began
With steamy organs on display. How good
It was to taste a bit of tail, or gnaw
A scrap of ear, cooked on the cellar stove			160
By mother as a special treat for me
While Dad and Granddad probed, and cut, and did
The work that took a man's strength. I watched
All afternoon as they reduced the body
To hams and shoulders, chops and ribs,
Bacon and hocks. And then
Granddad brought the grinder out.
He clamped it on the table's edge, and turned
And turned the crank,
And father dropped the meat					170
Into its quiet maw, and soon I saw
Sausage expand into a floppy casing,

5

Book I

A promise of aromas and good tastes
To come. After that Granddad layered
Pork chops in salt, in a wood barrel,
And then our work was done. He would make
A smokehouse in our yard next day,
And as I romped in the snow
Fabulous aromas would leak out
And drive me crazy with desire 180
For meals of smoked pork chops and sausages
Not yet to be. But that would be tomorrow.
For now the bloody men
Washed the bloody table off
And washed themselves as well.
Grandma and Ma composed a steamy pot
Of stew that had a most amazing flavor,
Made from fresh pork,
A reward for our work.
And once their work was done, 190
We sat down at a wooden round table
In Granddad's basement, and relaxed together.
I thought it must have been the same in Europe
When farmers could enjoy a hard day's work,
And after that a hearty meal, and time
Together as a family in peace.
Soon after, we came home, and clever Dad
Showed me some sausage casings he had saved,
And made balloons of them by blowing hard
Until they almost popped. I took a bath, 200
And played with sausage casings in the bathtub
Until I had to go to bed—balloons
Organic and peculiar, with a smell
I did not want to smell for long.
Mother soaped away the soil of day;
I watched the suds and water drain away.

My parents loved me more than I could know
Because my mother's pregnancy was hard
And she had almost lost me near the end.
My parents treasured me and played with me 210

Borealis

And taught me all they could. Even so
They were both alcoholics, and that problem
Produced deep trauma in my later youth.
Still, when I was very young our home
Was a place of love, and was a haven.

A cold October sky, cloudy gray
Overhung my afternoon. I waited
Outside a store on North Zane Highway
Until Johnny Mason showed up.
He had a bag of coins that he would trade   220
For stamps my father's boss had given me.
We squatted on the sidewalk
And poured over treasures
From far away and long ago
Because his coins were old
And my stamps were from abroad.
They showed American cargo planes
That looked like Air Force planes to both of us
(They carried mail during the occupation
After World War Two). To all of us   230
That war seemed only yesterday, although
America had won the war and peace
Had been declared around the wounded globe
Before any of us had come to be.
Johnny took a number of my stamps
And gave me coin for stamp, until we both
Declared ourselves content, and went back home
Because our mothers had our suppers ready.
Now at last I had a bag of coins—
A hundred year old centime made in France,   240
An eighty year old penny made in England,
A threepence with a ship on its backside,
Some Swedish coins with Gustavus Adolphus,
Who I thought was German, on the front,
And German coins as well, a Mark, a Pfennig,
And many other coins long since forgot.
At suppertime I showed them to my folks.
Mom and Dad congratulated me

Book I

And showed me how to use a metal polish
To remove any tarnish from the coins   250
And make them look resplendent, almost new,
Without damaging them, and so I did.

On summer days I sometimes took a walk
Alone or with a friend along an alley
Behind our house—a narrow access road
Of slag and gravel, short and seldom used.
The alley ended at a well paved street
Lined with wooden houses like our own,
And across the street lay a graveyard
That seemed to cover the green hill above   260
Almost to the top. I carried lunch
Packed in a World War One knapsack
And wore a World War One canteen
That dangled from a canteen belt
Strapped around my waist. The canteen
Had a date inscribed on the back
In numerals: 1918,
So I knew it had to be authentic
And issued by the U. S. Army.
My father, who was often on the road   270
As a travelling salesman, brought them home
One April afternoon after school.
When I heard his car door shut
I jumped up and ran outside.
I saw him walking up the front path,
Knapsack and canteen in his arms
And a very broad grin on his face.

So now, when I walked up that hill,
Sometimes alone, or sometimes with a friend,
I could pretend to be an allied soldier   280
Going up a hill in Germany,
On the lookout for our enemies.
A paved road wound up the hill
And halfway up, a concrete bunker
(Made in honor of the Civil War)

Borealis

Housed a cannon on two wheels,
Painted silver long ago, but rusty.
Once or twice I straddled that cannon
Because it made me feel like a commander
Who oversaw artillery—and saw,   290
Outside the bunker, an advancing foe.

Outside the bunker on the open road
I lacked the cover that a soldier wants
But I still wandered boldly up the hill
And came upon a flat concrete housing
Four yards by three or so, and low enough
To make a comfortable seat for lunch.
I sat down and opened up my knapsack
And looked across the valley as I ate.
I had a view that easily commanded   300
The whole broad Ohio, from North Wheeling
Southward, in one grand sweep.
I saw a blast furnace, where the workers
Made pig iron, and Wheeling Island,
Where Mom and Dad used to stop and eat
A snack at a sandwich shop they loved,
One that stayed open after midnight.
Back then Dad played saxophone
And Mom performed as solo vocalist
For a band in Wheeling, Niles Carp's band,   310
Before the government took Dad away
To war in Africa and Italy.

After lunch the afternoon was open
With all sorts of places to explore
Beyond our industrial valley,
Open fields and lonely forest paths.

On a broad slope behind the concrete housing
A dirt road wound toward a meadow;
Many times I looked across that field
And wanted to explore it on my own.   320
One afternoon I walked across

Book I

To a wall of bushes on the far side.
I passed through the bushes and could see
Houses in a valley far below,
Scattered all about, small and white.
A sea of trees in motion all around them—
Branches moved by winds I could not feel—
Made it seem almost another country,
A place of wonder and of fascination
Over the hill and far away from home. 330

When I was older and not so afraid
I went down the southern slope and found
A place where public grills and tables stood
On four acres under leafy cover—
A spot our family sometimes enjoyed,
Where Dad cooked out and I could play with friends
Or just whoever happened to show up.
Beyond those picnic tables lay a path
Travelled on by people who rode horses;
Not far down the path there was a spring 340
My uncle showed me once, and there I drank
The coldest water I had ever tasted.
I was amazed the hillside could produce
Water so cold and fresh, for anyone
Who travelled that way, just as we had done.

From that spot one could turn and follow
The same bridle path as it descended
Beside a shallow stream that gurgled on
And made stony music all the way
Down to the Ohio. I would walk 350
Along that path and sometimes could enjoy
Pawpaws that I found at summer's end
As they dangled yellow–black and plump
Just within a young boy's reach.
The path played out not far from them
Onto a quiet road with wooden houses
And I would amble up North Seventh Street
And end my journey where it had begun.

Borealis

Although I had become a wanderer
And loved and enjoyed so much good   360
That nature put before me in those days
(Just as anyone of my age could)
I took in far more than I understood.
When I was older I would come to know
A truth that could apply beyond myself:
A youth who spent long days among those hills
And was amazed at some far distant town,
And knew that cold spring water was a good,
And more than good, a wonder to be had,
Could one day come upon a better landscape,   370
Another shore that was his destiny,
And taste a very different sort of water.

As a second, third, and fourth grader
I wanted to learn about dinosaurs.
I watched dinosaur movies on TV
And read all of the dinosaur books
In our modest town library.
I got to understand how mud or silt
Could gradually cover their dead bodies
And how minerals could replace their bones   380
Until those bones became solid stone;
So a fossil skeleton was formed.
I also understood how a plant
Buried under mud could become
A fossil plant, with leaves and stem intact,
Wonderfully articulate in stone.

At nine years of age I dared imagine
I could find a fossil if I looked.
One cool September day after school
My uncle came and found me, and we drove   390
Across the broad Ohio into Wheeling.
We parked on the river bank and wandered
Back and forth among a world of pebbles
Large and small that had been washed ashore.

Book I

We turned over some pebbles carefully.
All were shapely, smooth and full of color,
But I could not care about their beauty
Because I wanted fossil bones or plants
And there was not a fossil bone or plant
Among them. Our flat river bank   400
Was not a place congenial to fossils,
And all at once we both understood
We had to find a spot more remote
From strong Ohio and his waves and currents
And water action that would smooth all stones;
We had to find a spot more isolated,
A quiet place for stones under pressure.

We drove up river two more miles
And came upon an old tool factory
Built snug against a West Virginia hill.   410
We parked in its gravel parking lot
And walked toward the base of the hill
And soon we found a trench half exposed
Under some leafy bushes. I jumped in
And dug into the clayey soil, and found
Soft shale stones that came apart
Almost miraculously with a tug.
As they broke apart each surface showed
A fossil fern articulated clearly,
A few black stems and spreading leaves   420
Against a flat background of brown stone—
Almost as though a very clever artist
Had painted black ferns on the brown rock.
We packed them carefully into a bag
And drove away amazed at our good fortune.
After I got home I washed them off
And put them lovingly into a box.
I had no idea how old
Or rare those fossils might be;
But I was happy to have dug up   430
Fossils as a nine year old
Just across the river from my home.

Borealis

Maybe one day I would become
A man who knew a lot of ancient lore,
An archaeologist or paleontologist.
For now I was just a boy, and happy
To have a box of fossil ferns at home.

I had a paper route after school
And carried twenty newspapers or so
To houses scattered over several blocks.　　　　　440
I loaded them into a canvas bag
And brought the Martins Ferry *Times Leader*
Home to many households, who would read
The latest news about the Cold War
And other news, national or local,
Because I brought it to their front door.
A lot of people counted on me then,
And I delivered faithfully to them.
Every week day I would deliver,
And every Saturday I would collect　　　　　450
The money due for those deliveries.

On Saturday mornings when I made
The rounds to collect for the papers
One of my customers, an older man,
Would show me how, on his kitchen table,
He had arranged two small stacks of coins,
One for the milk man, and one for me.
Another customer, a distant cousin,
Led me to a kitchen full of smells
From some exotic cooking she prepared　　　　　460
For her son and daughter and herself.
She was pretty, but she was not happy
Because her husband had abandoned her.
When I came, she often gave me food—
Some special treat that she had just created—
And I was glad to have it any time
Although I sensed the sadness of the heart
That had created it, and would create,
Because she had the soul of an artist

Book I

And cared devotedly for her young.   470

On Fifth Street, just a block away,
Stood a large house that was unequalled
Among the residences of our town,
A doctor's house made of red brick
And three stories high. It was colonial
With white wooden window frames and doors.
Every floor had its own kitchen,
Although I never saw the doctor's wife,
Or anyone at all, at work there.
The doctor's son was a friend from school   480
And showed me through the house one day.
He showed me a large toy machine gun
His father had just bought him for Christmas
That shot ping pong balls across the room.
In the backyard a blue tarpaulin
Covered their large pool, and we had hopes
Of water sports there on summer days,
But that June I moved to Florida
And never saw or heard of him again.

Every afternoon I brought the paper   490
To his and other houses on my route
And every Saturday I would collect
The money due from all my customers.
They were a microcosm of our land
(Although I did not know that word just yet).
So, in a very small way,
I had become a young business man
And grown a little bit beyond my parents
And all that I had known at home and school.

Although I had a paper route and schoolwork   500
The private world of my imagination
Was full of dinosaurs and rocket ships—
Monsters from the far distant past
Or visions of our future and space travel.
The science fiction movies back then

14

Borealis

Showed rockets that were mostly V–2s,
Ones that we had captured from the Germans
Or copies we had made and tested here.
I thought about such rockets every day
And drew them in my spare time at school. 510

Soon I got to know the major stars,
And all the planets of our solar system—
How many moons each one had
And how far away each one was
From the sun. My teachers were all books
Borrowed from our town library
Because there was no mentor or instructor
Who would tell a boy about the stars;
But I absorbed a lot, because I loved
Space and all that had to do with space. 520
The planets always captivated me:
Mercury, so close to the sun,
And Venus, always shrouded in hot clouds;
Mars, with its canals and snowy poles
That seemed to offer life but never could;
Giant Jupiter so far away,
God of all and largest of them all,
And Saturn, whose broad rings composed of dust
And floating rocks made such a spectacle;
And finally those travellers far off 530
In darker space, Uranus, Neptune, Pluto.
I loved those wanderers of our solar system
Named after Roman gods, and for a goddess.

I also borrowed dinosaur books
From our library and loved the pictures
Artists had made of them, and so I saw
In pictures and in my imagination
Those giants. I could say their powerful names,
Brontosaurus and Diplodocus,
Pterodactyl and Terranodon, 540
Allosaurus and Icthyosaurus,
And, of course, Tyrannosaurus Rex,

Book I

Tyrant lizard over all supreme.
I saw their habits and their habitats
And fell in love with them; on some days
My mind was full of swamps and dinosaurs
More than parents, teachers, or homework.
Before we left Ohio, that last year,
Astronomy and paleontology
Would play a tug of war within my soul   550
Because I wanted to do both, but saw
No way a human being could do both.

I entered fourth grade and fell in love
With a slender blonde girl who sat
Two rows across from me all day.
Her name was Joanna Jarvee.
Although I truly loved her, honestly,
I loved her golden hair almost as much:
Long and loose or in a ponytail
It seemed a sanctuary of the sun.   560
I wanted to go out with her, or some day
Hold her in my arms on the school grounds
With no one else around and kiss her once,
But I was much too shy to dare try.
I hardly ever got to talk with her.
Joanna knew I loved her,
Because I told a friend who told a friend.
One day another girl, a nice brunette
Named Karen, came to my home as a guest.
I don't know how our date had been arranged   570
One autumn afternoon after school
But I remember sitting on the wall
That bounded our front yard, alone with her
And talking about things that didn't matter,
And looking out across the Ohio Valley
And wishing that instead Joanna Jarvee
Were at my side and happy to be so.
A melancholy ache nagged at my soul
But I was nice with Karen, and I talked
As though I had no cares and was free   580

Borealis

To look out across our industrial valley
And talk with her about all sorts of things.
One time I saw Joanna in an alley
Behind her home a block from my home.
She was with a friend and I was, too.
We talked some and then we laughed some
But nothing came of it and I walked on,
Unhappy with myself. I often thought
Of her, and often wanted to be with her,
But afterward we moved away for good;　　　　　　590
Imaginary love travelled with me
Alive but unfulfilled in any way.
I had a half articulate awareness
Of some more powerful significance
To what had happened with Joanna Jarvee,
Or what had failed to happen, but I was
Only a boy who just awoke to love
And not mature enough to understand
The long and deep significance of it.

I fell in love with stones and always hoped　　　　　　600
To find unusual ones as I wandered
Along the roads and paths of my home town.
As often as I found one I would clean it
And place it with a few other stones
I cared about. Some of them I purchased:
An amethyst quartz crystal for a quarter
In Pittsburgh, at the Carnegie Museum;
An amber cat's eye topaz that would change
From amber striated to dark brown
And back again as I rotated it.　　　　　　610
I also had a prize my uncle found
In Arizona on a holiday:
A chunk of milky quartz, blessed with a vein
Of silver running dark across its center.
When he handed it to me he told me
How those substances were sometimes found
Together, and gave hope to prospectors
Of silver to be dug, or even gold.

Book I

Stones offered a long developed tale
Of geological glory   620
And I hoped I would discover more
In walks around our town, or in the country,
Or maybe in another museum shop.
I had developed a pure love for them.

Mother told me all of us had souls
And I supposed that must be true, although
I never wondered very much about it,
And no one (and no book) taught me to know
What form a soul should have, or what behavior.

Maybe it was my soul, or something more,   630
That moved me in a way I could not fathom
When I wanted far more than I could find
Among the stones and fossils I had found,
Or in a taste of pure cold water,
Or in a classmate's golden ponytail,
Or in the cornucopia of good
That constituted our household's world
And was a wonder—our Ohio home.

Book II

Solitude, Art, and A Night to Remember

God was all alone when he awoke
Our world and the whole cosmos into being
Without the help of counselors or friends.

So I would have thought, if I had thought
Much of God, or that there was a God.

I could be alone, and solitude
Could be a coach of sorts—one who enabled
A young boy to imagine other worlds
And fill a solitary afternoon:
A guide who could prod those creative powers   10
Dormant until someone awakened them.
I can remember hours full of fun
Even when I had to be alone
Because my parents had to go on errands
Or all my friends had other things to do.
I hardly ever murmured or complained,
Although I could feel lonely for awhile
Until I found some form of work or play.

Book II

One summer afternoon I took a walk
Along a red brick path through our back yard,   20
Where mother had a small vegetable garden,
And found a large, dark, oval rock
Among the smaller stones and slag and gravel
On the access road behind our house.
I set that rock apart and made believe
It was a monster spacecraft, and a danger
To the planets, colonies and outposts
Of a future human space empire.
I focused on my target, and I hurled
Smaller stones repeatedly against it,   30
And made pretend I was a space commander
Who threw our forces at a common foe
To smash and blow away its outer hull
Until it broke apart and came undone.
I could occupy myself that way
An hour or more and produce a war in space
That did no harm to any other one
But only broke a monster rock apart.

Anyone who saw me then could see
How solitude encouraged a small boy   40
Whose young imagination could conjure
A cosmos from an alley full of slag.
Generations of young boys before
From ancient Mesopotamia and Egypt
Who played among date palms by the Euphrates
Or by the Nile among papyrus reeds,
Or boys who grew up in the Middle Ages
And played at chivalry with broken branches
Had all discovered how to be alone
And find good ways to pass a careless hour   50
Without a toy or manufactured thing
But only what the landscape offered up—
Stones, or mud, or maybe fallen branches.
My parents made enough to feed and clothe us
And pay our mortgage and our other bills
And buy a toy or two for me—toy soldiers,

Solitude, Art, and A Night to Remember

Some modeling clay and small toy cars and trucks—
But normally I loved to play outside
And use what came to hand and make it work.
To be a boy like those already gone   60
Before our state or country had been born
Was to be part of something that endured,
An archetype far older than us all.

As we sat in school and autumn leaves
Added color to our local landscape
I dared imagine I could be an artist,
Probably because my uncle was.
I had seen a canvas full of color
On an easel in his upper room,
And a palette daubed with pools of color   70
And a palette knife, and many brushes
Arranged from large to small on a table
Along with tubes of paint in one corner
And that was how his room always looked.
Although he never was a noted artist,
My uncle had an eye for what was good
In nature and in art, and he could copy
Picasso with considerable care
As a sort of study for his art.
Once he did a good still life,   80
A vase full of flowers in the sun,
Not wild and dynamic like van Gogh,
But unobtrusive, like a vase of flowers.

Our class had an art contest
To see if anyone could produce
A large Halloween watercolor.
Another boy, named Eliot, and I
Became the only artists in our class
Because no one else dared try.
I sat at home one Saturday and planned   90
A large picture of a haunted house
On a low hill with blasted trees around
And racks of torn clouds under a full moon.

Book II

I came to class and started to produce
A watercolor version of my vision
On a large, white paper canvas
A yard wide and two feet tall.
Our teacher, Mrs. Jones, set up an easel
For Eliot and one for me as well
And every afternoon we stood and painted　　　　　　100
For more than half an hour in unique freedom
While our poor classmates labored on
Doing grammar or arithmetic.
Halloween day arrived at last
And the haunted house won the match
But only by a fluke and by default
Because my friendly rival made an error.
He painted a magnificent black cat
With raised hair, standing on a fence,
About to cry in fear or scowl in anger　　　　　　110
But—the cat was standing upside down;
Her stiffened tail pointed to the ground.
Mom and Dad were proud of me that day
But I could hardly feel I had done much,
Because I knew that Eliot's creation
Was better, and his cat was wonderful
Even though it was upside down.

Autumn passed, and when December came
Another opportunity arose
To show artistic prowess. Before Christmas　　　　　　120
Our Sunday school announced an art contest
For pictures based on Yuletide events,
Drawn with crayons or with colored pencils.
After my successful Halloween
Watercolor of a haunted house
I should have had some grounds for self-assurance,
But I could hardly start another art work.
I had a vague, melancholy sickness
Located somewhere in my stomach area,
A sense of nausea as I took my crayons　　　　　　130
And large white poster board into my bedroom

And laid them on the floor. I lay before them
And pondered what I ought to draw, one day
Before our class submissions were all due.
Because it was a Christmas contest
I thought a manger scene with baby Jesus,
Joseph and Mary and the local shepherds
And turbaned kings in robes, with valuables
Arrayed before the baby boy in homage,
Would be appropriate. Once they were drawn   140
I placed a guiding star above the manger;
Its glow illuminated all of them.
I thought that I had done a piece of work
Less valuable than the haunted house
But maybe good enough to make some show;
So I was embarrassed to be told
On Sunday morning at the end of class
My humble manger scene had won the contest.
My Sunday school teacher handed me
A small cardboard box that contained   150
A pen and pencil set by Papermate
In two toned olive green and stainless steel.
I came away uncomfortable that
Someone could win a Sunday school contest
With such a mediocre work of art,
Although I did have some artistic pride
After I won two contests in a row.

My grandfather never was an artist.
He joined the Army as a young man
In the Coast Artillery Corps
At the Presidio in San Francisco.   160
Later in Ohio he worked
In a local mill, and rolled hot steel,
Or "hot plate," as they called it in those days.

On days off he loved to bait a hook
And he showed me how to do the same.
When they could, he and Grandma took us
A forty mile journey over hills

Book II

North northwest of the Ohio Valley
To Cadiz and beyond—to Tappan Dam, 170
A neighborhood of lakes, woods and farms.
We bounced along a narrow dirt road
Until their black Chevy carried us
To a spot they loved, called Brushy Fork.
They parked under a large oak tree
And made a camp on the flat bank;
Then they cast their lines into the water
And sat and waited patiently for nibbles.

Above the dirt road there was a pasture
That had a few cows and some cow pies. 180
When I was older and allowed to go
Alone across that pasture and explore
The whole of it, and amble with the cows,
I was careful to avoid those pies.

On a day when I was very young,
Only five or six years old, I walked
With Mom and Dad one sultry afternoon
Along the dusty road of Brushy Fork.
Granddad had gone around a bend
To a favorite spot, to be alone; 190
Although he was there for over an hour
He only caught a few small carp;
He said he probably would throw them back
Because they were too boney. He still hoped
To catch some bluegills or some channel cats:
Those were better sport, and tasted better.

Mom and Dad and I walked slowly back
To our shady spot under the oak tree;
As we saw the tree, we also saw
A cane fishing pole—my fishing pole— 200
Where we had left it propped with its hook baited.
The pole moved back and forth (almost as though
Some water demon had got hold of it
And wanted to dislodge and drag it off

Solitude, Art, and A Night to Remember

Toward a cave submerged in deeper water).
We all ran together, and I saw
The cork bobbing up and down, the line
Tugging at the pole and then I grabbed
The pole and pulled and pulled, and soon there was
A five inch bluegill dangling from the line.   210
He looked so beautiful, flapping around
In desperation just above the water;
But I had no compassion for his quandary.
The only thought I had as I gawked at him
Was how miraculously it had happened—
How I had just hooked my first fish.

I could be a young rapscallion
Although I never would have harmed a soul.
One hot summer day when all of us
Were in Granddad's basement, and Grandma   220
Was busy at her old gas stove
Cooking up a mess of fish for us
(And scallions and pan fried potatoes)
I tiptoed up the basement stairs alone.
Stealthily, I turned the brass door knob
And walked into a quiet, empty kitchen.
I closed the door behind me, and then locked it.
I put the key down on the tablecloth
And walked quietly to the back door;
I turned the lock in it, and left the room.   230
Then I went out the front door,
The only one that I had not yet locked,
And set the door to lock after I closed it.

Now I stood alone on the door sill
And saw that I had got myself in trouble.
Earlier that day, before our visit,
Granddad had given his front porch
A fresh coat of dark green paint.
The porch was more than twelve feet wide
And ten feet deep; there was no way   240

Book II

To cross it without stepping on the paint
And leaving footprints as I walked across.

Four broad strides carried me over
And then I was on comfortable ground.
I walked around the house to the back yard
Where a set of double doors lay open;
I went down some concrete steps
Back into the basement, and behaved
As though nothing unusual had happened.

But then my mother noticed on the floor   250
Some small, green footprints I had made
As I so innocently walked around.
Soon the truth was out and I was warmed
And reddened by a strong embarrassment.
My poor Grandfather, and my father too,
Were just as stumped as I had been before:
I had accomplished such a perfect lock out
That no one could get back into the house.
After an hour Granddad found a neighbor
Down the street who owned a skeleton key;   260
Soon he had unlocked his own back door
And brought the house back under his control.

All told it was a moderate disaster
And nobody was put out very much
But I had just become aware of something
Within my self that made it much too easy
To act alone and without any forethought
Of consequences that I might produce.

I was far too young to understand
How many ways one thoughtless act can bring   270
Unforeseen harm or sorrow to another.
I only saw that I had been a fool
And hoped that I would not be one again.

Solitude, Art, and A Night to Remember

One day our next door neighbor came outside
And saw me standing on the patio
Unoccupied, just staring at the clouds.
He asked if I played marbles or would care
To have some marbles he no longer wanted.
As a younger boy he had become
A formidable shooter, and had won   280
Scores of marbles off the other boys.
He had saved them in a dark green vase,
Large and round, and full up to the brim.

I saw the vase, and I was overwhelmed
To have so suddenly a large collection
Of marbles: cats eyes, agates; swarms of others
Full of swirls and colors, blue and brown,
Green and red, and some that we called boulders,
Gigantic and dark green—a cornucopia.
I had never thought so many marbles   290
Would come into my hands, but I accepted
His offer with transparent gratitude
And took the bowl inside, to sort and see
How many kinds of marbles I now owned.

I found a sizeable array of agates,
Thirty six of them, and six of them
With dark olive green on one side,
A narrow belt of white around the center,
And brown or orange on the other side;
But on the other side, just two of them   300
Were an imperial purple. They would be
Commanders in an army I would form.
Also there were eight blue marbles
With swirls of reddish brown among the blue
So that they looked like planets with blue oceans
Embraced by oddly formed arms of land.
All of those would soon become commanders
And so would eight more cats eyes—all noble
Because they had soft purple flowers

Book II

That had a look of aristocracy   310
Protected for all ages in pure glass.

Among a sea of marbles I discovered
Five dark, transparent green boulders
And fifteen cats eye boulders, colored so:
Creamy white; red; yellow; blue; and green;
And just one triune yellow, blue and red.

It was an almost dizzying array,
But I was happy with my newfound toys,
And soon I marshaled all of them and formed
Two armies: cats eyes and transparent marbles   320
Against all marbles of a solid color.
Those mobile armies fought in many battles
And gave me hours of simple fun, both there
And later on in Palm Springs, Florida;
When we moved from Florida to Georgia
(And after that, whenever I would move)
I always brought the marble armies with me
And still today I have them in a closet,
Although unused for many decades now;
And if I spread them on the floor today   330
It comes upon me as a sudden shock
How simple the world was, and what it is.

Even before we moved to Florida
I loved all of the ocean I had seen.
I could have no idea at the time
How large a role the ocean and some lakes,
The moon also, and stars and galaxies
Would play as I grew older—how they would
Color and shape some of my strongest thoughts.

Our town had a large public pool   340
Bordering on South Zane Highway;
My parents took me there one summer day
To swim, snorkel, and play under the sun.

Solitude, Art, and A Night to Remember

My parents both had stories they could tell
Of what had happened to them in the water.

When my father was a boy he swam,
When school was out, in the Ohio River.
Even then some river boats had paddles;
He swam after those paddles manfully
And rode the waves that surged away from them   350
Although his dad had told him not to do it
Because the currents made by river boats
Were strong, and dangerous for a mere boy.
Because my father never cared much
About his father's warnings on this point
He soon became a very good swimmer.

My mother on the other hand did not.
When she was only ten she took a plunge
Into the far end of our public pool,
So much out of her depth she almost drowned.   360
As a result she never learned to swim
But always had a horror of deep water.

That summer afternoon at the pool
As mother lay warming in the sun
My father gave me a small swimming lesson:
He made me hold on to the slippery poolside
And kick until I made a lot of waves;
He thought I would become a good swimmer
As soon as I could kick like a master;
And that was what he taught me about swimming.   370

After I had made enough waves
I was free to go away and play.
I strapped on my green face mask
And sank under the water, just as though
I was a diver on a coral reef.
As I looked around below the surface
I saw a shoal of local denizens—
Summer bathers playing, swimming, walking

Book II

In colorful swim suits. All of it
I saw as through my own picture window   380
Because the water there was very clear.

Later that afternoon when we changed
Our clothes in the men's locker room
I put the mask down on the bench beside me.
When I was fully dressed I turned around
To take my mask, and found that it was gone.
At such a young age I could not grasp
How common such an act could be
In any public place where anyone
Could pick up an unguarded item   390
And take it home, and have no qualms about it.
That afternoon I got some tutelage—
A lesson forced on me about our culture;
Maybe no one then could have imagined
How innocent that poolside culture was
Compared to what our country would become.

Because I loved astronomy my parents
Bought me a reflector when they could,
The sort that Isaac Newton had once used
When he explored the night skies over England.   400
It had a four inch parabolic mirror,
Aluminized and wonderfully bright.

One evening after supper we went out
And stood the tripod on our patio;
I turned the telescope toward a moon
That floated round and creamy far above us.
We took turns at the ocular and saw
A large and radiant surface, pockmarked
With craters we had never seen before.
We saw enormous mountain ranges, too,   410
And broad expanses of dark lunar dust
Observers long ago had thought were seas.
Our souls absorbed the splendor of that globe;

Solitude, Art, and A Night to Remember

We saw now that our world was not alone
And saw it in a way we had not done.

On summer nights, when street lamps woke at eight,
I had to pack up toys and go to bed,
So then we brought the telescope indoors;
But now I thought more about other worlds
That floated far above and out of reach   420
And I anticipated many hours
Full of observations of the moon
And other objects far away in space.

The next morning I saw a speck of dust
On the mirror of the telescope.
I took some tissue paper from the bathroom
And tried to wipe away the small offender,
But on the very spot where I had rubbed
A large, dark gray oval appeared
And fine metallic dust covered the tissue   430
I had used to wipe the mirror clean.
I had a queasy feeling in my gut.
Worried and afraid I showed my father;
He took a look and then assured me
That he would take the mirror to the store
And ask what could be done. When he did
He was told he had to buy another
Because the surface of the one I rubbed
Had come without an optical coating
(Something a mirror could have to protect it   440
From any random contact or abrasion).
That day I got another hard lesson
About the transitoriness of things
Although I did not learn that long word,
Transitoriness, until much later.

At ten years of age I owned a wagon
Given me when I was only seven,
A red Radio Flyer with black wheels
And a black metal handle I could pull

Book II

Or use to steer the wagon where I wanted. 450
Sometimes I would carry it downstairs
And place it on our level front sidewalk
And settle onto it—then brace myself
For a headlong ride down the hill.
Not many yards beyond, our sidewalk sloped
Swiftly down and planed off below
Under a copse of trees not far from where
An old friend, Curtis Armstrong, lived.

Curtis and his mother had a house
Painted yellow, with a front porch 460
Over a garage, next door to Mrs. Jones,
Our fifth grade math and grammar teacher.
One snowy morning as I walked
Down our hill to school I saw her coming
Gradually up the slope toward me.
I waved hello and offered her my arm.
She was old, and happy to accept
My offer of support. Carefully
We made our way together down the icy hill,
Across North Zane Highway, to North School. 470
A snowy walk with her took much longer
Than I would have liked, but I could manage;
It made me somehow feel more virtuous.

Back then I did not understand
What had happened to my good friend
But Curtis was a thalidomide baby.
He only had one arm and one leg
And always used a wheelchair or crutch
When he had to get around outside—
At school, or when he played with me or others. 480
Later, after I had graduated
From Yale and was in Georgia with my parents,
I read he was arrested in a car
With some young man and woman, and the car
Was full of drugs. The Martins Ferry paper
Described him as a young, one armed musician.

Solitude, Art, and A Night to Remember

I also heard his mother lost her mind
And ended her days in some institution;
As for his father, an insurance salesman,
He had left the family long ago   490
And no one seemed to know where he had gone.
But as I settled onto my red wagon
The only thing I could anticipate
Was a rough, dangerous ride down the hill;
So I braced myself, and I shoved off,
And soon I was careering like the wind.

A month before we moved to Florida
We sold our house, and on a sunny morning
In June under some small cumulus clouds
That floated past and looked like tufts of wool   500
I handed over my old paper route
To a younger boy I did not know.
We said goodbye to our bungalow
And moved to my grandparents' house on Pearl Street.
The house was large and white, and only one
Of several such houses on a street
That looked more peaceful and respectable
Than any I had known in Martins Ferry.
Oak trees lined the road and stood tall
And cast their shadows on the way below;   510
So they formed a quiet, private world.
I could have stayed there happily all summer,
Especially now, because another friend,
Bill Jarvis, who had gone to North School
Until that very month, had moved close by.

One morning Bill and I got together.
I wore my World War I canteen and knapsack.
We walked up a hill above his house
And made our way along a forest path
Until we came across an open meadow   520
With tall yellow grasses in the sun;
Beyond being soldiers on the prowl
I cannot now remember what we played.

Book II

Around noon we came back down again
And found our way to Bill's back yard.
His mother gave us sandwiches for lunch,
And lemonade. We sat and talked, and took
Our time, and watched a small cloud pass by,
And lazed away a June afternoon.

Every sunny day was paradise 530
Once school was out. My only obligation
Was to act my age and play about.

One especially warm afternoon
I sat and watched the Mickey Mouse Club
In the cool of Grandma's living room.
Suddenly I felt a strange itch
And saw a rash where none had been before
On both my arms and legs, and on my hands,
And if I scratched, I only made it worse.
Granddad took a look and knew at once 540
That I had contracted poison ivy.
He brought some alcohol and wiped me down
And opened up a soft plastic bottle
And poured a creamy pink liquid out,
One dollop at a time, onto a pad
And daubed it on those numerous locales
Where sturdy bumps of the invader stood
Like well deployed soldiers on my flesh.

Morning and afternoon for seven days
I was a servant to the same regime 550
Of lotion and ablution, and always
A prohibition against scratching ruled.
If I scratched, the problem would grow worse:
Provoked, the rash would rally and advance
Across my body like a powerful host
And capture all my outer territories.
So for that whole week I was a hostage,
A prisoner at home. I could not play
Soldier with my friend, or go outside

And wander in the woods. I did not want 560
To let those bumps advance across my body
(Or bother someone else as I was bothered)
And yet, I wanted more than anything
To see my friend and play outdoors once more,
And see that meadow on its sunny slope.

Our family did not have many days
And then we would depart for Florida.

My parents and grandparents had to work
So I was left alone most of the week.
I passed some hours on the front porch— 570
The same front porch I walked across and marred
When I had locked the house against all comers
And tracked telltale green paint into the cellar.
I read some stories in a *Reader's Digest*
And drank a glass of iced tea on the swing
And as I did I caught an inspiration
And thought that I could write a story, too.

Not many months before, my mother bought
A copy of *A Night to Remember*,
A book by Walter Lord about *Titanic* 580
And her catastrophic maiden voyage.
Bill Jarvis owned it as a paperback
And told me that it was a good book;
Mom had bought it for me not long after
From a department store across the river,
Stone and Thomas, where we used to go
And do our Christmas shopping; there I saw
American Flyer and *Lionel* trains.
The book was one among a few volumes
The store held in a library for patrons. 590
When we asked the store librarian
She sold it as a favor to my mother;
She was touched that someone so young
Was interested in such a serious book.

Book II

Once I was alone again at home
And saw the photos in the book, and read
About *Titanic* and her majesty,
I was just astounded by that boat.
Titanic was a noble work of art
Judiciously assembled and appointed   600
With ornate staircases and chandeliers
And staterooms and ballrooms that were superb.
The passengers were glamorous; so, too,
The cargo hold, with treasures old and new,
From costly autos to an ancient copy
Of Omar Khayyam's *Rubaiyat*—although
I thought that was just some old ruby yacht.
Titanic was a monument to man,
So clever with her watertight compartments,
Constructed magisterially for ocean,   610
And yet, by some inexorable doom,
Unprepared to meet a random iceberg
That caved her hull and sent her to the bottom.

I thought that I, too, could write a story
About a ship that made a fatal voyage,
And so I did, and long ago I lost it,
But often after that I thought about
The art of composition and the role
It ought to play as I became a man.

The joy I had as I looked forward to   620
Our approaching move to Florida
Was dampened by a tragedy at home.

In April I had bought two turtles,
A female slider and her younger mate.
I put them in a shallow plastic holder,
An oval with an island at the center,
A ramp up to the island, and a palm tree
That crowned the island. I bestowed on them
Names I thought would be appropriate
For a god and goddess: Neptune and Venus.   630

Solitude, Art, and A Night to Remember

Every afternoon I fed them worms,
So I thought they ought to be content;
But Neptune made a bold escape somehow
And frightened mother when she saw him crawl
Under the couch, and thought he was a mouse.

I loved the turtles so I had been careful
To keep their water clean and feed them well,
But now I was about to move away;
The turtles had to have another home.
I entrusted them to Curtis Armstrong							640
But that turned out to be a big mistake:
He only had them for a couple of weeks
Before they clambered out of their safe place,
And after a few days he found them both
Dead outside his house. It was now obvious
I should not have entrusted them to him
Because he could not care for animals;
But now it was too late, and they were gone.

On warm spring nights at Grandma's house
There were always lightning bugs around							650
The bushes, or out in the open air.
One June night I took a jar
And perforated its metal cap
And tried to capture some of those bugs.
I thought if I could catch enough of them
I could make a lantern of the jar:
A lamp of bugs that would flash on and off
And show my way across the lawn at night.
Of course it was impossible to do
Because the wary insects were too fast.							660
Although I caught a few of them I knew
My small collection would not fill a jar
Or make a lantern. Now that I had caught them
And watched them crawl around inside the jar
I had to let them go, because I knew
They would feel like prisoners in a jar
And I would not be happy holding them.

Book II

Our move to Grandma's house would also mean
Another loss I could not have foreseen.

My father won a stuffed elephant   670
When I was four years old.
He won it at a local carnival
And as we walked away toward the car
Under the stars I had a happy feeling
Because he gave the elephant to me.
I gave my new won pal the name, Mo,
And as a boy I played with him a lot.
Often I would lay him on his back
And make pretend his body was a boat,
And use his trunk as some sort of rudder   680
To guide us on a journey full of danger
Across the ocean of our kitchen floor.
On other days the kitchen floor became
A scary swamp of brown linoleum,
And then I guided him through that.
I loved Mo very much, but a day came
When he was just too old to keep around,
So he had to go. After we moved
To Grandma's house I would remember him
And all our happy hours on the ocean   690
Or in the swamp of brown linoleum,
But when I thought of Florida and palm trees
Ohio things became much less important
And once we finally moved to Florida
Mo became a faded memory
And I seldom thought of him again.

Sometimes I ponder how our days flowed on,
Those youthful days on North Seventh Street:
How many hours were just full of joy,
How many days were passed just as a boy   700
With only boyhood troubles or assignments
To occupy my soul outside of play,
Or walks along our hilltop (or maybe

Solitude, Art, and A Night to Remember

A random hunt for Indian arrowheads,
Because there had been Indians in those parts),
Or hours spent at night under the sky,
Grateful just to watch the moon and stars,
Or afternoons, when I could spend what seemed
And endless span of time flat on my back
In our front yard, and stare up at the clouds   710
That looked as though they were in sky so deep
A boy could become dizzy watching them.

It was a world so simple and so good
That I could want to enter it today
And make it all my very own once more;
And yet, I know it never was my own,
My proper world, but only a small place
In which I lived and moved and had my being.

Sometimes it felt so much a part of me
That I could hardly know where I began   720
And where I ended, only I did know
That I was not the world, and that the world
Which offered so much ordinary goodness
Could also offer harm to my young soul.

Book III

Australis

Florida like a naïve lass was open
To tourists from abroad and those who came
From our own land on business or for fun.

Uncle Bob had moved to Florida,
And he was partner in a business
That made awning and jalousie windows
And sold them to a growing building trade,
And now our family travelled south to join him;
But when I saw those palm trees in Palm Beach
They were trees that I had seen before.   10

When December blew and Martins Ferry
Saw the snowflakes that we loved so much
We left them all behind so we could spend
Our Christmas holiday with Uncle Bob
And see how Florida would look to us
Before we cast our lot to move down south.
He had bought a house in West Palm Beach
On an unfrequented road that ended
Close to the Intracoastal Waterway.

Book III

His house was like a Spanish hacienda 20
With stucco walls and ochre roofing tiles,
And set far back onto a generous lot.
The front yard and the back yard had palm trees
That arced into the air with slender grace
From rounded bases on the sandy ground
And coconuts hung clustered at their tops.
All of it seemed miraculous to me,
As though, by some strange fate, I had just landed
Upon another planet, full of family
Who had arrived by plan ahead of me 30
And welcomed me with love and gratitude
Into a world of palm trees and warm breezes.

Uncle Bob's road was long and flat
And Carla, my young cousin, was allowed
To ride her bicycle along that road
As often as she wanted, and alone.
One day she let me ride her bicycle
Along her driveway and then on the road
And as I did I found that I could balance
And travel well, almost as though, somehow, 40
My body and my soul had become formed
To have such an encounter and succeed.

Back in Ohio I had often sought
To ride a bike on our back patio
But our small patio was much too cramped
And I could never get up enough speed
To get and hold my balance, so I faltered.
But now in West Palm Beach I had the room:
A flat road in a quiet neighborhood
So obviously safe that Mother would 50
Allow me to go out on Carla's bike
And I was not at all concerned about
The fact that I was on a young girl's bike.

Carla took me through their back gate
Past hibiscus bushes in full flower

Australis

And pale ficus trees with peeling bark
That pulled away like paper if you tried.
We followed a bare path that was all sand
And suddenly the bushes gave way
Onto a golf course, green and manicured   60
And quiet in the afternoon sun.
It was as though we had come on a quest
Through a tropic jungle and had found
A world that we had never seen before.

Beyond all former glory was the day
My uncle hired a wooden cabin cruiser
At Boynton Beach and took us deep sea fishing.
Before we got on board my father bought
A captain's hat with gold braid for me.
Boyish importance welcomed me aboard   70
Although I knew that I was not the captain.
The proper captain started up the engine
And guided us toward the larger ocean.

Turquoise blue waters flowed between
The inlet walls as our small boat chugged forward
Among traffic of other cabin cruisers
And motorboats, all bound for deeper water.
Both inlet walls had long rows of folks
Who stood under the sun and baited hooks
And cast their lines into the turquoise waves   80
And even there a person could look down
And see small fish or watch a shark meander
His lazy way along in lucid water.

Proper coastal water was less clear,
Opalescent green, and that gave way
To water more profound, a deeper blue;
Our captain told us we had found the Gulf Stream,
A broad, dark current that was strong
And even kept the British Isles warm
Beyond what their cold latitude deserved.   90

Book III

We dropped our anchor there and also cast
Our fishing lines although I had no rod
Because I was too young for deep sea fishing.
The Gulf Stream was an ideal place to stop
Because of all the fish who called it home:
All sorts of them would come and go below
And snoop around and look for easy food.
We floated several hours in that spot
And as our boat rocked mildly to and fro
And as the sun shone warmly down on us   100
I watched the clouds pass by and watched the sea.

I stared over the side and once I saw
Two large jellyfish come bubbling up,
So slow and languorous they almost seemed
Unreal—a life form from another world,
A world that I could never be a part of.
Later on we saw a small sea turtle
Much larger than a boy stroke languidly
Just inches from the surface, on his way,
Maybe, to eat those jellyfish for lunch.   110
Meanwhile my parents and my aunt and uncle
Caught more bonita than we ever wanted
But not much else all day, until my mother
Hooked something obviously large and strong.

Our captain showed her how to pull hard back
And then lunge forward and at every lunge
Reel in more of the wiry fishing line.
Mother struggled to obey and soon
Far away—a good half mile it seemed—
A sailfish broke the water with some fury   120
And thrashed magnificent in open air
And hit the water with a mighty splash
That told us she had hooked a champion.
She must have battled him for over an hour
Before she finally brought him to the boat.
The captain and his mate took a large net,
A gaff and club, and soon they netted him

Australis

And hauled him up the side and to the deck.
He flapped and struggled 'til they clubbed him down
And put him in the hold, and after that 130
We all decided to go back to port:
The afternoon was growing late and cool
And Mother's catch had made our day a triumph.

Florida was a wonderland to me
Not only geographically remote
But powerfully exotic in her landscape
And full of marvels I had never known.
She offered mangoes, guavas and cumquats,
Fruit I hardly ever got to see,
Let alone taste; and then there was the sun 140
So radiant and warm even in winter
A boy could run around as though in summer.
Such matters now seem commonplace to us
But they were paradisal to a boy
Who had just moved far south to make a home.
The land around us seemed almost untouched
Compared to what it has become today:
Human inhabitants had scarcely made
An impact on the land they occupied.
West Palm Beach was merely a large town
And felt almost a part of sand and sea, 150
And one could easily escape from it
And be on sandy paths in some pine forest
Or among cabbage palms minutes away
By car, off Okeechobee Boulevard.

After we drove to Florida in June
We took a small apartment on South Olive,
A very ordinary sort of place,
Flamingo pink in color with white gravel
Across the roof and lizards all around.
A block away the Miramar Hotel 160
Stood tall beside the intracoastal waters,
An old majestic pile in white stucco
With crimson trim, and palm trees on her grounds.

Book III

One summer day I walked along the road
That passed in front of her not far from home
And stopped and stared admiringly up
At a hotel that must have dated from
The days of Al Capone and Herbert Hoover.
However many decades had gone by
The Miramar had stood up very well;　　　　　　　170
She was a landmark and a hotel, too,
And every day her parking lot was full.

The Miramar Hotel was one of those
Structures among palm trees that could evoke
A bygone Florida that won my love.
Now they hang in halls of memory,
Portraits of beauty lost to us for good.

The Banyan Restaurant was one of them.
It was a small, unprepossessing place
And probably its food was not so good　　　　　　　180
But it, too, was a landmark, and it stood
Close to an ancient banyan tree that spread
More than twenty feet from side to side.
The banyan was a ghastly looking tree,
And one that never seemed to stop its growth:
Its branches groped out and dropped roots
Almost like drapes, or coarse slate-brown cascades.
It looked almost as though it had a mind
To spread its dominance by patient growth
And overpower all of West Palm Beach.　　　　　　　190
A few years later workmen cut it down
And trucked it off because it was too large:
It started to encroach upon the sidewalk
And would soon be a danger to South Olive.
Shortly afterward the restaurant
Closed down—almost as though the little place
Could not go on without its sturdy namesake.

Another building, one I loved at once,
Was a U.S. Post Office that stood

Australis

North of us, and not far from downtown. 200
During the Great Depression workers built
A classic structure out of blocks and stucco
And red roof tiles—a local undertaking
Funded by some public works program,
One of many such that sought to help
Our nation struggle out of its malaise
Under Roosevelt before the war.
The public hall was simple but exalted
As any work of art, perhaps, should be:
Its counters had been formed of polished wood 210
And tall panels of varnished wood embraced
The lower portion of its creamy walls;
All of the mail boxes were old brass.
Up above a mural coursed around
The long and narrow hall and on the mural
We could all see the Barefoot Mailman,
A bag of U.S. Mail slung over his shoulder,
As he walked along a lonely beach
Accented by sea shells and grey driftwood
Or rowed a boat deep in the Everglades 220
Among dead trees festooned with Spanish moss;
Not far from him an alligator sat
And watched him with its toothy mouth agape.
He looked so sturdy and so purposeful
That anyone who looked at him could see
The moral fiber of our youthful country
Apparent in his walk and firm outlook.
A decade later other men tore down
That noble monument to former days
And in its place they put a modern thing, 230
A structure of aluminum and glass,
A product without any character.
But what those prior men had once constructed
Had left a mark on me that would not fade,
And I was always grateful to have been
One of those who saw that Post Office
When West Palm Beach was small and when the traffic
That passed along her major thoroughfares

Book III

Included some adults on bicycles
And people used to walking in the sun.   240

Our first summer in Florida was grand:
I learned to swim, and we bought a good house.

Carla, Paul, and Robby were first cousins;
I saw them almost every day that summer
Because their house was only blocks away
From Walton Boulevard and our apartment.
On every Monday, Wednesday and Friday
Aunt Ellie took them all for swimming lessons
To Lido Pools on Ocean Boulevard
In Palm Beach, a coastal town of splendor.   250
I loved the ocean and the sandy beaches;
I had one major limitation, though:
I was not yet a swimmer—far from it.
One day Mother asked me if I wanted
To go to Lido Pools with my cousins.
I jumped at the chance to go with them
Where I could learn to swim under the sun.
Swimming there was easier because
The Lido pumped their water from the ocean
And we were all more buoyant in salt water.   260

Our swim instructor gave us at the outset
Blue or red paddle boards that we
Had to hold always in front of us;
Then we put our faces down and kicked
From one end of the pool to the other.
I could kick and not bother to breathe
Because my Dad had shown me how to do it.
After that we practiced many strokes
And soon I became competent, and swam
Australian crawl or butterfly, or just   270
Swam like a happy bullfrog underwater.
I had a summer full of fun, splashing
And learning how to swim, but most of all
I loved it when our teacher would toss pennies

Australis

Into the water at the deeper end
And challenge us to fill our lungs with air
And plunge, and stroke our way down to the bottom
And bring up any coins that we could grab.
Once or twice I captured all of them
But often I would have to come back up   280
With only one or two, or none at all.
But even when I could not fetch a penny
I loved the water, and I loved the game.

It took less than a month for me to learn
How to swim in Florida. At home
(Back in Ohio) I could never learn
Because the pool was far away from us
And summer was too short for me to start.
I found no swimming school until I came
To Lido Pools, where water from the ocean   290
Supported me in every new found stroke.

Florida was a boundless Paradise,
A world of open sky and open sea
And open opportunities for me
To come out of my cold northern cocoon
And let myself be molded by her charm—
To understand myself in terms of her
Warm atmosphere and what she offered me:
How I could plough my way through salt water
Or stand alone on sand and watch the waves   300
Roll constantly ashore, and in their sport
Suggest a sort of comradeship to me
I never would have thought was possible.

Our old Ohio Valley was a cage;
My soul was like a parakeet uncaged,
Or like a parrot gone to southern air
After her northern owner set her free.

Although I was youthful and ignorant
I was still more than happy to come home

Book III

To Paradise—and Paradise was good 310
Enough for me. I wanted nothing more.

After we moved to Florida my parents
Thought they would buy a brand new house for us
South of West Palm Beach, in Lantana;
But soon they found another place to build,
Also south of West Palm Beach
But not as far south, called Palm Springs.
We had a house built on a corner lot
And angled so that it would face the corner.
A concrete footpath led to our front porch; 320
A concrete driveway led to our carport.
Every day we came from our apartment
And walked around our house as it became
More of a home, with large awning windows,
Jalousie doors, and white stones on the roof
(A standard way of roofing in south Florida
Because white gravel would reflect the sun
And keep the houses cool and comfortable).

Many months later I observed
How stones would fall to earth after strong rain 330
And form a line of gravel that grew denser
Under the overhang the more it poured;
But there was so much gravel on the roof
No one ever thought about replacing
The fallen stones as they accumulated.
Our house was low and flat, a bungalow,
And beautiful to me: it looked so modern,
With concrete block construction and new windows
Made by my father's company, Bellhouse,
On Okeechobee Boulevard. The name 340
Of our new company was a composite:
The "Bell" was for "Red" Bell, my uncle's partner,
And "House" was taken from my uncle's name,
Niehaus, a name that means "a new house."
It seemed more than appropriate—poetic—
To buy windows from our own company.

Australis

For a month or two there was no lawn
Around our house, until a flatbed truck
Arrived one day with tons of grass rolled up
(Bundles of grass that people there called sod;   350
Unrolled, they measured two feet by one foot).
Four sturdy workmen took them off the truck
And laid them side by side around our house
And in one afternoon we had a lawn.
It only wanted water every day
And it would send its blades upward, and roots
Into the ancient sand that lay below.
Although it came in one afternoon
It looked as though it had always been there.
There was a cheaper way to build a lawn   360
On top of barren sand, and that was called
Sprigging: an owner took small clumps of grass,
Planted them in a careful quincunx pattern
Around the house, and watered them each day.
They could produce a lawn with careful coaxing
But laying sod was much the better way
And we spared no expense, and went for sod.

To my surprise our lawn was soon endangered
At Christmastime, when from an open lot,
Across the street, a wave of sand blew over   370
And covered up a corner of our grass.
When I got home from school I watered down
The rogue sand and shoveled it away
And rescued that small section of our lawn.
All through Christmas break I took my stand
And worked against those waves of winter sand.
I felt like someone on a wild frontier
Who had to battle nature in the raw
In order to maintain a modest plot
Of cultivated lawn, and so establish   380
A human outpost against sand and wind.

Book III

When I was young I partly was aware
Of some interior good that was my own,
A virtue that would surface now and then
When opportunity arose to show
Those portions of my soul. I never sought
Occasions to be good, and never thought
About what sort of goodness lay within,
But when I showed some loyalty, or sense
Of duty, or would help someone unasked,   390
I was aware of some internal motion,
An impulse that would lead me to do good,
Or to be good for someone. And impulse
Is hardly a good word, for it was more
A subtle growth that rose out of some depth—
A fundamental something, true and pure,
Though often I was out of touch with it.
Normally my days flowed on without
A thought of it—more full of various moods
And ways of thought that one would not call good.   400
Ordinary people thought of me
As a young man who was too solitary,
Who verged on arrogance because he kept
Apart, and read so much, and looked as though
He thought he was quite smart and knew a lot.

Are we what we do, or do our actions
Flow from our character, and so mold us
That good behavior makes us even better
And bad behavior makes us even worse,
Or is there more than that to what we are?   410
I never thought about such matters then,
And if I had, I never would have grasped
Those deeper truths untouched by smarter men—
Friedrich Nietzsche, say, or Sigmund Freud,
Or many of their spiritual descendants
Who sought to form some basic understanding
Of what it was to be a mere mortal.

Australis

I was still a boy and was in love—
Truly at home in Florida—and happy
To be a boy with only boyish tasks					420
And boyish opportunities for play.

I started school that autumn in Lantana
Because we planned to purchase a house there,
But then I moved to Meadow Park School
Because that school was closer to Palm Springs.
Before I left Lantana, though, I met
A boy who would remember me much later
And be a friend at Lake Worth Junior High.
His name was Allan Kramer, and I must
Have made a strong impression on him somehow,			430
Because he would remember me long after,
Although I had forgotten all about him.
Allan was a very smart boy
Who had received some tutoring at home
And who would outperform us all at school.
Later on, in high school, he and I
Would often exchange hasty notes in Latin
Under our teacher's nose, and love the risk.

At Lantana School I only learned
That I was not so talented at softball;					440
We often played softball in the morning
During our short class break,
But I could never hit the ball well
And never caught it as an outfielder.
I left Lantana School after a month
Without a happy memory to speak of,
Except I would nostalgically recall
The old wooden desks and wooden floors
(They seemed so friendly and so comfortable)
And there was also music I would hear					450
On mornings as it drifted down the hall
From someone's office—instrumental music
With sea gull cries and a flavor of the ocean

Book III

And freedom that contrasted very much
With books and study and my morning class.

Meadow Park School was a good place.
Like our house it was a modern structure,
Made of concrete blocks and awning windows.
It had four buildings, set in parallel
And joined by open walkways that were covered 460
By flat roofs supported by thin poles.
It was a more contemporary sort
Of school than I had ever seen before,
But I was glad to be there; I was open
To any good that Florida had to offer,
Including unaccustomed architecture.

I had a sixth grade classmate, Jimmy Graham,
Whose buzz-cut hair was platinum blond.
His blonde mother always seemed to me
A pure embodiment of proper good 470
Around the home. Even as she wore
Her apron and was chopping vegetables
Or doing any mundane kitchen work
For her family, she looked to me
Almost austere, and always beautiful.
I saw his father less, but once I saw
A German Lugar and a German flag
That he had captured during World War Two
In Europe when he found a damaged Panzer
Abandoned by her captain and her crew. 480

My father, who had fought in Africa
And landed with our troops at Anzio,
Also brought a wartime trophy home,
An iron cross dated 1939.
Somewhere south of Rome a German soldier
Lay in ambush with two other troops
Behind a shrubbery in the open sun
And watched the Roman road for any foes.
That afternoon my father drove northward

Australis

Along that road, alone with his own thoughts; 490
But as he drove along, he felt unsure
About the road ahead; so he stopped,
Picked up his carbine, circled slowly around,
And found the Germans lying with their eyes
Astutely on the dusty way below
But unaware of him. They turned around
And saw him there, and all four shot at once.
My father never knew who they were.
He wondered if they had loved ones in Munich
Or just outside Berlin, not far from where 500
Our family had its own ancestral roots.

Dad would often quote Douglas MacArthur,
Who said that war was hell, and as a boy
I seldom heard him talk about the war
Beyond that one encounter south of Rome.
Only rarely would a funny story
From somewhere in north Africa command
Our wonder and our laughter, and we saw
That war could also wear a comic face.

A famous war movie from long ago 510
Soon aroused my curiosity.
Jimmy was allowed to stay up late
And one night he saw *Gunga Din*,
A movie about England and her efforts
To subdue and hold her Indian Empire.
I never got to see the movie then
Because I had to go to bed too early.
Only later when I was a grown-up
Did I see that movie on my own.
But often after school we got together 520
And played at being soldiers in some war,
Because no matter what our fathers told us
We were young, and thought that war was fun.

We had hardly grown or seen enough
To know our world or understand it much

Book III

And back in the late 50s that was not
A problem that occasioned much concern.
We were young and free to play as boys
And let imagination run amok.
Adulthood and the world would surely wait   530
And let us have our moment in the sun.

A casual encounter in our classroom
In late December took my thoughts away
From war and all that had to do with war.
A boy in our class, named Maurice
(Also nicknamed Junior) was a rascal,
And far too much so for us to grow close;
But one day as I wandered by his desk
And saw a portrait elegantly drawn
Of Goofy, Disney's cartoon character,   540
The art work made me want to know the artist.
That lanky dog stood on a corner,
Apparently without a single care,
But with a "Hulk, hulk" scrawled in a bubble
Over his head, and that was how Junior
Wrote the sound of Goofy's unique laugh.
Nobody thought the laugh was true to Goofy
But we were all astounded by the drawing
And most of all the face; it was so good
We thought a Disney artist could have done it.   550

At home that night I lay on the floor
And tried to draw a Goofy face as well
But every time I did it was a failure.
I could not draw a mouth that was correct
And so I gave up on the mouth and drew
A smooth round head and a long nose
That looked more like a loaf of French bread
Than anything Walt Disney had produced.
And yet—that was the start of something good,
Because I soon added a rounded body   560
And now I had a creature of my own
Who stood a yard tall and had small arms

Australis

That barely hung as far down as his tummy
(The arms were cute but hardly practical).
I also gave him large, staring eyes
That looked so innocent and so naïve
That, although some would figure he was odd
Nobody would have thought my creature dangerous.
Once that was done, I added three small hairs
To crown a tall, domed, bare head. 570
Then I gave my new discovery
A name: it was a Dounae, and I helped
All of my friends pronounce it properly
So they could say it as I did: "Doun nuh."

Those Meadow Park days saw the start
Of a long and happy road of adventures
Because I caught a wind of inspiration
That carried me out of our solar system
Into another one—to the home world
Of Dounaes, who were blue and orbited 580
A blue giant far away from us.
All through junior high school I made up
Dounae stories, and I wrote them down
In study hall, whenever I could not stand
To spend almost an hour doing homework.
A decade later when I was a student
At Harvard doing graduate research
(I wrote a thesis on the English poet,
Percy Bysshe Shelley) I stole hours
From scholarship to write two Dounae novels. 590
Those Dounae books could never carry me
To Florida where it had all begun
But they could transport me away from Harvard
And to an ideal world that I had formed
Where all adventures turned out very well
Because the ones who had them were all good.

I was much too young to understand
What made a man an artist but I saw
A part of me that loved to lounge around

Book III

And let imagination ramble on, 600
Luxuriant and unpredictable,
And let a story come, or maybe draw
Something that had to do with space, or Dounaes;
But such preoccupations would not blossom
Until another year or two had passed
When I attended Lake Worth Junior High.
As long as I remained at Meadow Park
I did whatever I was told to do
And, when I could, I found some time to play
With Jimmy Graham, or I played alone
With marbles or whatever came to hand. 610
I wrote another short story once
About a liner elegant and doomed,
But mostly my imagination ranged
Over a world of play like any boy's.

Jimmy Graham had a few good friends,
One named Roger, and two Hatfield boys
(Their family had come down from New York
To Florida only a year before).
The four of them had planned a camping trip
And I, too, was invited, so I asked 620
And got permission from my Mom and Dad.
A camping trip required that our folks
Should outfit us with grub, and pots and pans
And two pup tents, and we could add our comics
And maybe games or some binoculars.
We put our stuff in Jimmy's station wagon;
His mother was our beautiful chauffeur.
She drove us down a sandy, bumpy path
Until we reached an ideal camping site
A mile or two away from Jimmy's house. 630
Our camping spot was at a distant boundary
Of a large, sandy acreage just opened
By contractors. They had not yet begun
To pour those concrete slabs that would become
The floors and outlines of so many houses

Australis

That soon the area would be transformed
Into a sort of model Florida village.

Jimmy's mother dropped us at our spot
Just below a long and lofty slope
That had not been there two weeks before.   640
A yellow crane had come and dug far down
And dredged a brown canal along that way,
And dumped all of the sand it excavated
Along the newly formed canal bank;
So in one day our slope had come to be.
I had no idea that afternoon
How soon a wave of bulldozers would come
And push our slope away and make it flat
And form the basis of a waterfront
For several houses that would take their stand   650
On green lawns among palm trees and palmettos
With handsome docks of pressure treated wood
For motorboats along the brown canal.
I was so new to Florida that I
Could not imagine how a sandy waste
Could suddenly become a settled place
And look as though it had always been so.

I clambered up the sandy slope and stood
Alone in the cool air and watched the sunset
And saw, in shade below, nothing but sand   660
As white as sugar, and some coral fragments
And ancient shells so blanched and desiccated
That anyone who looked at them could see
They had survived long ages out of water.
The white sand was an ocean vast and cool,
A novelty to someone like myself,
And I had never seen such shells and coral.
I thought they must be relics of those days
When all of Florida was under water,
And now I got to see them as I gazed   670
Across the sandy landscape where we camped
Millennia after they had come to be.

Book III

Although I was so taken with the glory
Of all that I surveyed, I also thought
That sleeping on the sand would be a challenge
To someone who had never slept outside.

But now, as that day's sun began to sink,
We knew the time had come to make our supper,
And someone thought we ought to try our luck
At catching fish, and make a meal of bream;   680
But that would be a messy job. We had
Some hamburger and other food from home,
So we voted instead to start a fire
And cook some burgers in the open air.
We found twelve hollow reeds and made a grill
By laying them at angles to each other
Over the flames; but very soon the fire
Devoured the reeds and also swallowed up
One hapless hamburger that I had placed
Upon our makeshift grill, and it was burnt   690
And sandy once I finally was able
To pluck it from the coals where it had fallen.
We cooked our other burgers in a pan.

Our campfire blazed and warmed us as we ate
And talked about those things of small importance
That made a schoolboy's thoughtworld in those days.
Then I unpacked some Uncle Scrooge comics
That I had found on comic book stands
At gas stations, and one convenience store,
And settled down to read and fall asleep.   700

My favorite character in all the world
Of Walt Disney cartoons was Uncle Scrooge.
He had adventures all over the globe
And I could journey with him as I read.
I saw the "Seven Cities of Cibola,"
Discovered by a family of ducks,
Come crashing down in ruin, all because

Australis

A crew of gangsters who had followed them
Across the desert as they had explored
And hoped to find those fabled Seven Cities   710
(The Beagle Boys) had fought among themselves
Over a statue made of solid jade:
A statue on a pedestal, set up
To trigger self-destruction of the towns
And bury all their gold and jewels in rubble
If anybody tried to move the statue.
I saw the Flying Dutchman ride the clouds
With blood red sails arrayed against the wind—
What looked to be a spectral apparition
And made old Scrooge's duck hairs stand on end   720
Until a journey to Antarctica
Exposed it as an optical illusion:
A ship in truth, encased and raised in ice
Above the water's surface, but refracted
By some strange play of lightning among storms
Across the ocean and to distant ports,
Creating among sailors quite a stir
Because they thought they had just seen a ghost,
A spectral ship afloat among the clouds.
Only a decade later would I learn   730
That Wagner had composed a tragic opera
Based on the legend of the Flying Dutchman;
But when I was a boy in Florida
I learned there had once been a "Seven Cities,"
Or rather, there had been a story of them
Told by the Indians to *Conquistadores*
Who always had a hunger for more gold.

Shortly before ten our blazing fire
Subsided into coals. We closed our tents
And hoped to get a good night's sleep;   740
But now I had to pay a sorry price
For my own willfulness. I had a cold,
And it had bothered me for several days.
My mother told me I was not allowed
To join my friends on that first camping trip

Book III

Unless I made it through the day at school.
I had made no secret of the cold,
So Jimmy and his mother knew about it;
But all day long at school I did my best
To wrestle down each telltale cough and sneeze 750
And make a show of being better off
And feeling better than I really did;
And maybe I believed that I was well,
Or well enough to join my friends that night
(Or half believed it) but when darkness came
And colder air, all my bravado flagged.
I had to face the fact that I was ill
And could not last the night. I was so ill
I could not fall asleep on the hard sand.
I had to face the fact that I had been 760
A fool to force my way among my friends;
And now (although it was past ten o'clock)
I had to go. My friends could not help much
Except to offer some encouragement
And watch me pack my things and see me off.

The long trek to Jimmy's house began,
A two mile walk. The moon was full,
The air was clear and cold, and even though
My head was stuffy and my throat was sore
I could admire the vast, abandoned stretch 770
Of moonlit sand that lay so still before me.
As I trudged on under a milky moon
The pale, white sand seemed frozen in cool waves;
It was as though I walked across a sea
Of waters some magician had enchanted
To bar them from their customary play.
Even in my illness I could tell
Sublunar Florida was beautiful;
Her beauty comforted me as I walked.

A half hour later I arrived 780
At Jimmy's house, and there a babysitter
Allowed me to come in, and offered me

Australis

Some temporary bedding on a sofa
Until the Grahams got back from a show,
A musical not far from where they lived.
Soon after, they arrived and took me home
Where Mom and Dad were, thankfully, awake,
And very soon with little more ado
I was asleep in a familiar bed.

Winter was mild in Florida, and soon   790
My first Florida spring enveloped me,
Almost as warm as an Ohio summer.

After a year in Florida I was
Transformed from much that I had been before.

Whatever I had been back in Ohio—
Whoever I had known—seemed far away
And almost faded from my memory.

It was as though the hot Florida sun
Had blanched those images lodged in my soul
Until they were as pale as old white sand   800
Or faded shells, or coral from long ago.

Book IV

Lake Worth and Junior High School

How many families had travelled south
Before my parents moved there to embark
Upon their journey to a better future?

How many voyaged from nations far away—
From Spain, from England, or from Germany?
How many came from further south yet?

Our nation thought it was a melting pot
But Florida was not that complicated.
Only along the coast and in Miami
Could I see many people in one place,   10
And even the Atlantic coast had room
For unbuilt townships and new populations
And much of the Gulf Coast was just a place
For seagulls and sea turtles and sea grapes.

Florida back then was mostly Yankees
And Florida crackers, people born in state,
And there were also Cubans and some people

Book IV

From Puerto Rico and from further south,
But they were only rare phenomena.

Our family was part of one migration,   20
A flock that had begun to grow much larger:
The many who flew south to find a hope
Of opportunity and fuller life
In warmer weather, far away from all
The winter gloom and factories of the north.
Our own household was not our family's vanguard
And others of our clan would follow us:
Uncle Bob had moved two years before
To become partner in a window business
And uncle Emil moved a year later   30
And bought a small house close to Coral Gables;
My grandmother and grandfather came down
Not many months after we found a home
But that was for a very different purpose:
My grandmother had jaundice, and her liver
Was beyond hope. She only stayed with us
A month or two, and then she passed away.

Although her passing saddened me, it was
No tragedy to me, because I was
So young and full of sap, like some young tree.   40
But I was old enough to understand
That older people do not live forever.
They could not be expected to remain
For many years among us. Grandma's death
Was harder for my mother, who had loved her
More deeply than I understood and who
Would mourn for many months and grow an ulcer,
A symptom of a profound agony,
And carry it around with her for decades.
I could fathom some portion of her sorrow   50
Because I had sorrowed myself so much
Only one year before in Martins Ferry
When mother had been carrying a baby,
A boy who would have been my only brother.

Lake Worth and Junior High School

He was my brother, only not for long.
Gregory Brett was born three months too soon
And only lived one week after his birth.
I sometimes thought his death was what had moved
My folks to make our home in Florida
And leave behind his grave, if not his memory.   60

But Florida was not a place for sorrow,
Not for one as young as I and eager
To sample all that nature had to offer.

Before I went to Lake Worth Junior High
My parents bought a bicycle for me.
Sometimes I rode that bike around a lake
And stopped where I saw lily pads, and waited.
Soon I would be rewarded by a "Ronk"
And then another "Ronk" and a "Ronk, Ronk"
A call from some large alligator hidden   70
Under the lily pads. I was astounded
To see how close those 'gators dared to come
To houses in a new development,
And every now and then I saw a photo,
In our local paper, of some policemen
Who labored manfully to bind a 'gator
On somebody's front lawn or in a driveway.

I always loved reptiles and dinosaurs
And now in Florida I got to see
Not only alligators in the papers   80
But also many of their smaller cousins
Around my uncle's house and our apartment.
More lizards darted in the flowery bushes
Than I had ever seen. A few of them
Were colored blue and black and looked unsafe
(Somebody told me they were poisonous)
But most of them, American chameleons,
Were green fellows that looked for all the world
Like tiny dinosaurs. I often tried
To catch them as they flitted among leaves,   90

67

Book IV

But they were normally too fast for me.
One afternoon I captured one bare handed,
And held him carefully as he looked up
And stared at me. His rib cage was wonderful.
It rapidly expanded and contracted
As (full of fear) his little heart and lungs
Worked overtime to calm him or prepare
A sudden getaway if he could manage.
I wanted to observe him a short while
But soon it became obvious I could not.   100
Although I was infatuated with
The wondrous architecture of his body,
I saw he was unhappy, and I knew
It would be cruel to hold him any longer;
So I let him go and watched him scamper
And lose himself among a leafy forest
Of tall hibiscus bushes. It struck me
Just how much happier I was to lose him
Than I had been to hold him in my palm.

I was not yet mature enough to grasp   110
That love is at the root of everything—
That love supports the smallest animals
And holds the cosmos in great harmony—
But now I found that I could love a lizard
(An animal my parents would not care for).
I found my love for him was so unhampered
That I would rather let him run and play
Than hold him in my power and at my whim.

I met another boy at Meadow Park
Who loved to model objects out of clay.   120
His name was Jerry, and when I found out
Our common interest, I felt glad—and challenged.
Not long before we moved to Florida
My Mom had bought a pound of modeling clay.
On winter afternoons I sat alone
In our kitchen at a small sash window
And formed it into soldiers on a board

Lake Worth and Junior High School

One yard long and one foot wide.
That board became a field of battle as
The men shot at each other from the cover   130
Of straggly rock walls formed out of clay.
The officers had swords that were not clay
But straight pins that my mother loaned to me;
And I could also use the pins to punch
The bullet holes in soldiers who were shot.

So now in Florida I had discovered
A soul mate who was willing to engage
Our armies in apocalyptic battle.
We chose the Second World War as our motif,
A topic I was happy to attempt   140
Because I had only just discovered
A clever way to manufacture warplanes
Out of my clay, and load them up with bombs.
Jerry chose to lead the allied forces,
So that left me commander of the Germans.
We made a date: one Saturday away.

A week before we met, my bedroom floor
Became an armory, where I constructed
A fleet of aircraft—fighters for one man,
Or dive bombers for two. I also made   150
Four rocket launchers for a strong attack
Against the army that my foe would draft.
Because a war is ultimately won
Not only by an army's armory
But by foot soldiers who fight door to door
I formed an army of a hundred men.
That may not sound like such a powerful force,
But it was probably beyond compare
For magnitude among all powers made
Of modeling clay when I was a young boy,   160
At least among the boys I knew at school.

On Saturday we met at Jerry's house
And I deployed my army against his.

Book IV

I stood my troops behind a rocky wall.
He stationed his across an open waste
Dotted with monster boulders that were scattered
Randomly on the field. I launched my planes
And dropped so many bombs on his positions
I thought he must soon be obliterated;
But somehow many of his troops held on 170
So it was not yet obvious who would win,
Although I ruled the air and had more troops.
Toward the end I launched a ground attack,
But only after I had sent a huge
Barrage of rockets that I hoped would further
Soften up his troops for my assault.
A number of those rockets randomly
Found the boulders that he had arranged
Apparently for mere topography
Or maybe for some troops to hide behind; 180
But as the rockets pierced those massive boulders
My friendly foe showed signs of undue anguish—
Apparently undue, until I found
His crack troops were hidden in the rocks
And every rock was hollow camouflage
With soldiers in it, ready to attack;
So now instead of targeting his soldiers
Who stood across the way, I shot the boulders
In front of me, and soon I had destroyed
A major part of his combative force. 190
After that my enemy collapsed
And I swept all before me with no effort.
I came back home in triumph. I had made
A brilliant stroke, like those the Germans made
In the early days, before the course of war
And history turned against their fierce ideal.

I was still a boy and young enough
To make up boyish wars with modeling clay
And fantasize about the glamor of war;
And there were other contests I could join, 200
Such as knights errant had been wont to have

Lake Worth and Junior High School

On chargers in mediaeval tournaments,
Or on the field of battle for their ladies,
Or on the road or in some lonely vale
Against a foe encountered just by chance.

One day I saw a Technicolor movie
Based on the novel, *Ivanhoe*, by Scott,
And came home with a head full of ideals
Of chivalry and valor and the call
Of knighthood and the splendor of it all.   210
I looked around my neighborhood and found
All sorts of boards and smaller bits of wood
Abandoned by local construction men.
I brought my lumber home and got a hammer
And saw and nails, and soon our family's carport
Became a mediaeval armory.
I chose a piece of plywood for a shield
And nailed two straps of clothesline on the back
So I could slip my arm through one and grasp
The other in my hand, and hold it firm.
But now I had to have a trusty blade.   220
A two foot length of pressure treated wood
Would do the job. I cut the narrow board
To angles at one end and made a point;
I hammered home a shorter piece of wood
Across the base to make a good hand guard.
Although a sword and shield were normal gear
I still wanted one more appurtenance.
I had to have a mace and chain to swing.
I took a foot long section of wood pole
And nailed a two foot long segment of rope   230
Onto one end. Then I took the rope
And forced it through a soft rubber ball
And tied a sturdy knot at the far end.
Now I had a mace and chain to wield
And clobber any enemy who dared
Assault my knighthood or impugn my honor.

Book IV

Many afternoons I played with Jim;
He brought his sword and shield along with him
And we did noble battle in my yard.
I swung that mace (as David must have swung   240
His sling when he stood, small, against Goliath)
Around, around, around, through hissing air,
And when the rope could not be seen for speed
I hurled it hard against my challenger.
It slammed against his shield and made a bang
That shook our neighborhood, and so much so
That one good neighbor, who wanted a nap,
Ambled across the street and bade us stop,
But only after we had swung and banged
Our wooden swords athwart strong plywood shields   250
(And mace against a deftly wielded armor)
For over half an hour. We were in truth
Exhausted, and happy to have to stop
But we would hardly say so; *au contraire*,
We moaned about adults who could not know
How carefully we fashioned all our weapons—
How long we labored on them—and how much
Our sport was not just play, but chivalrous.

Our knighthood was the flower of a summer
And then we parted ways more than we knew   260
Because we were assigned to different schools
(He went to West Palm Beach; I went to Lake Worth)
And soon we would encounter other souls
And over time our friendship would decay.
When I was older I would see how normal
That pattern was for us Americans,
And how our mobile nation would encourage
Much that was temporary, so that even
A close friendship could be disposable.

Before that day, however, and while summer   270
Still had a number of hot days to offer,
I hoped that I could make some extra cash
By setting up my own lemonade stand;

Lake Worth and Junior High School

One summer night I lay in bed and reckoned
That I could also add some soda pop,
And keep it chilled, and offer it in bottles.
My mother was at home, and she could help;
She happily provided me some ice
And loaned the family cool box for the sodas.

Our whole village was still under construction   280
And we were just the second family
To have a house completed and move in;
All around us contractors were busy
Laying foundations, setting concrete blocks,
Installing reinforcing rods, and leaving
Rectangular holes in the concrete walls
For doors and awning windows soon to come.
Some of those workmen wandered by our house
And saw the lemonade stand on our lawn
And gladly paid a quarter for a glass,   290
Or for a bottle of cold soda pop
As they stood sweating under a hot sun,
And so my venture prospered for two days;
But after that the novelty wore off
And I abandoned it. I can recall
How on the day after I called it quits
A workman came around the corner, stood
Confused a moment, and looked for the stand
He thought had been there just the day before,
And asked me if the stand was thereabouts;   300
I told him it had been, but I had only
That day abandoned it, and he walked off
Hot, thirsty, and annoyed; I felt ashamed
Because I felt that I had let him down.

Of course I could feel sad, but I could feel
What another poet born in April wrote
A hundred years or more before my birth:
In nature there was nothing melancholy.
An open sky above with sunny clouds,
Those solemn and majestic cumuli   310

Book IV

That stood like giants underneath the moon
(So pure and white under the sun or moon)—
An open sky like that could make me happy
And more than happy as I walked alone
Or with Mother on a nocturnal stroll.

Sometimes on a starry night I stood
And watched the Milky Way, a path of stardust,
Our galaxy then visible above
Because our local populace was small;
No urban glare mounted to hide the stars.   320

One cloudy night I had a sudden shock.
I took the garbage out as usual
And brought a flashlight from the kitchen drawer
To show my way; as I ambled along
I played its narrow beam across the grass.
By chance I turned it upward just in time
To spot a massive web one foot ahead
Spun by a giant spider between bushes
In our back yard. I watched its hairy form
Suspended at the center of the web,   330
And my heart skipped a beat as I stood there,
So grateful I had not walked into it;
Even in my shocked state I could observe
A few small dragonflies and other prey
All hopelessly ensnared in that great web,
Unable to do more than stay and wait
Upon its architect's inexorable pleasure.

In nature there may be no melancholy
But I recall a melancholy mood
One cloudy afternoon as I came home.   340
I was alone, because my mother worked
In West Palm Beach for two insurance salesmen.
On week days after school I made a snack
And read some comic books and maybe watched
The Popeye Show (I loved the old cartoons).
One afternoon I felt lonely and glum,

Lake Worth and Junior High School

So I got on my bicycle and drove
Around our neighborhood, and soon I found
Sandy soda bottles abandoned
By workmen who had gone home for the day.   350
Not many months before I had bought
A basket for my bicycle and as
I saw those empty bottles suddenly
I got a good idea: I would gather
What others left behind and make some money.
I could collect those cast away bottles
And take them to a local gas station
And get a nickel refund for each one,
And so I did. Now after school each day
I picked them up and made some extra money;   360
But once the Palm Springs houses were completed
The carpenters all went to other jobs
And my good source of cash evaporated.

I needed a large basket for my bike
Because I had acquired a paper route,
A small one, close to our home in Palm Springs.
The morning paper was the *Palm Beach Post*,
The evening paper was the *Palm Beach Times*,
And I delivered them six days a week,
And on the seventh, Sunday, I would carry   370
The Sunday morning paper—always fat
Because it was the paper for the day
And full of extra magazines and ads.
In Martins Ferry I had carried papers
For nine short months before we moved away;
But I had learned a lot, and I was ready
To take the challenge of another route:
Today I had to serve more customers
And work at hours that made me feel adult.
At four o'clock every weekday morning   380
A truck drove by and dropped a heavy bundle
Of papers at our corner, that day's *Post*.
I woke up and got out of bed at five,
Put on my clothes and shoes and hastily

75

Book IV

Prepared a hot dog breakfast for my father;
I wrapped the newspapers with rubber bands
And put them in my basket, and drove off.
When I got home my father was long gone
And mother was usually still asleep
So I cooked my own breakfast, wolfed it down   390
And gathered up my school things in a satchel.
Mother was up by then and saw me off
And left for West Palm Beach and her day's work.

I can remember many of those mornings
Before the sun came up, when a full moon
Sank large and creamy in the west
And cast a pale and fading luminescence
Across the pure, cool sand of many lots
Where houses would be built. The yellow orb
Produced a temporary world for me   400
Where palm trees cast their shadows for the moon,
Not for the sun, and where a placid pond
Gave back the moon her image like a mirror
As she floated serenely among clouds
She would soon abandon in the west;
And then the sun rose up and overpowered her,
So opposite, so radiant and hot,
And cast his bolder shadows on the sand.
But for one moment between moon and sun
I saw a world few folks would ever see,   410
A world of subtle shadows that soon passed
Beyond that hour and deep into my soul,
Suspended long in halls of memory.

Although I had a paper route and carried
The world's latest to more than twenty people
So they could have the news in printed form
Our family was never much concerned
About the world's problems; they always seemed
So unresolvable and far away.
We only rarely watched evening broadcasts   420
On the three major networks, and we read

Lake Worth and Junior High School

Our newspaper only occasionally;
There were no cell phones or laptop computers
Or other media for private use.
We knew more about our own neighborhood
Than we did about the latest news
From Washington or Moscow or Berlin.

One family came to Palm Springs before us
And we became good friends. We often shared
A meal—a cookout in our open carport   430
Or pizza made by the Papaleos.
Afterward we played a game of hearts
Around their kitchen table or around
A redwood picnic table in our carport;
We laughed and talked and played the hours away.
Our conversation and our jokes were simple;
No harsh or coarse remark was ever made.
All our antagonism was in the cards.
Dominic Papaleo often tried
To "shoot the moon" and outsmart everyone,   440
Although he seldom made it. I looked on
And saw his plan unfold play by play
As he accumulated hearts and took
The Queen of Spades and surged from goal to goal,
Until his wife destroyed him with one card.
Such evenings became an institution
And soon I found my way among the cards
Until I "shot the moon" (but rarely made it).
The taste of victory was good as was
A sweet release of tension that built up   450
As I labored to capture every card
That counted, on the road to victory.
After two years our card games tapered off
Because the Papaleos opened up
A pizza restaurant in the Farmer's Market
Just north of us on Congress Boulevard.
The pizza they sold there was not as good
As what they made at home because they skimped

Book IV

On some ingredients to make a profit
But that was business, and we understood.   460

The Papaleos owned a mongrel dog
Called Smokey who was black and brown and wandered
In joyful freedom all around Palm Springs.
He had a slender tail that often curved
Upward and wagged unflaggingly because
He was beloved and loved us without pause.
One afternoon as I sat with Granddad
Beside the picnic table in our carport
Smokey wandered across our front sidewalk
And stopped to sniff the base of a royal palm tree.   470
I got my trusty bb gun and just
For our amusement shot his right hind quarter.
He bounded with a startled "ki–yi–yi,"
And ran off down the street. The spectacle
Provoked a storm of laughter from us both
But I loved him and in less than an hour
I found him and made up with him. Although
I knew I caused no harm to his young body
I was profoundly wrong to scare him so.

At once I understood how much a man,   480
By someone called so aptly *homo faber*,
Man the maker, had enormous scope,
Because of his ability to *make*,
To alter any animal's condition
For good or ill depending on his purpose
Or understanding of the power he holds;
And it was wrong for me, a boy with power,
To force my way against the way of nature
And traumatize (for my own idle sport)
An animal so capable of love.   490
Although I garnered much from Dominic
About the game of hearts, I gathered more
From his young dog about the human heart
And when after another month had passed

Lake Worth and Junior High School

A car on Congress Boulevard collided
With Smokey and drove on without remorse
And left his carcass sprawled among sand spurs
A mile away from home I mourned and wept
Along with Dominic, who found the body
And brought it home with sorrow and warm tears.   500

Paradise could become a place of sorrow
Produced by humans who would make it so—
A lesson I would learn as a young man.

Florida could instruct me on the land
But also brought me lessons from the sea.
Her oceanic wisdom tutored me.

Lake Worth public beach was popular,
A twenty minute drive from Palm Springs,
And often I would go there with my folks
Or with a friend and spend an afternoon.   510

On summer days we ran across the sand
As fast as we could go and splashed our feet
In shallow waves, because the sand above
The water line was hot and burned our soles.
I loved the beach: it was stable and warm
And offered a true contrast to an ocean
That was moody and unpredictable
And could be cold below the thermocline;
And yet together they composed a vision
Of sand and water in a close embrace   520
So faithful no power could separate them.

The roll of constant waves enchanted me;
They always brought an offering of shells,
Some broken, some still whole, all beautiful,
And cast them carelessly along the shore
For anyone who wanted to enjoy them.
I often walked and found so many shells

Book IV

I could not take them all, but had to choose
The very best among them.

                I could snorkel
And make my way out to a shallow reef   530
Not many yards from shore and find new treasures—
Conch shells, scotch bonnets and a few small cowries—
And crowds of fish that darted here and there
Silver and luminous in broad daylight.
I passed my hand through undulating weeds,
Some gold, some green, some ochre or burnt umber,
That sprouted from the reef and formed a haven
For inch long fishes who sought refuge there
From larger predators roaming about.
All of them were both predator and prey,   540
Alert and hungry, always on the prowl.

Ocean's menagerie told me a tale
Of coral shallows and a sanguine sea.

One afternoon I played close to the ocean
And built a sand castle I hoped would stand
The ocean's worst assault before I left.

I paused and looked across the placid water
Toward the wooden pier at Lake Worth Beach
And saw a form so large I had to stop
And watch a wonder that slowly arose   550
And glistened in the mid–afternoon sun.
It was a giant brown animal
And looked much like a massive tarpaulin
Only there was more shape: it had a head
And broad wings some forty feet across.
He hung suspended large and motionless
Along one side of the long fishing pier.
More minutes passed and more folks stopped and stared.
Gradually we saw a manta ray
Emerge in slippery solitary splendor   560
As those who stood along the pier combined

Lake Worth and Junior High School

The muscle of a dozen arms to pull
His vast, almost unmanageable bulk.
Another hour's work and they could hold
A large hook that snagged him when alone
And harmless in the water farther out
He swam around the deep end of the dock.
Soon after our newsmen and camera buffs
Had taken all the photographs they wanted
The ones who captured him lowered him slowly   570
And happily he found his element:
He gave a mighty thrash among the waters,
Sank below the waves and swam away.
The next day's *Post* told about the man
Who hooked the manta ray at one a.m.
And battled him two hours all alone
Before others had come and helped him out.
More hours passed before the sun came up
More hours still before those men could see
The dark, gargantuan outline of the monster   580
Whose territory and whose freedom they
Had compromised as they combatted him;
But now he was at large in his vast home
And maybe wiser after his warfare
With one who hooked him, whose small race had built
The wooden pier from which the line was cast.

I was no salt water fisherman
Although I tried my hand one afternoon
Just down the road from Uncle Bob's house.

I sat with Carla on a concrete wall   590
Beside the Intracoastal Waterway.
The sun was high, the water brown and wavy
And we had cast a baited hook and line
As far into the water as we could.
We hoped to catch our first salt water fish;
We sat alone and watched the choppy waves.

Book IV

My aunt had given me a piece of shrimp
And I had sunk my hook deep into it.
Would it become a morsel for a mackerel
Or for a larger fish, a snook maybe,   600
And bless our supper table with a banquet?

We sat and talked and enjoyed the clouds
That floated over Palm Beach east of us.
Twelve years would pass and I would scuba dive
Off Lake Worth Beach and in the Florida Keys
And Carla would be living in Atlanta
But also scuba dive in the Bahamas
With someone she would marry and divorce.
But on that day we were only two cousins
Who sat together on a concrete wall   610
And let our feet dangle above the water
And hoped our bait would lure a goodly fish.

Our vigil was rewarded soon enough.
I felt a tug and saw the rod turn down.
Something obscured by the murky water
Pulled at our hook and would not (or could not)
Surrender it.

        Now I started to work
And spun the reel and after a few moments
A form emerged out of the dark brown water
Almost as dark and brown—as though it had   620
Been compounded of intracoastal water.
It was a toad fish and well named because
It looked almost as though it *was* a toad
With a round torso and a stumpy tail.
Somehow in nature one can often know
Just by a glance at some repulsive form
That to furnish food for human beings
Formed no part of its primordial purpose;
Our fish was such a one although we found
A decade later that someone who broadcast   630
Evening news about the day's sport fishing

Lake Worth and Junior High School

Concocted a new recipe he dubbed
"Tasty Toadies" for his audience.
He told us every night *who* had caught *what*
And what local inlet welcomed their catch.
When mother caught her sailfish he announced it
And we all squealed with pleasure when we heard
Her name broadcast to all of the Palm Beaches
As we sat down around the supper table
At uncle Bob's after we had returned   640
From that day's fishing trip. Some twelve years later
When our family moved back to Florida
I saw he had a television program
And showed fresh photographs from Boynton Inlet
And also from the inlet at Palm Beach:
Photos of people standing by board walls
Where all the fish they caught were hung on spikes
And dripped cold blood—a photogenic catch,
And happy smiles adorned the anglers' faces.
A few years after that the program ended   650
Because the host had gunned his motor launch
And careered dangerously around the harbor
In West Palm Beach. He was so full of liquor
He thought he could do whatever he wanted.

A year or so in Florida had made
A different boy of me—a boy who loved
The broad Atlantic and her many moods
And waves that rolled reliably and would
Cast shells upon the sand for me to choose;
She also caused the underwater plants   660
To sway luxuriously back and forth
For local fish who darted in and out
And found safe harbor in those sea weed jungles.
I loved the sandy shore where I could be
An architect of sumptuous sand castles
And coastal cities fortified with walls
Multiple inches thick that could withstand
The warm, relentless waves before at last

Book IV

Collapsing and subsiding into nothing
As water swirled around and overcame 670
(After a long, inexorable assault)
Any construction that would take a stand
Against the constant power of the sea.

I had been told she was formidable;
I had not seen the ocean in her power.
I simply loved her as a part of nature.

Because she had such beauty and such power
I could not help but fall in love with her.

I loved the sand, the palm trees and the sky
Almost as though they were a part of me. 680

A year in Florida had set me free,
Had given me a sense of open borders—
A landscape open to a southern sky—
A world of sun and clouds and forms of beauty
Unknown to me before but now adored.

The palm fronds seemed to rattle in the breeze
For me on winter nights; the moon shone full
For me, and sailed among cumulus towers
And cast a silver glory on the landscape
Before the sun came up and washed my soul. 690

The sun bathed Florida in light and warmth
And showed a landscape of unequalled forms—
Of passing beauty unsurpassed—for me.

All nature lay before me, and it seemed
An obvious conclusion that for me
All nature was the present and the future.

Although I had not put it into words
Or thought of it as a philosophy,
I wanted to be one with frond and sand

Lake Worth and Junior High School

I wanted to be one with cloud and sea. 700
I was at home with them more than I thought.
I had no other home or other place
To be, or want to be. I was in love,
And moved in love among my elements
Of earth and sky and sea, all tropical
And all as constant as the sun or moon.

Book V

A Florida Boyhood

O Muse, conjure my aquatic days,
Aquamarine days at Palm Beach.
The noon sun blazed as I sat on the sand
Above the water and absorbed it all:
A sunny strand of subtropical leisure,
A friendly public shore populated
By tanning Snowbirds and Florida crackers,
Adults who came to spend an afternoon
And boys and girls all bronze and full of play.
As starfish scattered on the ocean floor   10
Seem to lie in harmony with nature
So people lay on the open sand
Scattered at random under a hot sun
As cooling waves pulsed along the shore,
Every thought in harmony with All
(If any thought beneath a torrid sun).
In Eisenhower's day a public pier
Stood upon the spot. Man and boy
Combatted rod and reel against all sharks,
Amberjacks, bonita, manta rays,   20
Stingrays, pompano and barracuda,
Jack Cravalle, porgies and guitarfish

Book V

Who were our local submarine companions.
I was a youth and saw it as a youth.

O Muse, conjure my aquatic days,
Aquamarine days at Lake Worth.
At noon the sand was hot so I ran
Across the beach and comforted each sole
In cool and welcome shallows. Orange snorkel
And Squalé mask in hand and Cressi fins   30
I saw among the waters vast and calm
That asked me to attend and sample all
True joy. I was a true Sea Hunt boy
Young and full of adventure.

                        Mask and fins
And snorkel on I sank and swam along
A shallow reef. I saw another land,
Abodes of coral contour old and soft
And green with algae, Davy Jones' suburbs.
Solar rays, watery and bland,
Glanced off myriads who swam along,   40
Sea minnows and some baby barracuda
Who darted in and out of nooks and crannies
Always goaded on by appetite
Or *Angst*. I saw them all and swept my hand
Among them and my joy was unalloyed.

I swam toward the rocks and saw a lobster,
A so-called Florida lobster without claws,
Ochre and still under a slimy outcrop,
Antennae hanging limply as he rested.
Aroused, I swam ashore, pounding water.   50
I ran across the sand, snatched a towel
And ran back, splashing as I came.
I plunged into the sea, towel in tow.
What a rare trophy he would make
What a reputation I would have
What a glory for my father's table
When I brought him home. So I swam:

A Florida Boyhood

My towel dragged and my young pulse pounded
As I wondered how to lure him out,
A noble young crustacean, from his home   60
(Or catch him unaware while he dozed).
He was soundly in his habitat.
I was an intruder full of hope
Who lacked the strong counsel of the old.
Still I took him on, and I was cagey.
I grabbed his languid tail from behind
But suddenly he was a dynamo.
Armored musculature hard at work
He thrashed, and yanked, and swam away. Amazed
I stood up dripping and alone, a towel   70
And one forlorn antenna in my hand.
All was over and I waded back
Awash with loss and strong embarrassment.
My catch was one abandoned antenna.
What a rare trophy it would make.
What a reputation I would have.
What a glory for my father's table
When I brought it home.

I sought my own salvation in the sea.
I was young; I had no understanding.   80
I was a budding hedonist who found
A land of cabbage palms and sun and sand
And thought it was all good and all for me.
Under a full moon beside the sea
Palm fronds made faint music in the breeze
And blue Atlantic in a tropical mood
Lay like a woman warm and amorous
Who had accepted me and would accept
And take me in a tender, deep embrace
Forever. And forever was enough.   90
Forever was a mood, and I was young.

One ordinary evening with my folks
I shopped around in West Palm Beach
And saw a telescope, a small refractor.

Book V

It cost as much as I made in a year
From household chores and my small paper route
But soon I was a boy astronomer.
One balmy evening as I went outside
To set my telescope up in our driveway
A crescent moon floated overhead.   100
When I looked through the ocular I saw
Enormous craters, some with central peaks
Whose sharp shadows lay on the lunar floor
And mountain ranges, vast by earthly standards,
Also umbrageously articulated.
Lady Diana was so opulent
Magnified that night by telescope!
She was a goddess; I was an explorer
Enamored of a pale and distant world.
She never saw decay (or hardly ever)   110
Upon her holy surface. She was such stuff
As dreams are made of on a summer night
When flush with the horizon she arose
And lay upon the waters far away
For couples lost in love to gaze upon.

I was young and was a true romantic
Although I was not yet aware of it.

I turned a bold refractor on the sky
And sought to master all the Pleiades
And probe Andromeda's far galaxy   120
Shaped like a flying saucer full of suns.
I saw Orion's sword and nebula
(Formed like a horse's head and dark as coal
Among a blaze of interstellar gasses
Illuminated by the stars behind them).
I found Trapezium, a group of stars
Millions of decades younger than our sun,
A trapeze for some lofty acrobat
To sway under a sublime cosmic tent.
I located two double stars that orbit   130
A common center locked into a dance

A Florida Boyhood

So gradual they looked frozen in space.
I saw globular clusters close to us,
Those densely packed balls of stars that seem
Pale snowballs framed against the dark of space.
I noted carefully all that I found
And drew them as I saw them—galaxies,
Star clusters, double stars and nebulae—
And made a notebook of my observations.

Astronomy opened a door for me   140
To all I ever hoped for or imagined.
My soul was full of science fiction stories.
I longed for travel far beyond our globe.
I would gladly have explored other worlds
And many winter nights as I observed
A heaven full of wonders far away
A huge frustration, almost agony,
Consumed my soul because I knew that I
Was born before those voyages could be,
Though late enough to know that they *could* be   150
In some far distant future, granted only
That *Homo Sapiens* (so proudly named)
Could manage in his slow Darwinian progress
To blast from swamp to stars and not to blast
Our world and all our hopes into the dark.

In Florida I also came to love
The art of cinema in certain forms.
A world of older movies came to me
On television. In those simple days
We only had the three major networks   160
And not all stations broadcast round the clock;
But late at night some stations showed old movies.
I was too young to stay up very late
But once I was a few years older, then
I got to see some films my mother saw
When she was just a girl in Martins Ferry.
I also went to local theaters.
I saw *King Kong* with Jimmy Graham once

Book V

(For the first time) and watched in blank amazement
To see what cinematic art had done 170
So long ago and with so few resources.
I watched a lot of science fiction movies
And horror movies, too, and soon I made
A record of the ones I got to see
In one black, marbled composition book.
The drama and the science of those movies
(Or quasi science) captivated me
And gave my soul some potent images.

On Sunday afternoons in Miami
M. T. Graves sat in a gloomy dungeon 180
Under the aerial of Channel 7
And broadcast horror movies to the young
Across south Florida. Boys such as I
Could watch a bat afloat in a boudoir
Flap, until its wings became a cloak,
And watch a small dark form become a man—
Bela Lugosi as Count Dracula.

I saw Dracula movies old and new
And soon they came together in my thought
And formed an ideal Dracula collage. 190

I saw the Count advance toward his love,
A woman young, asleep, and unaware.
He crouched slowly beside her, bared her throat
And gazed upon her. Now those ancient eyes
Glowed with a fierce, immortal appetite.
About to taste her blood, his face aghast,
The noble Transylvanian staggered back.
He lifted up his cloak and turned away.
Around the woman's throat a magic charm,
A golden cross, had done a holy work 200
And shocked the ghastly suitor from his course.
Count Dracula, abashed but not undone,
Approached once again and made his cloak
A wall between himself and that gold cross.

In low seductive tones he wooed his lady
And moved her by his eloquence to loose
Her one defense. Enchanted fingers moved
And fumbled at the latch and soon the cross
And chain slid soundlessly under the covers.
Count Dracula advanced with a smile   210
And bared his canine fangs and sank them deep
Into her throat and drank his fill; and soon
He owned her and now she was like her lord,
Not dead, but undead. I looked on enthralled
As Harker and van Helsing tracked him down
From smoggy alleys of Victorian London
Across the waves and mountains to Romania
And Castle Dracula, that stood alone
Above a foggy valley by full moon.
I saw the coffin lid undone, I saw   220
The fatal shafts of dawn land hot upon
That pallid face, I saw those eyes of hate;
I saw Jonathan Harker raise his mallet
And watched a hammer and a wooden stake
Undo the spell of centuries. I saw
The body age and crumble into dust
In seconds, and I saw Count Dracula
Become a story to amuse the young.

After I saw the movie, *Dracula*,
I bought the book and was soon taken in.   230
Bram Stoker was a master of his craft.
He portrayed what no author ever had
As though it were a palpable occurrence
A good observer could report to us
Such as a scene where Dracula crawled down
The castle wall by moonlight like a fly
Or like a spider as Jon Harker watched
Almost unable to believe his eyes.
Although I loved the book that did not make
Me emulate (or try to emulate)   240
What Stoker had accomplished in his novel.
I scribbled science fiction now and then

Book V

(Mostly in study hall when I was bored)
But I was more a watcher than a writer
And I always looked forward to next Sunday
When I could watch "The Dungeon" on TV.

Boris Karloff played the man-made monster
In *Frankenstein* (I only read the book
Years later as a Harvard graduate student).
Lon Chaney Junior would become the *Wolf Man*; 250
I saw his facial hair grow wild and wolfish
And then his fangs grow long, and heard a poem
That echoed in my soul: "Even a man
Who's pure of heart and says his prayers by night
Can become a werewolf when the sun goes down
And the moon shines full and bright." I always hoped
He would be cured, but that was not to be.
Only a silver bullet could redeem
A man who had become a lycanthrope
And it could only save him by a shot 270
That ended both the man and wolf at once.
As he passed on his wolfish hairs receded,
His fangs vanished, and he became a man—
The man he was before the curse had found him;
So now he could be buried as a human
And mourned as one who had returned to us.

The motion picture industry made me
An acolyte. In West Palm Beach the Surf,
The Florida and the Palms were holy temples:
Movie theaters where I often went 280
To see the newest works of William Castle
And Hammer Films—and also humbler products
Such as the latest movies from Japan:
Godzilla, Rodan, and a horde of monsters
Somehow connected to the atom bomb.

There never was a monster like Godzilla,
Larger than any known dinosaur.
Godzilla shook the landscape as he walked

A Florida Boyhood

And kicked Tokyo to shreds like rotten cardboard.
Atomic exhalation came from him   290
And melted power lines and made them droop
And set large storage tanks of oil or gas
Ablaze and turned the waterfront to cinders.
The armor and the rockets of Japan
Assaulted the gargantuan in vain:
Godzilla just became the more enraged
When any bomb or rocket flashed and burst
Around him (they could never do him harm).
Japan had formed a cautionary tale
Out of her own misfortune for us all.   300
Our human race had climbed out of the swamps
And found a power just penultimate—
Atomic power that could blow us up
Or could produce a monster like Godzilla.

"What hath God wrought," asked Alexander Bell.
"What hath man wrought," asked one Japanese movie
And had no answer, though it posed the question.

With every horror movie I took in
I saw my young imagination grow
Almost as though I gave it food and drink   310
(Although I had not done so as a plan).

I loved especially the combination
Of concepts old and new, in thoughtful ways
Never before attempted in a film.

One movie struck me as a work of art
Far more than any other in my youth.
I watched with joy as Henry Frankenstein
Worked in a modern, secret laboratory
Housed in a windmill from the Middle Ages.
He laid a stone cold body on a table   320
And carefully secured the hands and feet
With manacles, and placed electrodes where
They had to be in order to assure

Book V

The lifeless body—body not a corpse
Because it had not died, nor yet a babe
Because it was not configured by God
Within the womb of an expectant mother
But by a man in his rash arrogance
Compounded out of human body parts—
Would get a surcharge of electric voltage   330
Strong enough to make it come alive.
I gawked entranced as he tossed a switch
And incandescent bolts arced through the air
Between two Van de Graff generators.
An ancient watchtower was rocked and shaken
By modern power unimaginable
To those who had constructed those stone walls
So many centuries before. And now
A monster came to life and raised a hand,
Opened its eyes and saw a brave new world,   340
One it had never looked upon before.
The doctor almost lost his mind with joy
At what he had accomplished and he shouted
As though the world could hear him, "It's alive!"
And very soon the world would come to know
What Frankenstein had done as a new creature
Stumbled among the vales and villages
Of Germany, unstoppable by man,
And wrought a bloody vengeance on our race.
One man had made it but that man had not   350
The wisdom or the character to love it.
Young Frankenstein had hoped to make a god
Or demigod—a higher form of human;
But out of body parts and borrowed brain
He made a monster, and a monstrous end.

His story was a cautionary tale
Appropriate to Romantic Germany—
A land of castles from the Middle Ages,
Of Father Rhine and ancient Mosel vineyards,
But also populated by a folk   360
Of many talents who would soon produce

An elevated culture in the vanguard
Of science and technology in Europe
And in the world. So Mary W. Shelley,
Who wrote the book, produced a prophecy
(Though such was not her intent) of a people
Who would step forth like Frankenstein and fashion
Out of a land of old Romantic notions,
Out of a land of Zeppelins and rockets,
A new colossus to bestride the world.   370

Only as an adult would I discover
How formative a role Germany played
In modern life and culture, and what danger
Reposed in people of enormous talents.
As I grew older I would come to love
The music of Beethoven and of Brahms
And Wagner's operas and read Kant and Nietzsche
And understand the German contribution
To modern physics, industry, and war—
Max Planck and Krupp and Messerschmitt and Hitler—   380
But now I was a youth who saw a film
Drawn from a book that was a prophecy.

I had a friend named Rodney Politano.
I met him in sixth grade at Meadow Park.
Because his house was not so far away
We got to know each other well. We rode
To Lake Worth Junior High on the same school bus.
One evening as we stood outside my house
And talked and wondered how to pass an hour
An orange ball of flame ascended slowly   390
Above the distant lights of West Palm Beach.
I thought it had to be a UFO
And ran indoors to grab my telescope;
Although it was an awkward job I managed
To nudge the telescope through our front door.
I stood it on its tripod and could see
The ball had arced much higher; its color
Had mutated from orange to white; it moved

Book V

Much faster with a flattened trajectory.
Father had taught me how a shooter ought   400
To gauge a mobile target's speed and aim
Somewhere ahead of it to hit the mark;
So I took care and moved my telescope
Ahead of what I saw, and soon enough
The ball of flame swam into view for me.
But what I saw surprised me—not a ball
Of flame but only a broad fan of white
Powerful exhaust that flowed from small hot spots
I had not seen before; as I observed
The ample fan began to dissipate   410
And suddenly a burst of fire above it
Showed me the motor of a second stage
Had now ignited and assumed the job
Of transporting a payload into space.
I watched the rocket vanish into darkness,
And told poor Rodney what I had observed
Because it had unfolded much too fast
For me to share the view with him—I offered
The ocular to him once I had seen
The stages separate but he was no   420
Astronomer and unfamiliar with
The telescope and all of its controls
And never could have tracked the soaring missile
As it pursued a course into the dark.

When I folded my papers the next morning
I saw an article on the front page
About a missile launch from Cape Canaveral:
The Air Force had launched a "Jupiter C"
(A large ballistic missile) far down range
To plunge somewhere into the south Atlantic—   430
A trial made for national defense.

I was more privileged than I could fathom
To be a dweller in south Florida
Where I could watch a drama in the heavens:
Faustian man threw flame and thunder upward

And brought unnatural luminescence there.
He tore apart the solitude of night.
South Florida was now my habitat
And all I had to do was walk outside
And look toward the north to see a wonder 440
Of human accomplishment in our day
For rocketry had made it possible
To hurl an atom bomb against a foe
But also gave us hope that we could flee
Earth's gravity and put someone in orbit
Or one day put a man on the moon.

Not long after Grandma was under ground
Granddad had sold his home, left Martins Ferry,
And moved to Florida to stay with us.
He bought some bushes and small trees for us 450
And planted them around our house. Our yard
Soon underwent a happy transformation,
Full of accents and color. We were glad
To see him so engaged with earth and plants
Because they would bear fruit and had a future.
Granddad also purchased a strong cane pole
And reckoned he would catch some southern fish.
He was not interested in ocean fishing
Maybe because the ocean was so large
And not a place he was accustomed to. 460
But soon he found a comfortable spot
At Lake Osborne a couple of miles away
From Palm Springs—a public lake where people
Could swim and waterski or catch a fish.

In Florida in those days whoever owned
A cane pole could go fish without a license
So Granddad got a long cane pole, some hooks,
Some fishing line and corks and a sharp knife.
He located a gas station that sold
Large earthworms in white cardboard canisters 470
For fifty cents a canister. He bought
A couple and drove off with me to try

Book V

Our luck at catching something in Lake Osborne.
I owned a cane pole, too, and Saturdays
We drove together to our lake and parked
Beneath a cluster of Australian pines,
Baited our hooks and cast them in the water.
We caught a lot of blue gills there and later
When I had money from my paper route
I bought a rod and reel and thought I would   480
Try to hook a catfish. Granddad taught me
To bait my hook with rotten chicken liver
(A delicacy for your local catfish)
And after that I caught my share of them:
Mud catfish, channel catfish—and one time
I caught a turtle (not what I had wanted),
A slider who had scrounged around the bottom
And found the rotten liver to his taste.
When I took him slowly off the hook
He turned his head and bit me on the finger.   490
I tossed him in the water in a hurry
And I was glad to watch him go back under
But I would carry on my index finger
A strong impression his young beak had made,
A memory of him for years to come.

One sunny summer afternoon we sat
Beside the lake and watched our corks for hours:
The afternoon was lazy and the fish
Must have been lazy, too, because our corks
Sat motionless upon the dark brown water.   500

My father thought that fishing was moronic
Because you sat so long and only waited
And hoped some random fish would come along
And take an interest in your soggy bait.
That afternoon I found I understood
His attitude, because it was a chore
To sit and sweat under the summer sun
With all my soul focused on one small cork.

A Florida Boyhood

I looked around and saw a cloud or two
That floated very slowly over us   510
And then I looked across the lake and saw
A stand of pine trees on the farther shore;
They stood breathless that sultry afternoon.

I finally looked once more toward the water.
Our favorite spot for fishing at Lake Osborne
Had one small concrete wall. I sat there now,
My feet above the water as I mused
And watched my cork; but as I hung my head
And stared below me suddenly I saw
A water moccasin meander by,   520
Dappled and beautiful below the surface
An inch or two under my naked feet.
I saw his head, flat and triangular,
So full of venom and so full of death
And suddenly could sense that I was mortal.
I did not want to inhale or exhale
Because I did not want to make a sound.
How could something so deadly be so lovely?
I did not care; I did not want to know.
I only sat as still as I could be   530
And watched the serpent form meander past
Until it disappeared in dark brown water.

The water in Lake Osborne was so brown
Because of tannin in the plants; but I
Was told that in the intracoastal portions
It had become dark brown because men dredged
White sand that formed the underwater bottom
And uncovered an old organic substrate
That turned the water brown as it seeped upward.

Brown water told a story on the land.   540
On any ordinary avenue
Of West Palm Beach, or Palm Beach, or Lake Worth,
Sidewalks turned reddish brown and looked Floridian
Whenever someone dug a well to water

Book V

A lawn from Florida's artesian springs.
The water that came up was iron rich
And after many months of watering
Any lawn would grow robust, and sidewalks
Would turn a dark red brown because the iron
Deposited by all that surfaced water   550
Would rust under the hot Florida sun.

After a couple of years in our new home
My parents thought it would be a good move
If we, too, sank a well for our own lawn
Because it was a waste to use tap water
To water grass. My father telephoned
A local drilling company, and soon
We had a well some two hundred feet deep
And ready to pump water on demand.
Our apartment on Walton Boulevard   560
Had been supplied with well water; at school
All of the fountain water was from wells;
Although I loved the word, artesian,
I had a strong distaste for any water
That came from underground in Florida
Because it was so strong. It had a flavor
Half rotten and half bitter, and it made
Our kitchen sinks and water fountain basins
Turn reddish brown and look just like our sidewalks.

Our well provided ample water for us   570
And made our lawn so effortlessly green
(Even through the most torrid summer weather)
That we were glad to have it. Only rarely
Loose sand would clog the filter far below
The surface and our pump would not produce.
My father had to blow the sand away
And he would ask a worker at Bellhouse
To loan him a bolt action .22.
He stood above the back yard access pipe
And aimed the rifle carefully straight down;   580
One gentle squeeze, and Bang! a bullet found

A Florida Boyhood

The filter far below and blew away
The sand that clogged it. Once or twice my father
Was blasted by a sudden jet of water
That shot back up the pipe as he stood over it:
He could not jump away in time to dodge
A shower from the water he had freed.

Our home was now a Florida home in truth:
My grandfather had planted many plants
Indigenous to Florida or the tropics— 590
Yellow hibiscus and pink oleanders,
Young ficus trees with bark that peeled like paper
Or like papyrus (and as we were warned
The sap was poisonous), a banana tree
That gave us hands of Florida bananas,
And evergreens that guarded our front door.
He added, at the corners of our lot,
Two royal palms that would grow straight and tall
And stand majestic in the years to come;
And now to crown it all a subtle rust 600
Had just begun to show up on the sidewalk
That curved around our fruitful property.
After a decade, as I was to see,
Our pavement would become dark reddish brown
And look as well established and as old
As any length of pavement in Palm Beach,
Or West Palm Beach, or Lake Worth, or Lantana.

A young, transplanted man, I was secure
And happy in my subtropical soil.
I loved the waters of south Florida: 610
Artesian waters for a healthy lawn
And waters of Lake Osborne full of fish
And the long Intracoastal Waterway—
Salt water full of toadfish, starfish, snook
And other fish that swam the ocean paths.

I flourished in a land of many waters
Almost as though those waters watered me

Book V

And made me one with that wet molecule
From which all life arose in ancient oceans.

I could have made a poem or a song   620
To Florida, garden subtropical,
So full of water—from the Everglades
(River of alligators, snakes and sawgrass)
To the Atlantic or the Caribbean
And Gulf of Mexico—peninsula
Surrounded by the flow of many waters,
Full of abundant life and formed for us,
Well watered people of south Florida.

Book VI

Paradise and Old Masters

Paradise lost, how can I sing of you?
How many hours under silver moons
How many hours under torrid suns
How many hours at the water's edge
Or hours underwater among corals
That look like human brains or branch like trees
For wary fish or men to swim among,
How many hours form a human soul
For Paradise and qualify a man
To sing of what can never come again?   10
I sing of one who came and walked in beauty
And passed away into the halls of memory,
A museum that holds her now forever
Complete and unpolluted by our world.

Is she more valuable now to me
Because she cannot fade from memory?

I could not understand back in those days
How rapidly the work of human commerce
Would make her gaudy and transform her soul

Book VI

From something simple yet ineffable
To something full of crude vulgarity,
A state of crime—drug traffic, prostitution,
Murder, abuse, and rape, and rapine, too,
As men fulfilled a mandate to subdue
The world around them, but in such a way
As to undo the world they would subdue.

I ponder such matters as now, a man,
I understand them better, even see them
For what they are; but then I was a youth,
Who thought that he was coming up on manhood,
As biologically he was; yet he
Was still so much a boy that he imagined
All that he saw around him would endure.

Her beauty was both natural and social
As humans balanced their environment,
Lived happily within it, and developed
A world of pleasant lawns and fruitful trees,
A world of angling and of deep sea fishing,
A world of snorkeling and of scuba diving—
A world so human and so natural
That every day seemed like a celebration
Of Adam's place in that subtropical garden.

One morning as my uncle drove me home
After a stay with him at Coral Gables
I looked and saw a mass of remote clouds,
Cumulus towers; one after another
They marched like purple giants dark and huge
Against a pale blue heaven in the east.
A golden fringe of sunshine bordered them
As (far beyond) the sun above the sea
Cast morning splendor over all it touched.
The beauty and the power of that moment
Endowed it with the stature of a vision:
I saw the splendor of a rack of clouds
More grand and lofty than our architecture,

Paradise and Old Masters

More vibrant and alive than human art,
More full of power and movement than some souls—
Almost as though those clouds were giants in truth
And marched across the sky to forestall dawn
And tower above man, and show how they 60
Could blot the sun and cast their shadows long
Over the human landscape far below.

That was a holy moment for my soul:
I loved those clouds; I gazed upon them long,
As though by looking I could make them stay
Suspended in a purple majesty
That was so superhuman and dramatic . . .
But now they live in memory alone
For their tall march was ended long ago.

I loved to look at cloudscapes as a boy, 70
From puffy clouds above the Ohio Valley
On summer days as I sat on our porch
To cumulonimbus clouds in Florida—
Those masses that could float above the sea
And form gigantic towers in just moments
And flatten into anvils at the top.

One afternoon on Lake Worth's sunny shore
I waded in the shallows and could see
Thin silver fishes dart around my feet,
Illuminated by refracted sun; 80
Then suddenly a shadow overcame us
And I noticed a giant overhead
And not far off. Cumulonimbus rose
And warned us by the gusts he conjured up:
He would advance and rain all over us.
He gathered warm air unto his flat base
And sucked it upward and it made him strong.
Puffs of white cloud erupted loftier
And dazzled those below who watched him grow—
A titan who flexed muscles nebulous 90

Book VI

As he pursued a course inexorable
And bound to flood our overpowered shore.

I grabbed my mask and plunged into the waves
Because I wanted to be underwater
And observe from a spot below the surface
When he poured down upon us from above,
Warm cloudy water pounding on the ocean.

I worked my hands and feet to stay below
And my back touched the sand; then I looked up.
Rain drops began to fall and pelt the surface,   100
A thousand watery dimples. They appeared
And disappeared and were as soon replaced
By many more that vanished in their turn,
An endless rush of drops onto a surface
Metallic gray because the cloud above
Was gray and somber as he dropped his load—
Almost like numerous small envoys—
Droplets from heaven joining ocean water
And losing their identity among
Extensive acres of the salty deep.   110
I could have owned it as a metaphor:
A boy who came from upper atmosphere
And who could fancy he communed with heaven
Was fated to be one with salty shallows,
Communicant with Florida's warm sea.

For anyone to be at one with ocean
A snorkel or a scuba tank would serve.
On Saturdays I loved to watch Lloyd Bridges
Who played Mike Nelson in a show called *Sea Hunt*
About a brave and mature scuba diver   120
And his superb adventures underwater.
We only owned a back and white TV
But I could still enjoy the panoramas
Of underwater wonder as my hero
Combatted any malevolent foe
Among dark stands of kelp or far offshore,

Paradise and Old Masters

Or helped a stranded diver find a refuge
After his boat had sunk, as both of them
Attempted to avoid a killer whale.
Mike Nelson always was a good man   130
Above the water or below the waves.
I was an avid follower of his
And as I watched I gathered lore about
The sea and scuba diving, and I hoped
One day to emulate him and to have
Adventures of my own with Davy Jones.

Another day I snorkeled at Lake Worth
And swam along in warm and lucid shallows;
I saw the ocean floor had sandy waves
That undulated far off in the distance   140
And soon were lost in deeper, darker water.
The vista made my heart work doubly hard
Because a sudden fear came over me
Of ocean depths I had never explored,
A prospect I found dangerous and somber.

In shallow water I looked downward now
And saw the ocean floor close to my hand.
I focused on its sunlit, wavy sand,
And saw it was in fact a mirror image,
A copy of the waves that passed above.   150
I was astounded that those waves could do
A godlike act and transform the loose crystals
Below them into sandy undulations,
An image of themselves as they passed over.

I thrusted forward with blue Cressi fins
And forced my youthful body to move faster
Than any man could do with just bare feet.
Then two small bumps (or maybe two small stones)
Came into view only four feet below
Half buried on the beige ocean floor.   160
I slipped below the surface and went down
To have a closer look. I poked and probed

Book VI

And hoped to loosen them from where they rested
But suddenly a sandy cloud erupted
And made the water murky all around.
Slowly the water cleared and I was shocked.
The objects were not stones—they were aware;
They were the eyes of a disgruntled stingray
Who bolted from the sand (where he had burrowed
To take a postprandial nap, maybe) 170
And whipped his tail around and up and down
While warily, but also languidly,
He flapped away toward the deeper water.
He looked much like a large aquatic bat
Or underwater version in our day
Of Pterodactyls who once soared above
And ruled the atmosphere of our young earth.
I was grateful I had not encountered
The wonderful but dangerous animal
At closer quarters, and that I had come 180
Upon him from the front and not the back;
For if I had come at him from the back
He could well have lashed out and wounded me
And even brought about a sudden end
Because he had a barb that he could sink
With brutal power into a careless foe.

My granddad had once hooked a young stingray
Shortly after he moved to Florida.
One sunny afternoon in late September
He stood hard by the shore and cast his line 190
Far out into the murky Intracoastal.
He passed most of that sultry afternoon
Under the dappled sun and shade provided
By large Australian pines and cabbage palms
And at the end his patience was rewarded.
He felt a tug. His rod began to bend.
Granddad was sure that he had hooked a fish.
Soon he would reel it in and win a supper
Out of the dark brown waters of Lake Worth.
But Florida surprised an interloper 200

From the Ohio Valley who had come
To show his prowess in her waterway.
My Grandfather was ignorant of stingrays,
So he did not know what to make of one.
It was not like a catfish or a bluegill
Or any sort of carp, or bass, or trout,
Or other goodly fish that he had seen.
One look could tell him it was truly ugly
And probably not very good for supper.
But that was all he got—one startled look—   210
Before he felt a whiplash, and a sting
That filled his chest with sudden agony.
Some helpful standers by and anglers
Severed the helpless stingray from its stinger;
They drove Grandfather to a hospital
And soon a good physician took the barb
And cleaned the wound and bandaged it so well
Granddad recovered rapidly and then
Could laugh with us around the supper table
About the odd encounter he had had.   220

Florida's untamed nature could harbor
Stingrays and other dangers for a man
But that would not deter my love for her.

She captured my whole adolescent soul:
Her pale, flat landscape was a Song of songs;
Her warm Atlantic was a love affair.
I doted on the clouds that floated over;
They watered us or just adorned the sky.

As a young man I loved not only nature
But also all the good that books could show me.   230
One lazy summer day I strolled around
Lake Worth and in her public library;
I came across a book by Donald Keyhoe
About a topic strange and new to me:
Unidentified Flying Objects, or
UFOs for short. Keyhoe had been

Book VI

A major of Marines and had become
A thought-provoking author on the topic:
He gave accounts of flying saucers, told
By reputable officers and pilots, 240
All trained observers in our armed forces,
And also by police, highway patrolmen
And public and commercial airline crews
Who saw unusual objects up above
And dared to talk about them and report them.
He got to know the Air Force officers
Commissioned to study the UFOs.

The U.S. government had a project dubbed
"Bluebook" located at Dayton, Ohio
(An air base where Mother had been employed 250
As secretary to an Air Force colonel
Shortly before the end of World War II).
The project sought to understand what caused
So many to observe phenomena
Cigar shaped, saucer shaped, or more globose,
And how those apparitions could perform
Phenomenal maneuvers over us.
Although they were officially "unknown"
Almost anyone on the street you asked
Could say what UFOs were thought to be. 260

I read about the day that Kenneth Arnold,
A private pilot over Oregon,
Saw silver saucers coast around the mountains
Just like a squad of war planes in formation
One year after the end of World War Two.
Arnold's account produced a small sensation
And afterward the volume of reports
Began to swell as, all over the country,
Numerous folk who never heard of him
Or saw his story in the newspapers 270
Reported unknown objects overhead.
In those hot summer months I read a lot
While I sat in a chaise lounge in our carport

And sipped iced tea and turned page after page
And got an education on the topic;
I even wrote some letters to the Air Force
And asked for information about saucers.

Far more than any other UFO story
One close encounter seemed, to me, substantial:
A pursuit over Washington, D.C.   280
Capitol radars had triangulated
A group of UFOs above the city.
Our Air Force interceptors took the air
To locate and if possible force down
Any unusual airfoils they encountered.
The fighter pilots saw seven round objects
And radioed them but got no response;
Once they offered chase those luminous discs
Veered away abruptly at right angles
And flew off faster than the speed of sound.   290
Two summer nights in 1952
The same scenario played out—the same
Triangulation and the same pursuit
And just the same result: our fighter planes
Embarrassingly outperformed by something
No one could understand but that the Air Force
Accounted for as temperature inversions
When asked to give a public explanation.

I even built a UFO detector,
A foolish thing I read about somewhere.   300
It used a magnet, battery, and doorbell
Connected by some naked copper wires.
The wires were organized so that if ever
A strong magnetic force passed over us
The magnet would respond and sway around
And make its wire touch another wire
So that the doorbell rang and gave a warning.
Whoever had prepared the prototype
UFO detector obviously thought
The UFOs had magnetic propulsion   310

Book VI

And that made sense to me; so I made one.
I took it to our science fair that winter
At Lake Worth Junior High and when the judges
Asked after me and asked me to declare
The purpose of my unusual submission
I enthusiastically told them about it;
But once they understood the apparatus
They all thanked me politely and moved off.

During that final year in junior high school
I saw *The Time Machine* starring Rod Taylor, 320
A movie based on H. G. Wells' novel;
The movie made me want to read the book.
I bought a copy of my own downtown
And devoured it one summer afternoon.
It was a bold and fascinating story
Although it was so dark: it showed a world
Where ice and snow had covered all the land
As earth slowly rotated underneath
The glow of a dull, moribund red giant
(For that was what our sun had then become) 330
And in that most unfavorable *milieu*
All human life on earth had passed away
And life itself would soon no longer be
As anyone could tell who read the book.
Although I shunned his vision of our future
I loved the author who had thought it up
And wanted to read more of what he wrote.

Science fiction would become for me
Religion. I collected paperbacks
And made a small library in my bedroom. 340

Once a week, on Friday, we ate out
At Morrison's, a cafeteria
In downtown Lake Worth. I would leave the row
Of folks lined up outside the restaurant
And go exploring in a small newsstand
Across an alley. The newsstand became

Paradise and Old Masters

A favorite haunt of mine for I could browse
A wall of science fiction paperbacks
All new to me and sometimes if the gods
Favored my youthful hunt for fantasy, 350
A book by Wells. I bought such novels as
War of the Worlds and *When the Sleeper Wakes*
And an anthology of his short stories.
More than my parents knew I loved to go
Downtown to Lake Worth and to Morrison's
Because the food was good, but even more,
Because I would be able to explore
My favorite shop and with any luck
Add to a growing library at home.

Above all other authors I loved Wells. 360
I loved the flow of words that he produced.
He fashioned narratives so cultivated
And urbane that I stood in admiration.
His prose was holy treasure from of old.
England stood then atop a pinnacle
Of influence and power in the world
And had produced a culture unsurpassed—
A product of her unique sort of people;
The envy of a now forgotten world.
As those Victorian days came to a close 370
They gave us Wells' bold, fanciful stories.
He composed them to showcase his ideas,
His ruminations on our destiny
And on the universe we called our home.

Astronomers thought they had seen canals
Crisscross our closest planetary neighbor
So Wells imagined we were not alone
But under constant scrutiny from Mars
Observed by intellects immense and cool
Without a care for our primitive race 380
But hungry for our green and fruitful globe.

Book VI

Or he proposed that we were all alone
And our too human race would separate
Into an upper and a lower class,
Capitalists and Labor, and from them
Evolve over eight hundred thousand years
Into two separate races, one above,
The Eloi who lived in pampered luxury
Among fruit trees and luscious berry bushes
In something like a latter day Eden,   390
And one below, the Morlocks who had been
Labor in days of old but had become
A race of cannibals who fed upon
The Eloi above to whom they still gave care,
Rather like flocks of cattle whom they fattened.
The Time Machine portrayed our gruesome end
But *When the Sleeper Wakes* showed how it started
In future London days when the Elite
Played above ground and Labor slaved below.

Karl Marx, perhaps the father of such thought,   400
Foresaw a much more optimistic future
But Wells, more poet than economist,
Was happy to spin tales that would expose
An economic system that was founded
On values he concluded were inhuman.
He thought himself a literary hack
But seemed to me a master who employed
Ideas just in vogue, like Darwinism
And Marxism—two *Weltanschauungen*
That sprouted and bore fruit on English soil.   410
On them he based a metanarrative
Played out in clever novels that would show
How human ambition and human folly
Would put us on a path to slow extinction.

I found a volume of his shorter tales
And read them as I lounged in a deck chair
And sipped iced tea on summer afternoons
Under our carport's open, breezy shade.

Two stories struck me more than any others.
One story was "The Empire of the Ants,"   420
A morbid tale of insects that evolved
Deep in the jungles of the Amazon
And mastered metallurgy and warfare.
Soon they would conquer South America
And by the 1950s or 60s
Discover Europe in an outward journey
Of racial cleansing and colonization.
The other was "The New Accelerator,"
About a scientist who made a drug
That gave him power to accelerate   430
And move so fast that people on the street
Seemed to have stopped all movement and stood still.
He ran about the public ways unseen
And saw cart horses with legs motionless
And cart drivers with whips frozen in air.
Although he understood how criminals
Could use the drug if it were made public
He planned to patent it nonetheless
And leave the outcome to his fellow men.

A socialist from Bromley in Kent   440
Had made a conquest of an adolescent,
A Florida devotee of his fiction
(Who, though, would not become a socialist)
And often as I read those clever tales
I thought I had been born in the wrong era
And wished I had been born in Wells' England
Where all seemed cultured and morally sound
And lawns were mown immaculately well
And rolled by servants and all hedgerows trimmed
So that no line or angle was askew,   450
Where men wore suits and carried walking sticks
And women dressed in modest elegance
And boys wore uniforms to school and got
By rote their Latin and their English grammar;
They laid a sure foundation for a future

Book VI

As orderly and cultured as the present
They saw around them, which they would improve.

Although I authored science fiction stories
I could never rival H. G. Wells
And never tried to imitate his style. 460

At home and in our study hall at school
Whenever and however I could manage
I devoured science fiction. Once I got
A bizarre idea: I would gather all
The bold scenarios I had enjoyed
And form a future history of them,
One I could put together on my own
As though all of the novels I had read
Were parts of one gigantic jig saw puzzle
Made for a youth like me to put in order. 470

Although my idea was grand in scope
And promised to create a superstory
Or super history of our universe
It was the product of a youthful fancy
And doomed to fail because too many plots,
Too many worlds, and empires, and disasters
Were portrayed by those science fiction authors
For me to force them all into one canon,
One cogent narrative of future days.
I gave it up and soon began to draft 480
My own stories once more—all short accounts,
All science fiction, and all now forgotten.
I was just happy that I could compose
And let my young imagination travel
Untrammeled far away among the stars.

I could be anywhere I chose to be;
I could see any world or any future
And all of it seemed true and not made up.

Paradise and Old Masters

I floated in the depths of space and saw
A billion trillion stars shine bright and dim   490
Against a background of black emptiness
That was deep space, and I could feel the horror
Of being in a ship among the stars
With nothing but infinity above
And nothing but infinity below,
All of it cold and inhospitable.

There was another boy my age at school,
Also an avid science fiction fan,
And as we talked about our favorite novels
We soon found we both favored the same authors;   500
Once we got to know each other better
We formed a plan to meet on Saturdays
And work together in an extra room
That made a modest study for our family
Until we had produced our own novel.
I always played some music in the background,
Rachmaninoff or Rimsky-Korsakov
(Sergei Rachmaninoff's *Second Concerto*
Or Rimsky-Korsakov's *Scheherazade*,
So poignant with its plaintive violin).   510
My friend was a good soul: he only loved
Popular music; but he humored me
And labored long with me against that backdrop
Of large orchestral sounds. Gradually
The grandeur of the tones he was exposed to
Took hold and turned him from one world to another,
From rock 'n roll to music by Tchaikovsky,
Rachmaninoff, and Rimsky-Korsakov,
The titans of Russian romanticism.

The musical conversion of my cohort   520
Was our endeavor's one enduring fruit;
Our novel never got public exposure
Although we did complete and send it off
To Ace Books, a New York publisher
Of sci-fi paperbacks but they returned

Book VI

Our manuscript and said they could not use it;
And in the end I was not so surprised
And not so very disappointed either,
Nor was my friend. The two of us had had
A lot of fun together and my friend   530
Had come to know some music that endured;
Maybe that was accomplishment enough.

The musical landscape was not unknown
To me during our Martins Ferry days.
My dad had studied piano as a boy
And mastered clarinet and saxophone.
When he was a young man he joined a band
And played the jazz that he had grown to love.
Big bands were popular back then, and Dad
Performed for one in Wheeling 'til the war;   540
He joined the army then where he was able
To carry on his musical career:
The Army's First Armored Division
Had its own band that travelled with the troops
(Those soldiers who saw combat at first hand).
After the war and after the adventures
And traumas that my father left untold
Or only partly told Dad once more took
His saxophone and joined the band in Wheeling;
He hoped to earn his living as a player.   550

The band normally worked into the wee hours
And Father stuck it out until my mother
Pushed me into the world in Martins Ferry
And I became a toddler in short order.
Soon after that, Dad left the band for good
Because the way of life that it encouraged
Was not a good one for a growing family.
My parents never wanted me to study
An instrument. When they would think of music
They thought of band music, and the late hours,   560
And alcohol, and all that was unsavory:
A future they did not want for their son.

Paradise and Old Masters

Still, I was born with music in my soul.
Although I did not study formally
I had an ear for tones. I slowly found,
From snatches captured now and then by chance
On radio or on our television,
That there was music very different from
My parents' big band music (or love songs
By Frank Sinatra or by Perry Como)   570
And very different from the rock and roll
Made controversial by Elvis Pressley—
A music that awoke my whole being
Far more than any music I had known.
I wanted to explore it, and in Florida
I came upon a set of sixteen records
Sold one by one in regular installments
At our local Winn-Dixie super market.
I used the money from my paper route
And bought the records and a record player.   580
A doorway now stood open to a world—
A tonal architecture of the west—
Music by Bach, Vivaldi and Mozart,
Beethoven, Schubert, Schumann, Brahms—and Haydn,
Who once had been Beethoven's sole instructor
And called the father of the symphony.

Florida had become a world of tones,
A land of musical discovery
Where human music would join sounds of nature—
Dark thunder showers on the open sea   600
Or powerful waves that could devour the shore
(Or in a gentle mood with soft approach,
Caress the open sands of old Palm Beach)
Or palm fronds rattling in a friendly breeze
Soughing off a warm sea or from the 'glades.

Those natural sounds were music to my soul:
Pure movements in a symphony of nature

Book VI

Available to anyone who cared
Or anyone who had an ear for them.

Symphonic music sounded more exalted   610
And was more full of human mind and soul
But nature had a structure and a beauty
More powerful than any human work,
More orderly and better than a movement
Composed by Brahms or any symphonist.

Now in my youth all nature and her music
And music by some human symphonists
Began to come together in a way
I could not have explained or fully grasped;
For now there was a sense of unity,   620
A sense of holy unity in music
Composed by those who had a profound knowledge
Of what was true and lovely and sublime
Beyond what any mortal could express
(Unless it took a form of ordered tones).

Yet nature also had a unity
Of grand power and glory as I saw her:
An atmosphere I moved in every day
In love profoundly, and profoundly sold
To sun and clouds, to sand and sea and palms.   630

Book VII

Farewell to Florida

Could I return to Paradise once more?
Could anyone escape—to what you were?
O holy one who loved me and embraced me,
You took me as a boy and made me yours,
You washed me in your ocean and you warmed me
Under a constant sun on open sands.
You are the one who taught me how to love
As I had never known and made me see
All nature in her freedom and her splendor
As I had never seen her, clothed in glory,   10
As though our human race had not yet come
And made inordinate demands of her.

I loved. I loved all that I saw around me
That spoke of beauty and was beautiful.
As I grew more aware and capable
A strong desire, a rage for beauty almost,
Arose in me and took a larger role;
I was now old enough for love and wanted
To hold and value what was pure and true
In nature and in art. But human nature   20
Remained unfathomable and obscure
To someone who would fathom outer space

Book VII

And plumb the ocean depths with scuba gear
Or understand the structure of great music
By Beethoven or Brahms, but who had not
A faculty developed to embrace
Or understand the nature of our race.

"The proper study of mankind is man,"
Pope once intoned, but I was not a student   30
Of human nature even though I loved
Majestic works of power and of beauty
By artists or composers: those who seemed
Almost a higher order of our race—
A few who understood what was most true
And beautiful, and shared it with us all.

I was an adolescent and not yet
A man who understood his fellow man.
In part I was grown up, in part a boy,
And boy enough to want to be a boy
And do the boyish things I always had—   40
Go play at soldier with a friend or two,
Build armies out of clay or play with marbles
Or go out fishing with my grandfather.

But school was not to be unvalued. There
An unexplored country awaited me;
My science teacher urged me to acquire
A language I had never thought about:
Latin, the tongue of poets and of Caesars.
She thought it would be valuable for one
Who wanted to go on for a degree.   50

My Latin teacher was an older woman
Who also taught our ninth grade English class.
Her courses helped me understand our language,
And Latin strengthened my vocabulary
And grasp of syntax, although I would know
Some unaccustomed sorrows as I strove
To capture unfamiliar paradigms

Farewell to Florida

And hold them firmly in my memory.
After a half year I could compose
Short notes in Latin and send them *sub rosa*   60
To someone who would correspond with me,
A classmate, Alan Kramer. I had met him
In sixth grade at Lantana, where I first
Attended school in Florida. Alan was
Superb at Latin and at every subject
But later he suffered a mental breakdown
At Princeton University and left;
Much later I was told that he attended
An Episcopal school in the Palm Beaches
But after that I heard no more of him.   70
We took our Latin and our English classes
Together and we always had good times.

In English class our teacher had us read
Great Expectations, stories, and some poems.

One poem captured my young imagination:
The "Rime of the Ancyent Marinere"
By S. T. Coleridge. He collaborated
With William Wordsworth on a small volume
Of poetry when both of them were young,
Lyrical Ballads. I enjoyed his poem   80
Mostly because it was so strange and spooky.
He told us of a sailor who was doomed
Because he shot an albatross that was
Supposedly a bird of love, beloved
By an unknown spirit of the southern pole.
The *numen* brought a curse upon the crew:
Our sailor told of days becalmed at sea
And oily waters full of slimy creatures
Who slithered on the surface, and of ghosts,
And sailors who had died but rose again: 90
They drove the cursed ship back to its home
Before it broke apart and sank like stone.
Our mariner was placed on shore alone
To tell his ghastly narrative to one

Book VII

Who had been chosen to hear it (when he felt
A signal agony come on him he
Must tell his gruesome tale to every one
Whom Providence had made his audience).
I could not understand it as a youth,
Maybe because it was so oddly told; 100
So much of it happened without a motive
Or any cause that I could figure out.
It was as though our world had just gone crazy
Or part of it had just become a nightmare.

The poem's atmosphere both puzzled me
And captivated me. I was aware
The author of this work had to have been
Both talented and unusually formed:
A man whose bizarre thought world could produce
A south sea that was pure hallucination 110
Or almost so. I would be much older
Before I could do justice to that poem,
Both as a man of thought and as a man
Who thought he had the nature of a poet.

Coleridge's poem had a closing moral,
But I could not remember it among
A flood of imagery and strange ideas
That captured my imagination then:
"He prayeth best who loveth best all things
Both great and small," he wrote, "for the dear God 120
Who loveth us, he made and loveth all."
I was in love with nature and I loved
My home and life in Florida—and loved
The animals and plants that flourished there
But never thought of them in terms of God.
I understood the universe was matter,
Just subatomic particles and atoms,
And never thought beyond that bare idea,
Although I knew that there was energy
And energy and matter were related 130
And somehow formed a cosmos out of nothing.

Farewell to Florida

My own world was not so Olympian
And full of thought that I could not do sports.
I played sand lot baseball across the road
In Palm Springs, and my grandfather would stand
And pitch balls to me after school was out;
He hoped I would become a better batter.
My grandfather had been a baseball player,
An amateur when he was in the Army
At the Presidio in San Francisco. 140
He nurtured false ambitions for my future;
He hoped I would become the baseball player
He never got to be and make the majors.
But I was not much good at any sport
And never got much practice at the game
Or any other sport except football,
A game my friends and I would often play
In grass lots after school on sunny days
Or cloudy days, but not on rainy days.
That autumn I became a football player 150
On one school team. I had to be a tackle
Because I was the new man on the squad
And that was what they needed; so I strove
To manage at that spot although I was
Hardly large enough to make a difference
Against most tackles I had to confront.
Nonetheless I managed once or twice
To do some good and drop a running back
And even once to sack a quarterback.

Our football practice started after four. 160
It always took place on an open field
Our class would occupy every morning
During an hour of physical education
Playing sports and doing calisthenics.
A set of bleachers overlooked the field
And after school I sat what seemed like ages
Until the other players and the coach
Arrived for practice, armed and clad for battle

Book VII

In fresh white uniforms and pads and cleats.
Until they came I was alone and read   170
A science fiction novel or short story.
I loved the solitude. As autumn passed
The sun cast longer shadows from behind me
Across the open grass, a sign that fall
Was on the wane and an unwelcome winter
Would soon be here with short days and cold nights.
Strong melancholy overcame me then
Alone with autumn shadows and my thoughts
Of football—of how much it did not matter—
And Latin and my science fiction novel   180
And how the world seemed mostly out of joint.

I wanted to read Omar Khayyam then,
Because I saw a movie based on him.
He was so oriental and exotic,
So full of poetry and strange adventures,
I had to find a volume of his verses.

I loved our Lake Worth public library,
A modest building that looked classical
With several palms around it on small grounds.
It owned a good collection of volumes   190
And comfortable armchairs for its patrons
So when I could I drove from home and parked
And browsed among the stacks and looked for books
On UFOs, or science fiction novels.
I hoped to find a book of curses, too
(Probably because of all the movies
I saw at theaters or on television
I had unusual interest in such matters)
But I could not find a volume of them,
Not a single page, so one morning   200
I conjured up my Latin and produced
A curse all of my own—a foolish one
Which had no power over anything,
But then, who wanted magical power?
I only thought how much fun it would be

Farewell to Florida

To utter maledictions in the tongue
And the authority of ancient Rome.
My curse was elegant and almost potent
(Though not with occult power) at the start
But then it lost its verbal verve and punch
And dwindled to a modest flow of sounds.
Alan Kramer like the way it started,
And so did I, for it opened with thunder:
Omnibus ignibus Orci, potestate-
que maximae obscuritatis...
Then—what? I have forgotten, and my curse
Has long since found the deep obscurity
It so deserved. But for a day or two
It was a plaything that amused us.

I found a book of verses by Omar,
"The Tentmaker," Khayyam—*The Rubaiyat*,
Translated into English by Fitzgerald.
Omar Khayyam was an astronomer
But was a poet, too, and I absorbed
The oriental flavor of his poems:
A short abandon into worldly pleasure
But, over all, a doubter's melancholy.
Because he thought too much he had become
Discouraged, for *his* world was out of joint
And human wisdom could not make it good
Although his poetry could sing of it.

I often thought it was unusual
For someone of my age and situation
To read Omar Khayyam, and so it was.
None of my friends had ever heard of him;
But then, few of my friends had ever heard
Of Mozart, Beethoven, or Haydn, either.
I read his poems avidly and loved
The flair for beauty and the irony,
And above all a touch of hedonism
That looked so daring to a boy like me.
Of course, I did not know the Persian tongue,

Book VII

But I was happy with a good translation;
His poems put me more in touch with one
Who had a mind to question all he saw.
It titillated me to think that way
A little bit; I almost felt quite bold
And unconventional among my classmates.

Our school declared a Latin Day in April   250
And all the Latin students got to dress
In Roman costume (mostly mattress sheets)
And go to all our classes dressed as Romans.
The Roman girls wore tunicas and stolas;
The Roman boys wore tunicas and togas.
Although it was an awkward sort of clothes
The overall effect was worth our trouble:
We made a proud show, and afterward
We formed a small parade that wound its way
From Lake Worth High School into downtown Lake Worth
And to the Intracoastal Waterway.   260
Once the parade was over we were free
To go back home or wander through the town
Just as we wanted. I strolled thoughtfully
Past stores I knew and would smile inwardly
As ordinary people looked at me;
No doubt they wondered what was going on—
What bizarre apparition from past ages
Had wandered into sleepy downtown Lake Worth.

I walked casually down Lake Avenue
And past Morrison's cafeteria   270
Until I reached our public library.
I stood still on the pathway just outside
And watched the palms and palm fronds in commotion
As warm afternoon breezes made them sway.
For just one moment I began to feel
As though I were a Roman senator
Walking among the shrubs of some good *locus*
Of public learning for the public good.
I turned to face the old wooden door

Farewell to Florida

And slowly stepped into the noble hall.   280
I found myself in a most holy hush.
Books that would never say a word out loud
Spoke volumes to my soul and challenged me
To understand, to grow, and be a brother
To those who labored to improve our world.

How would it be if Florida became
A modern parallel to Rome's Republic,
A place where every citizen was sane
And managed his own business in a way
That only made our land become stronger   290
Because one made one's life and labor there?
How would it be if every citizen
Were such a human soul—both orderly
And masterly in every thought and work?
How would it be if those in Florida
Thought not of personal gain but rather thought
Of human honor and of charity,
Of noble poetry and lofty art,
Of all that made us what we ought to be
And would transform our land and make it good—   300
Not grand in arms or strong in industry
But good because it was the home of Goodness?
No such Florida had come to be;
No such Florida would come to be.
But for one moment I, a senator
Immersed in one library's solitude,
Could ponder such a Florida alone
Where all around me spoke of ancient Rome,
Her noble hours, her faithful senators,
Her halcyon days before the Empire came   310
And undid what was left of the Republic.

With Roman thoughts to ennoble my soul
And boundless splendor of quotidian skies
And pure undaunted music of palm trees,
Numerous starry nights that offered me
Astonished hours of astronomy,

Book VII

And Florida's ocean at my beck and call
So I could plunge into her tropic waters
As often as I wanted—and I did—
How could I be unhappy in those days? 320
There was enough in Florida to calm
And settle me into a peaceful mode;
And one form of adventure from my past
Was an unsullied good that I could count on:
I could go catch a fish with my grandfather
And be a boy once more with rod and reel.

One Saturday we took the road and made
An hour long journey to Lake Okeechobee.
The only lake I ever saw that large
Was Lake Erie. My folks had taken me 330
To see Niagara Falls when I was ten.
Of course, Lake Erie was the larger lake
But to a boy who stood upon the shore
Both lakes could look as large as any ocean.
Grandfather came along, so we formed
A plan to suit us all: we'd have a picnic
And see how many catfish we could catch.

As we drove along the shore I saw
A wall of earth that was a barrier
So no hurricane could ever come 340
And wash the lake out of its shallow bowl;
Such a catastrophe had happened once.
Polluted waters flooded all the fields
And overwhelmed the modest wooden houses;
Hundreds had drowned because there was no wall
To hold the water back and keep them safe.

We parked and chose a spot close to the shallows.
I checked my rod and gave my fishing line
A tug but as I did it broke in two.
Grandfather tugged it once and called it rotten 350
And said I ought to cast the old line off
But that would mean unwelcome extra work:

Farewell to Florida

To unwind all of it and then once more
Wind yards of pristine cord onto the reel.
I wanted to go now and catch a fish
So I ignored his counsel and went on
With my own plan. I slung my bait far out.

For one long hour I had no result
But then we had our picnic lunch; we lay
Some postprandial moments on the shore   360
And afterward loaded the car and drove
Like tourists 'til we reached a large canal.
Broad and slow it parted from the lake
And travelled calmly toward West Palm Beach
Where it would flow into the Intracoastal.
Someone once noted, "Still waters run deep,"
A proverb true of that dark brown canal
If it was true of any Florida water.
I got my rod and reel and took my bait
And put my chicken liver on the hook.   370
A leaden sinker sank the line far down
Close to the wall I sat on, and I waited.
It was not long at all before a tug
Announced an unknown animal below
Had taken interest in my rotten bait—
A large catfish, just as I hoped and planned.
The line was taut and anyone could see
A very large something was on my hook
And stood opposed to all that I would do
To haul it out of its dark habitat   380
And hold it in my hand triumphantly
And take it home where I could skin and gut it
And serve it on a table for our supper.
Now the rod dipped strongly toward the water
And I was seasoned fisherman enough
To know my hook was lodged unshakably;
It would only be a matter of moments
Before a trophy fish danced in my hand.
I felt him growing closer as I pulled

Book VII

But with a sudden snap the rod swung back. 390
The line was limp, and I now stood alone.

An older angler, Granddad offered counsel
To one bold youth who would have none of it.
I trusted to a poor and rotten line
To satisfy a momentary urge
And consequently missed a worthy catch.
Once we returned home my only thought
Was to go back to the same spot once more.
I badgered my poor parents frantically
And they obliged me. One more Saturday 400
We packed our car with picnic goods and drove;
But now I had replaced hook, line and sinker.
I was all set to catch a monster catfish
And yet we passed our afternoon in vain
On the same wall because whatever creature
Had found my rotten liver to his taste
Was either on an errand far away
Or lost his appetite for baited hooks.
My grandfather had known how much I'd want
To have another go at the same spot 410
And understood how foolish it would be
To make the effort but he came along
Because as Grandfather and angler
He understood the ways of boys and fish.

One Saturday morning I wrapped the papers
With rubber bands and put them in a basket
Over the front wheel of my bicycle
And as I carried out a routine chore
I saw an article about a land
We always hoped our family would tour 420
But what I saw aroused much doubt in me
Because Castro, the rebel who had toppled
The regime of Fulgencia Batista,
Had now avowed himself a communist.
He wanted to install on his large island
A "Dictatorship of the Proletariat,"

Farewell to Florida

A rule by dictate that abolished
Freedoms Americans mistook for granted
Under the pretense of a public mandate
To guide the nation to a better future 430
And to a day when government itself
Would atrophy and pass away unwanted
And be replaced by something much, much better:
A classless state, a free society
Where all who had would give to those who lacked
And all who worked would give to those who could not
Where every man would be every man's brother
And every woman every woman's sister
And ranks or titles or inheritance
Would not exist but only love and goodness. 440
Under a mask so humane and so bland
The human face of one dictator hid
And ruled all people by the will of one.

I saw how fallible one man could be
(And anyone who knew some history could)
In Mussolini, Hitler, Joseph Stalin . . .
I had a deep mistrust of Fidel Castro
And put no faith at all in communism,
A creed that promised everything to all,
An earthly Paradise, a brotherhood, 450
Man helping man and woman helping woman,
Only attainable at one small cost:
Pull down the edifice of centuries,
A social system that had slowly grown
(Forward and backward truly, but had grown)
Toward a way of life and polity
That gave a chance to almost anyone
To labor with a reasonable hope
Of improving his family and himself.
In homage to a supposed dialectic 460
Whose mandate all of history must obey
People were summoned forth to crush and maim
And let blood flow across the public square
In freedom's name and overturn all order,

Book VII

But all their efforts only came to this:
Rule by an iron and oppressive hand.
One could see in Lenin and in Stalin
And later in Nikita Kruschev's rule
The systematic inhumanity
Of dialectical materialism.   470
I thought it was insanity made legal,
Unholy appetite made into law.

I had no way to know, on that warm morning,
How much the fate of Castro and his land
Would complicate my life and shape my path
(Not into communist romanticism—
The sort of solidarity that led
Our college students to fly down to Cuba
And spend their Christmas holidays in fields
Shoulder to shoulder with a Cuban farmer   480
To harvest sugar cane with those machetes
They left behind when they flew north again—
But to a different place and other fate
Than I had ever wanted or imagined).
I harbored no illusions about Castro
Or Cuba or about his communism
But I could not foresee what it would do
To our own fortunes as a family.
Once Castro came to power and was known
To be a hostile power to our south   490
Just ninety miles away from old Key West
A lot of northerners who planned to move
To Florida decided to stay home.
A drop in new construction would result
And window sales would also be affected
And then my father's company had trouble
Nobody could foreknow and the two owners
Resolved to pull up roots and move the firm
Somewhere more favorable to the business.
Bellhouse had sold some windows in Atlanta   500
Where growth was underway and all looked good
For profit minded people and for housing

Farewell to Florida

So "Red" Bell and his partner, Uncle Bob,
Declared Atlanta, Georgia, was the place
Where we would relocate. It was as though
One sought to plant a tree by flowing water.

The news was a disaster for one soul.
Florida's landscape had become a part
Of me and I had grown to be a part
Of sand and sea and palms in Florida.   510
It was a Paradise, true Paradise
Of nature's bounty and unbounded joy,
Not the paradise Marx had concocted
When he sat warped and stifled at a table
Imposing constructs on the flow of history
In one London museum in rainy weather.
But I was just a boy so how could I
Conjure a way to stop the flow of history
As it affected us? We made our plans
Toward a day I never hoped to see   520
And hoped never to see; and yet that day
Would come inexorable as the dawn
Or as the glorious sunsets I adored.

Because the housing market was a shambles
We could not find a buyer for our house.
We had to rent it to a younger couple
Who soon after defaulted on the payments.
My parents had to ask me for a loan
Of money I saved from my paper route
To make the mortgage payments to the bank   530
But after that was gone they lost the house.

We packed all of our goods and left our home,
Our home of glorious years in Florida,
And moved to an apartment on Lake Osborne
Only a block or two from Lake Worth High.
I walked to morning classes and passed
My final hours with Florida friends.
I was still young and found I could enjoy

Book VII

Our new apartment and its situation
On that same lake where I had fished so often;   540
But in my soul I felt a sadness growing
Far more than I had ever known and knew
It would endure beyond our move in June.

There was a German couple there who owned
The small but comfortable apartment complex
Of which our small apartment was a unit.
We got to know the couple as we sat
On early evenings or late afternoons
Around a table with them on a patio.
They relocated from Berlin to Lake Worth   550
And hoped to make a new beginning here
After the war, and after years of planning
And steady industry they owned those flats
That stood across the road from Lake Osborne.
How often had I passed the same apartments
En route to fishing with my grandfather?
I never once imagined that one day
I would inhabit one with mingled joy
And sorrow at their lovely situation
Because I had good reason to suppose   560
That home in Florida would be my last.

I wondered as I ambled by the lake
What future should be mine and who I was—
What should I do and where I ought to go,
What my soul was and what it should become.
I undertook a literary work,
A novel thing for me because it was
Not fiction but autobiography.
I wondered if an account of that sort,
A true attempt to understand my past   570
And how I came to be what I now was,
Could be more valuable than any story:
A boy transplanted from Ohio south
Astounded to arrive in Paradise

Farewell to Florida

But without any idea at all
How utterly it would transform his soul.

I understood that I was hopelessly
In love with Florida as I had known her
Although I knew I could not hold that goddess
In my embrace forever or just once. 580

So I began and wrote a chapter there
Beside the dark brown waters of Lake Osborne.
After we moved to Georgia I became
Involved with other things—another life—
And soon forgot my autobiography
And once my college years were over with
I found that I had lost it in the course
Of all those moves that made a student's days.

One afternoon I stood beside the lake
And saw a thunder cloud accumulate 590
Above the dark brown waters; a sharp breeze
Morphed to a wind that whipped the water up
Until small whitecaps drove toward the shore.
A massive thunderstorm arose close by
Closer than any I had ever seen.
I thought if I stood tall before its power
Silent upon the shore as it progressed
I must be struck by lightning or drawn up
By howling winds into its dark embrace.
But then I had another, bolder thought: 600
Maybe a man could stand and shake his fist,
A bold young man could offer up his scorn
Against that mighty power and survive
And not only survive, but come triumphant
Out of whatever deluge it could muster
And pour upon him in its strong advance.
I thought how Beethoven on his last bed
Sat up and shook his fist in one grand gesture
Of romantic defiance as he heard
A thunderstorm burst loud over his house 610

Book VII

(Or so the story goes, perhaps a story
And nothing more—but if only a story,
A fable nonetheless appropriate
To the composer's unconquerable nature)
And so I stood before that thunderstorm
And saw it come upon me with no harm
As I communed once more with Florida waters,
Waters from heaven come to earth for us.

How long, O Florida, how long again
Before I would commune with you so well,   620
So happily under a spreading palm,
Or on a beach with waves that made no challenge
Composing one long rolling serenade,
Or under water with a myriad
Of scintillating fish among the corals,
Or standing boldly as a storm advanced
About to deluge me with stormy water,
And know once more that I was made of water
And made for water and for Florida?

Would Florida become my home again   630
Or would some fate call me to Paradise?
Such questions were unanswerable for me
The day we packed our car and took the road
With Paradise behind us and a world
Before us that was all unknown to me.

Book VIII

Atlanta and Cross Keys

How can I say what gloom hung over me
As we drove north and palm trees in our wake
Could only wave their fronds and fade away?
We drove toward the hub of the Old South
And as we passed through suburbs of apartments
Clustered in random unattractive bunches
Atlanta rose above us in the distance
In Faustian defiance of the sky.

She was immortalized by academics
Who chronicled the Civil War and told   10
About a northern general's progress—
Of Sherman's ruthless march toward the sea.
He trod upon a nation just defeated
And devastated the Confederacy.

The warfare and the passion had been brought
Before the public some decades before
By a movie (based upon a book)
Boasting Clark Gable and a famous cast:
Gone with the Wind.
 But no movie could matter
Or help me now. I was a Florida boy   20

Book VIII

Rudely transplanted to another state,
A place where land was rumpled and not flat,
Where upstart pine trees held the sky at bay
And people spoke in unfamiliar tones—
Accents so thick I could not understand
Unless I asked them to say one more time
What they had said; I came away embarrassed.

We moved into a duplex several blocks
From Cross Keys High School where I would study
For both my junior and my senior years   30
Before I packed my things to go to Yale.

Once I had hoped to have my own airfoil,
A World War Two attack plane, and commute
From home to school and back as I attended
Florida State University
In our state's capital, sweet Tallahassee,
Town of palmettos and southern live oaks.

But now I was on a long, shady street
Far from Florida's palm environed structures
In a red brick duplex among old wooden houses.   40

We never got to know their occupants
(Only the ones next door had a loud dog)
Before we bought a house and moved away.

A retired Jewish couple owned our duplex
And occupied the other half of it.
According to an old family tradition
They motored to Miami every summer
But on a hot July afternoon
As he loaded up their station wagon
The old man dropped dead from a coronary.   50
His wife ran out and tried to force a pill
Through his clenched teeth as he lay unresponsive.

Atlanta and Cross Keys

An only sister also lived with them
But after he passed on she followed suit
Partly because of some bowel condition,
Partly because of grief for her lost brother.
The widow lady was a Christian Scientist.
I lay in bed and her nocturnal tones
Bored through the thin wall that stood between us
As she instructed her sister–in–law   60
On a faculty she called "mortal mind."
She hoped to convince the moribund woman
Her malady was only an illusion,
A concept very hard for me to fathom.
The poor woman was obviously ill
And would not be another year among us.
In fact she died a month after her brother
And shortly afterward we bought a house.

Before we moved the school year had begun.
I can remember sultry autumn days   70
Walking to school across a hazy valley
Behind our duplex; before me the sun
Conjured up a cloud of golden mist
As I descended into our small vale
And out of it again *en route* to school.

I trudged down red clay slopes and up again
On many mornings and soon understood
Nature could be winsome in Georgia
With golden haze or skies of icy blue.

On two cool September Saturdays   80
Her skies *were* icy blue and looked so deep
I doubted any eye could fathom them.
Somehow the quality of atmosphere
Suggested I should take my telescope
And pass an hour in the cooler world
After the sun had set and look around
And see what deep sky objects I could find.

Book VIII

After supper I explored and saw
How many stars there were—how many hovered
Just at the brink of visibility—   90
And our own galaxy, the Milky Way,
Hung like a remote fog across the sky,
A cloud that spoke of stars uncountable
Thousands of parsecs from our solar system.
My ocular explored numerous regions
And found a number of far galaxies
And nebulae.

      Soon I began to feel
More comfortable in the Deep South.
Stars shone down on Georgia after all   100
Atlanta also had the Milky Way
September skies could be profound and blue
And all of it was there for any youth.

But now I had classes. I could not know
What sort of road lay just ahead of me
Or how it would lead to unequalled joy
And melancholy, and transform my soul.

When I was a young boy in Martins Ferry
And afterward in Florida I thought
I would grow up to be a scientist.   110
I had done well in math and science classes
And as I started school in the Deep South
I looked forward to my first physics class
And trigonometry and higher math.

One physics group at Cross Keys High enrolled
For a slow bus trip to Oak Ridge.
Our soporific journey could not dampen
My joy when I saw a nuclear reactor
Housed in a pool flooded with turquoise light.
The luminescence that so gorgeously   120
Shone forth below would be the end of me
Or anyone who ventured close to it.

Atlanta and Cross Keys

The Oak Ridge men gave dimes to us, exposed
To radiation so a Geiger counter
Would pop and crackle when held over them.

But soon I had more powerful encounters
That would contribute to a change of course.
I took my Latin from a youthful teacher
Who would become a scholar later on
And had my English from a lovely blonde   130
Who irritated me at first because
She seemed peremptory and self-important
But I soon felt a love for her beyond
Any emotion I had ever known.

She was a graduate of Vanderbilt
And valued good instruction. She assigned
Our class a twenty page long term paper,
A sort of work completely new to us.
She made us buy cards and produce notes
Drawn from at least five secondary sources   140
As a foundation for our compositions.
I chose a novel topic for my paper:
A poet, Ezra Pound. He had become
A powerful reactionary who
Was an expatriate in Italy
And broadcast propaganda for the fascists
Before the war erupted with those three
Axis powers who hoped to rule the world.
Although I had not heard of Pound before
I chose him as the subject for my paper   150
When my teacher proposed him to me.
She thought he would prove interesting to one
In whom she had begun to take an interest.
So I was introduced to Ezra Pound.
I soon discovered in his poems and *Cantos*
A world of intellectual stimulus:
Abstruse allusions, potent imagery,
Haiku poetry (he called it *hokku*)

Book VIII

And mastery of arcane languages
And literatures ancient and modern160
But his unruly verse could seem at times
Almost chaotic in its liberty
And sometimes hardly more than prosaic.

Pound could march along with obscure quotes
From older works and other languages
And leave an educated reader undone.
His composition dazzled me and soon
I came under his troubled influence
Although the world could boast better poets.

Ezra Pound had been a major help170
To T. S. Eliot when he composed
His masterpiece, "The Waste Land," even though
Pound himself was never to produce
Any work as luminous as that.

Although I had begun to study poems
Music was still the idol of my soul.

I found a record shop not far from home
And purchased six Beethoven symphonies.
They poured their holy music forth for me.
I sat before them with profound devotion.180
I also bought his piano concertos
And the violin and triple concertos.

I found an order, purity and power
Especially in the works for orchestra
That made his music unlike any other.

I borrowed a couple of biographies
Of Beethoven from our school library
And carried them from one class to another,
Exploring them whenever I was able
(Some lull in what a teacher had to say190
Or when I thought her point was unimportant)

Atlanta and Cross Keys

No matter what the class, except for Latin
And English where both teachers were superb
And one was young and captured all my love.

Beethoven's tortured days absorbed my thoughts;
The "immortal beloved" saddened me;
But as I walked around from hall to hall
His melodies and counterpoint encouraged
My lonely and uncomfortable soul;
I wanted very much to return home   200
And put a record on the record player
After supper and devote my whole thought
To one of his immortal compositions.

I was too young to understand back then
How one tormented artist could produce
Compositions that would comfort others
Long after the creator had passed on.

A boy named Geoffrey Hull also enrolled
In Mrs. Ramsey's English class with me
And as autumn sank and winter loomed   210
We talked about music and poetry.

We got together at his home on Friday
Around seven o'clock to enjoy music,
Classical recordings I had purchased
In Florida and later on in Georgia,
Compositions of Beethoven, Schumann,
Sometimes Tchaikovsky, Antonin Dvorak,
And several other major composers.
We sat together in his living room
And spent an hour or more before the works   220
And afterward compared our thoughts on them.
It was almost as though a concert hall
Under his roof had welcomed just two boys.
Afterward we often played a board game
Until it was so late I had to go.

Book VIII

Those were good evenings, memorable for friendship
And intellectual growth.

                We came to love
The symphonies of Schumann and a style
That was both grand and melancholy—but
When I first heard the "Rhenish" symphony   230
A sudden *Angst* swept over me because
I thought he had outdone my Beethoven;
But soon maturer judgment set me right.

One night we played the D Minor concerto
By Brahms and were both genuinely stunned
By what came forth. It was as though a mountain
Of giant tones fell suddenly upon us
Full of tumultuous sound without a pause.
The autumn term would pass before I fathomed
The opening movement or much of that work.   240
Long afterward when I heard its successor
I was amazed at how mellifluous,
Both calm and pastoral with all its power,
It was by contrast to the craggy first.
A record jacket told how Brahms had fought
To pull the first concerto into shape
And how he could know mastery when later
He turned once more to the concerto form
And wrote another large work for piano.

The same occurred with the *First Symphony*,   250
A major *opus* that took twenty years
Because as he once said, to undertake
Such a work after Beethoven was no joke.
The *First* was also full of powerful storm
And dark romantic thunder. Though titanic
It would be followed by a pastoral *Second*
So full of peace and fluent melody
One never would have thought its predecessor
Had won through storm and stress to sound a note
Sonorous and triumphant at the end.   260

Atlanta and Cross Keys

Music was now a haven for my soul,
A home of lofty structure, power and goodness.

I was in love with it and found it offered
Encouragement no one could countermand.

On the FM band one station broadcast
Classical music the whole day. For me
It took the place of one I found in Florida
A month before we moved to Atlanta.
At home I turned it on sometimes and listened
But more often I sat alone and played   270
A work and tried to fathom out its structure
As the record turned. I studied themes
With a focused soul as they unfolded
And followed variations as they came.
I loved the variations most of all
Because they formed an intellectual dance
Somewhat predictable though never wholly.
I was astounded when I later learned
The final movement of Beethoven's *Eroica*
Was just a group of theme and variations   280
But many months would pass before I saw
The same was true of Brahms' *Fourth Symphony*
Because it took me longer to love Brahms.
However, even without a profound grasp
Of all the wisdom of architectonics
I could absorb majestic power and goodness
Along with staggering simplicity
From those and other compositions,
A combination that enabled me
To look into a true artist's soul.   290

A cosmos of pure compositions
Could show the power of a lucid mind,
A strong will and a self under control
To anyone who would allow them to.

Book VIII

A true composer would let music flow
From sources deeper than a human mind
And any other human could commune
With those natural currents as they flowed.

Music captured Hull and me so fully
Our parents bought us season tickets so   300
We could attend the Atlanta Symphony.
We donned our suits and overcoats and hats
Because we thought it was appropriate
To show that we would honor by our dress
The noble nature of a concert hall
And the exalted music that should fill it.
The orchestra all wore tuxedos then
Or long black dresses. Their choice of black costume
Spoke of humility, we thought—like that
Worn by some pastors on a Sunday morning.   310
One woman always stood out in the crowd
Of concert goers. She wore a long gown
Of luminescent red, and seemed to be
Some bird of alien, outlandish plumage
Flown from a southern jungle far away
And out of place among a sober crowd
Of portly men in suits and other ladies
Who dressed more modestly for the occasion.

One day Arthur Fiedler came to town
As guest conductor of the orchestra.   320
He led them in a Haydn symphony
And other pieces I cannot recall.
I do remember though the quality
He conjured out of our modest ensemble,
An orchestra that sounded second rate
Compared to some more recently recorded—
Performances by Cleveland and George Szell,
Who understood the work of Brahms so well,
Or Philadelphia under Ormandy
(Whose Rachmaninoff symphonies were so lush),   330
Or Paul Paray conducting in Detroit

Atlanta and Cross Keys

Mendelssohn's youthful *Midsummer Night's Dream*,
Or Boston under the Teutonic wand
Of Eric Leinsdorf, who was disciplined
Beyond so many others on record.
Led by the Maestro's hand the work of Haydn
Resounded through our hall with stately grace,
Order, and intellectual clarity;
A dancelike quality came forth, unknown
To Maestro Henry Sopkin's performances.   340
My father speculated that the name
Of Arthur Fiedler was enough alone
To move common musicians to perform
Beyond their ordinary competence
Because he had flown all the way from Boston
And his fabulous Boston Pops to grace
Atlanta, cultural hub of all the South.
Because my father was a saxophonist
And had some knowledge from the big band era
I had to acknowledge he could be right   350
Although it seemed more probable to me
Arthur Fiedler was a good conductor
Who wanted and was able to produce
The optimal performance from his players
No matter what the town or orchestra
Because he had learned how to do the same
In Boston with his world renowned group.

Atlanta was a town that gave me music.
I loved it now more than I could have done
In Florida or anywhere before   360
Because I was more suited to absorb it.

Maybe I was in truth a refugee—
A teenage boy who was in love with nature
As he had once known her in Florida
But who with or without her beauty longed
For beauty of *some* sort and found it now
In music he had just begun to love
In Florida but grown to understand

Book VIII

Far more as he matured in Atlanta.
One could buy a record in the Hub   370
From a well-stocked record shop
Or some department store, or one could study
Classical music on the radio;
I could go downtown and hear a concert
Performed by a professional orchestra—
Something I could not do in West Palm Beach.

Good music, though, could be no substitute
For all the glory I had come to love
In Florida on land or in the ocean,
A world where nature wore a holy face,   380
Although in older music I had found
A paradise of tonal architecture,
Another, hidden home where I could enter
And know the company of noble souls:
Composers who loved order and gave birth
To works of lofty power and tenderness;
Creators such as Haydn who became
Almost an icon of spiritual soundness,
Logical clarity and strength balanced
With interludes of calm and sure repose   390
For a boy who profoundly needed them.
I loved his last symphony above all,
The *London*. One found there an ordered space
Where poignancy and power to spare
Found proper bounds and thus true freedom, too,
A classic value of the Enlightenment;
And who could forget Mozart, who announced
A powerful *amen* in the fourth movement
(A liquid fugal treatment so abundant)
Of his last symphony, the *Jupiter*?   400
And then of course Beethoven, Haydn's pupil,
Who on his own explored a sea of tones
Unplumbed by capable contemporaries
Who observed from the shore—Spohr, Ries or Hummel.
Beethoven was my hero in those days
And any who loved Haydn's symphonies

Could see Haydn's influence on his pupil
Although in the *Great Mogul* one could see
Worship of nature and a will to power
Fully Romantic and a love of freedom   410
That made him a Prometheus to man.

I was now in formation. It could look
As though I loved music much more than words
Although my major talent lay in words
And not in music. I implored my folks
To buy me a piano so that I
Could practice on the instrument beloved
By masters such as Mozart and Beethoven.
I took piano lessons for a year
But nothing came of it; only I saw   420
I would not be a concert pianist.
I did compose one very short *étude*
And Mother put the first four bars to words
But it was not in a popular style
So she could not accomplish much with it.

The autumn of our senior year Virginia
Asked me to play Instructor for two days
And offer a short course on music history.
She had conducted us through the *Inferno*
And thought we could enjoy some lighter fare;   430
Maybe a change of genre and instructor
Would offer us a modicum of comfort.
I brought my records and my record player
And gave my classmates samples much too short
From Mozart's *Eine kleine Nachtmusik*,
Beethoven's dancelike *Seventh*, and, from Brahms,
The *First Symphony*—dubbed Beethoven's *Tenth*.
I played some shorter pieces: one by Liszt,
Les Préludes, and a Wagner overture
And something from Stravinsky's *Firebird*.   440
Although it was a rag–tag course our students
Had been exposed to several good examples

Book VIII

Of music they were unaccustomed to
And maybe the exposure would do good.

Mrs. Ramsey also asked a blonde,
Marci Spencer, to conduct a course
In art because art was her private passion
As music had been mine; and Marci gave
A lucid introduction. So we shared
The honor of being student instructors. 450

(She loved above all Michelangelo's *David*).

I could have fallen in love with that blonde girl,
And she with me. One day we made a date
To play a round of par three golf. Because
I was so shy I never sought to kiss her
Although I wanted to. I wrongly thought
She was involved with someone else. However,
Our afternoon date had exposed my soul:
I was not free. I had fallen in love
And could not shake it off. I loved Virginia, 460
Our English teacher, who had offered me
Ezra Pound and world literature
And sparked an interest in the plastic arts.
Virginia had a passion for the arts
And almost seemed a work of art to me
Although her youthful and seductive beauty
Surpassed what any stone or metal sculpture
Or portrait made of brush strokes could offer.

I was in love with her and poetry.

All of my somnolent poetic nature 470
Was now awake although as yet unformed.
I authored short poems in my spare hours.
I hoped to write some sort of epic poem.
I worshiped at an altar new to me.

Atlanta and Cross Keys

Passion for poetry and for Virginia
Now flowed together like two powerful currents
And cut new channels deep into my soul.

Like ocean currents they would carry me
Toward the open ocean.

My road forward, though, was not *Appian*.
Poetry was not yet a well known world
Although I had explored Pound's curious *Cantos*,
Some works by Eliot and some by Whitman
Whom Pound once labeled a pig-headed father.

Those men and the tradition they produced
Became a sort of anchor for my soul.

They had a freedom I would emulate
Although I could not master it because
I was too young.

                I could not understand
A fundamental truth of my Becoming:
There ought to be a substrate in a poet
Profound and full of hope, but one our world
(Human and natural) slowly *confirmed*
Until it had become a sure foundation.

Good poetry could grow on that foundation—
Poetry full of love and sorrow, too—
Whatever form the poetry should take.

I was too young to understand how long
The preparation of such a foundation
Would probably demand given my nature—
What happiness and sorrow, awful tumult,
Foolish ambitions, thwarted expectations,
Apparent victories, comforts and wounds—
A troublesome rood of mortal variables
Would form my inner person and prepare me

Book VIII

To offer up a love song—one of sorrow
And solemn joy—born out of gratitude
For decades of tumultuous formation.

But I was lazy and naïve. I thought
Someone could produce poetry beyond   510
The sort of person he had grown to be.

A youthful soul could produce works of art
Superlative and worthy of attention.

I hoped to make an icon out of words,
A lofty work which others would applaud,
A monument more durable than bronze.

On ordinary evenings after supper
Upon the floor of our small living room
I lay alone and propped a notebook up
Against a large cushion and wrote poems.   520
Often I put music on because
I loved the flowing sound of harmonies
And counterpoint from our old stereo.
The music came from our one local station
That was devoted to the classics
Or from a record I had set to play
As a melodic background for my work.

Music and poetry had come together
And grown inseparable in my soul
Although I was frustrated that mere words   530
Could not accomplish what good music may.
I had no doubt any poet must falter
And come far short of what a great composer—
A good composer even—could impart
To an audience by music alone.

A smattering of poems was all I owned,
Mostly anthologies, but I began
To purchase volumes and explore the poems.

Virginia took a course on modern poets
At Emory University. She studied   540
W. B. Yeats and Wallace Stevens—men
Whose work was new to me and full of lore
And argument I could not understand.
We read "The Second Coming," and for me
The power and obscurity of Yeats
Were wonderful and frustrating at once.
Virginia loaned a volume of his prose,
A Vision, where Yeats proffered metaphysics
And opened up a world truly bizarre
And arbitrary. It had major cycles   550
Of history that were unprovable,
And reincarnations equally so.

It would be decades more before I saw
A problem faced by Yeats, a poet graced
Beyond so many others with a talent
For lyric poetry, a man who had
No world-view of his own, no *Weltanschauung*
(A word I later came to know and love).
He had no proper subject as a poet;
In truth, he had nothing to write about.   560
He had to cast about to find a topic
In Irish lore, or later in *A Vision*,
To form the subject matter of his poems.

He had a problem I would also have,
One I already had as a young man
Who wanted to write poetry in school.
I could not understand the problem then
(Although I was dimly aware of it)
Because I was not troubled by the fact
That as a youth I was not fully formed   570
And had no settled concept of the world.
I could not understand how very much
Music in concert halls, perhaps, but more,
Music in poetry must have a source

Book VIII

Not only in an artist's inner man
But also in that man as one who saw
And understood his place within the world.

Some of me wanted to explore all knowledge
And understand what others long before
Had fully understood and then passed on. 580
I studied sermons from the Buddhist schools
And opened up Plato and Aristotle;
But I was such a novice I could not
Make use of what they wrote even to start
To understand or value my own place
Within a larger world. I wrongly thought
I understood the place I had just found
In one old southern city and in school.

Our move from Florida had been a storm
For one young, naïve boy. My youthful soul 590
Was like a Gulf shore after a tremendous
Hurricane had whipped the waters up
And torn its fledgling architecture down.

Yet on that devastated coast arose
Another and a better architecture
After a hurricane in calmer weather.

Or someone could compare my youthful soul
To an uprooted, immature tree
Transplanted by a strong yet unseen hand
Close to abundant water that would seep 600
Under its roots and provide nourishment.
Perhaps I was a sapling who one day
Would produce fruit agreeable to some
Who found me under favorable suns.

Book IX

Cross Keys and a New Road

A passionate London poet once declared
Beauty and truth were one, and the same thought
Occurred to me during my senior year
Before I heard his name spoken aloud
Or found it in a book of poetry.

I had become just old enough to love
With passion that was strong and would endure
And I had found a woman who was young
And gorgeous. I looked into her eyes
And almost lost myself. I watched her moods   10
And her young, supple body as she moved
And all I saw of her captured my soul;
I loved her mature mind that was alert
And taught and challenged a young man to grow.
I wanted to know her with all of me.
I wanted to be one with her at once.

Autumn evenings I paced solitary
In our back yard and now and then I stood
And felt a gush of warm love

Book IX

Flow and flood my youthful soul.   20
I had never known such sweet pain
As love and hurt combatted in my chest.
I was immobilized by agony
And longing for a woman beyond me.

One part of me wanted to hold at bay
The tumult but the whole of me could not;
I fought a losing battle in a war
Of desperation, love and hopelessness
For (what was worse) Virginia had a husband
And so was wholly owned by another   30
And out of reach. She was a decade older,
So I could only be a student friend.
I wanted and adored her as a goddess
Who taught me some of what she understood,
A holy past of art and truth.

                    She was
A mistress of all that was beautiful
And as I looked at her I thought she was
Almost an incarnation of her lore,
Or "borrowed finery" as she once termed it.

So: full of love I thought I understood   40
Something profound about the whole of love—
How much one longs to mingle with the other,
Not only two bodies, but soul to soul—
As though two mortals could become one Being,
One essence far more wonderful than either
Could be, apart, although wholly in love.

A potent longing haunted me always
Although I never spoke it to another.

So I began my second year at Cross Keys
Flooded with sorrow, profoundly enamored.   50
Whatever class I happened to attend
Whatever subject matter I took up

She occupied my hope and fantasy;
Nonetheless I managed as a student
To study Latin and do good translations
Of Vergil, Catullus, and even some Horace,
And P. Ovidius Naso, whom I read
With mixed emotions when he counseled one
Who hoped to capture a married woman:
Draw her name on her own table—*in vino*. 60
I had not had a Christian education
Although my parents were conventional
In morals and behavior so I always
Assumed adultery had to be wrong
And I could not have ambled down that path.
Nonetheless I often hoped one day
Virginia would divorce and she and I
Could make our way together and know love
And purpose as a devoted couple.

Among the surges of a hopeless love 70
Music was now a harbor and a haven.
I sat at home and studied Beethoven
As often as I could and sank my soul
Devoutly into the commanding order
He conjured out of his own troubled hours
As he sought power and beauty no mere mortal
Had understood or brought before the world.
I also bought a recording of Schubert
Whose somber symphony left half undone
And called "Unfinished" spoke of sorrow 80
And awful loss. Much later I discovered
Schubert had died of syphilis acquired
By foolish youthful lack of self control,
A tragedy ironic in a man
Who managed such formidable arrays
Of notes and bars that moved at his command.
I bought a record of his "Great C Major,"
A symphony entirely new to me,
And was astounded at its modern sound—
The powerful rhythms as it strode along, 90

Book IX

A force unto itself. His smart allusion
To the last movement of Beethoven's *Ninth*
In his own final movement struck a note
Of bold Germanic wit because it made
An auditory claim to have accomplished
Something like Beethoven's mastery
The moment he paid homage to the Master.

In all my sorrow and in all my joy—
Sorrow in love and joy in modest growth
As I garnered more intellectual food   100
From school and books for my imagination—
Nature was still a comfort and a balm.

Close to our home there was a modest pond
With a small dock folks almost never used;
Maybe a fisherman or two would come
And cast a hopeful line into the water
But if one did I never saw it happen.
I had gone there one summer evening
And sat down on the dock and stretched my legs
And watched across the water as the sun   110
Sat radiant and calm among the clouds
Afloat over a distant stand of pines.

On autumn afternoons and early evenings
Once school was over for the day
I drove down to the lake and took a notebook
For composition as I sat and watched
Sun and clouds commingle in their sport.
Those clouds would not obscure an autumn glory
Of sunshine that shone strong around and through them,
Pink, rose and gold and full of distant warmth.   120
It was a glimpse of heaven far away
For me and those who stood below and watched,
If any stood; but I was all alone
On almost every visit to the dock
And grateful to be so, with all my thoughts
Of poetry, and love I could not have.

Cross Keys and a New Road

Although I loved and love consumed me so
I also had a family around me.
My grandfather had journeyed to Atlanta
From Florida. He passed his final years   130
With us before an economic change
Called us to Florida once more. During
My senior year as I prepared for college
Our small household would often pay a call
On *Catfish King*, a large suburban restaurant
That offered catfish from Lake Okeechobee
Caught and transported fresh from that large pond
Overnight, every night, for our delight.
It was an honest, homely joy to sit
And watch a waitress carry our portions   140
Deep fried and brown and crispy—towering
As though each plate supported a small mountain
Of catfish from our southern sister state.
Moreover, joy of joys, each one of us
Could reload his plate at no extra cost.
Our family parted from the *Catfish King*
Content to know that we had gormandized;
Maybe that made a full American
Of me. I thought of food as entertainment
And even more so when we had to pay   150
For just one course and got all one could want.

Sometimes I would improve a narrow round
Of comfortable routines by travelling
To famous Emory University,
A lofty seat of learning not so far
From Cross Keys High School. I first saw the campus
One cold November day when Virginia
Took some chosen juniors for events
Which challenged us to demonstrate in public
Our small command of histrionic art.
I conned a paragraph from Ayn Rand,   160
A passage I believed in thoroughly
About our freedom and the sacred will

Book IX

Indomitable of an individual.
Because I spoke with obvious ardor
Some judges awarded me good marks
Although I did not carry off a trophy;
Nonetheless I enjoyed the adventure
Though it was counterbalanced on the scales
By my poor showing as a sole debater.
Before that day I had never debated   170
And had no natural aptitude or skill.
As a young boy I often saw my parents
Argue—almost violently sometimes—
And as a youth I formed a strong resolve
Not to argue or be confrontative.
I disappointed all (myself included)
Who thought I ought to do well in debate
Because I had done well in declamation;
But I was more than glad to let it go
And turn my thoughts to poetry once more.   180

I saw Emory's campus in the spring
(I travelled there to use the library)
And I was taken with its southern beauty—
An island of classical architecture
Among spreading magnolia trees festooned
In masses of fresh blossoms, pink and white.
It stood on rolling lawns and seemed to say
Civilization had established here
An outpost that would not be shaken soon
Or ever, for it stood permanently   190
For human culture and the human mind,
And may that mind bring forth flowers and fruit
And more adorn the landscape of the future
Than those magnolia blossoms had adorned
The rolling lawns and buildings of a college.

At Emory I took a summer course
Offered by two professors who taught
Astronomy and astrophysics there.
One morning I brought along a notebook

Of my own drawings of celestial objects— 200
Star clusters, double stars and nebulae;
I had volunteered for ten minutes
To share some observations among classmates.
I made a large impression on the students
Although probably not on the professors.
The course was not a course for college credit
But only for enrichment; all the same
It stimulated me and made me look
Once more upon astronomy with favor
As a possible future vocation. 210
Before the course was over we were able
To use the college telescope. I saw
How much more light a larger instrument
Could gather, on a clear and starry night,
Than my refractor ever could have done:
How luminous deep sky objects could appear
Reflected by the large and polished mirror
Of Emory's Newtonian reflector.

At Emory one summer day, at noon,
I met with her for lunch. She seemed to me 220
A goddess with blonde hair, who sat opposite
On a plastic chair in a large common room.
I was in love with her and every moment
I got to spend with her was far too good
To last but never good enough because
It could not last beyond a confused moment.
I felt a growing sickness in my stomach,
A queasiness and sense of strong despair:
To be so close to one I could not have,
To love a woman who would not love back. 230
I sat in thrall and ate and talked with her
About poetry, and Eliot, and Pound,
And William Butler Yeats—about my own,
What I had written and how it was good
And not so good, and what I ought to learn.

Book IX

In Latin class I read saucy Catullus
And Horace's *aere perennius*,
And what Cicero said before the Senate
To pillory rebellious Cataline
But beyond all compare was what I found 240
When I read Vergil's strong hexameters;
They carried me from fallen Troy aflame
To Carthage and its queen, Dido, who perished
Forsaken by Aeneas on his way
To found the empire Vergil saw around him,
That grand imperium under Augustus,
That *pax romana* from a capital
Of red brick buildings clothed in gorgeous marble.

Long after Rome had fallen, and her glory
Became a spectacle of broken statues 250
And toppled colonnades for passers by
To gaze upon and take a moral home,
Rome's noblest poet found a brother Italian
And turned him from the wood of this dark life
To guide him through the agonies of hell
To better hopes of purgatory where
He found his Beatrice, whom he loved
And she would be his guide to Paradise:
Dante Alighieri, son of Florence,
Who for his love and sorrow would become 260
The greatest poet of the Middle Ages.
Our English class had studied his *Inferno*
For two long weeks as my Virginia sat
Adorable on a tall stool before us
And taught us all that we should know of Dante.
But what I thought of most was not the poem,
But rather Beatrice, Dante's love,
Who was, in God's large plan, another's wife.

Of man's first disobedience, and the fruit
That brought us all our woe, I read at last, 270
But on my own. I had acquired a taste
For epic poems after Homer and Dante

Cross Keys and a New Road

So now I turned to Milton, whom John Dryden
Had thought the greatest poet of them all.
I observed Satan as Milton portrayed him,
A grand Archfiend with vile combustion down
Tumbling from heaven accompanied by his host,
Beelzebub and all the other gods,
Onto a lake of fire in new formed hell—
Suffered to have dominion there by Him   280
Whose arms prevailed above on Heaven's *champaign*
(He proved himself Almighty against his foes).
I saw a man and woman in a garden
Undone by a foul serpent, known to us
As Satan who loquacious as he coiled
Seduced our mother to a mortal sin;
And Adam fondly joined her in her fall.
The scope of fallen history he unfolded
Until one Man regain the blissful seat
Our parents lost to follow a false lord.   290

Milton astounded me. In every line
The power of his mind was evident.
He was not satisfied with common thoughts
Or turns of phrase, nor was he neophiliac,
But rather: as an empire newly founded
Produces coinage proper to the realm,
A coinage never made or seen before
Although compounded of a common metal,
So Milton coined a language new to us
Although compounded from our native tongue.   300
He formed an idiom suitable for one
Who would explain the ways of God to man.

I read another work all on my own.
I saw how in the middle course of life
John Bunyan's Christian found a Book and got
Conviction and much trouble from its pages.
He chose therefore to flee his native town,
The *City of Destruction*, and his spouse,
His offspring and his neighborhood and journeyed

Book IX

Through many dangers, toils and temptations 310
Past *Doubting Castle* and *Giant Despair*
And the *Valley of the Shadow of Death*
Until at last he found *Beulah Land*
And that City so aptly named *Celestial*.
He was a citizen of that same Town;
It was not of this world—just as his faith
Was not of earth but came from God in heaven
And brought him to his Savior in the end.

I saw a faith I could not understand
Or rather, one that I would not embrace 320
Although it underlay such works of art
As Milton, Bunyan and others produced.

Those powerful affirmations sounded true,
Just as Händel's *Messiah* sounded true,
As though Jesus must be the "Lord of lords."
Once I heard other vocal works by him
It became obvious that oratorio
Stood at the apex of his compositions.
Noble *Messiah*, vast as any ocean,
Enfolded both in words and harmony 330
A truth Händel had understood and shared
(As any artist must share what is true,
What joy and suffering have formed in him).
He offered in a torrent of creation
An *opus* he produced in just one month.
I rose as did the audience in awe—
Or cognizant of that tradition
Begun when George II stood to honor
The "Hallelujah Chorus," when *Messiah*
Was first performed at London's Covent Garden. 340

His oratorio was German art
Composed on English soil by one who stayed
In London and was compensated there
Just as the symphonist, Franz Joseph Haydn,
Would come to London and his countryman,

Cross Keys and a New Road

Karl Maria von Weber, sojourned there,
For London had a public who would pay
Appropriately to artists who composed
Works that surpassed what any son of England
Composed or had a calling to compose.   350
Weber wrote to his friends in Austria
What luxury it was to be abroad:
To compose freely and be well rewarded;
To be so affluent he could afford
A haircut whenever he wanted one.
So now I understood why those composers,
Mozart, Haydn, Beethoven and Weber
And many other men of lesser fame
Adopted a long hairstyle In Vienna.
It was not genius made their hair grow long;   360
It was the specter of poverty that loomed
For men of genius who adored their art.

School and music could engage my soul
And poetry was always a young siren
But in July another door would open
To a chamber I had known before.

At Emory there was a young professor
Who taught his students to compose short stories.
Virginia knew him and put in a word
For me, so I was able to join in   370
And try to craft, under his tutelage,
A story that someone might want to publish.
Although I had produced so many stories
When I was still a boy in Florida
That was so long ago I had forgotten
How to be free and let imagination
Have its own way and spin novel adventures.
Back then stories just flowed out of my soul
And almost had a life apart from me.
By contrast now I pondered, struggled, wrote   380
To satisfy the standards of a course
But came up empty handed because I

Book IX

Had now begun to form personal standards
And could not satisfy them with a story
Or anything composed of common prose.

Over lunch I talked with my professor
In the same dining hall where I had met
And spoken months before with Virginia;
He knew us both and ventured the opinion
That poetry would often grow the best   390
Upon the strong foundation of a love
That was frustrated—like the love of Dante
For Beatrice, or the love of Yeats
For Maude Gonne, or such another love.

Many nights I lay down on the floor
After supper in our living room
And propped my notebook up against a cushion;
I had put a record on, Schubert or Brahms,
And now I would compose. Pencil in hand
I wrote—erased—and wrote—erased again—   400
And wrote 'til I was happy with my work.
I had a process that was comfortable,
One I would use for many years to come
As I composed poetry long or short.
My senior year I produced many poems
But only two I thought were any good:
"Six Tone Poems," and "Beowulf's Barrow."
"Six Tone Poems" sought to capture impressions
From before dawn to sunset in a city;
"Beowulf's Barrow" was a modest heap   410
Of verses placed as a memorial
To *Beowulf* after I read that poem.

Although I wrote those lyrics and I studied
William Butler Yeats and was so taken
With his insane Irish imagination
(And wondrous way with words and argument)
A larger, deeper part of me soon longed
To write a major epic of some sort

Cross Keys and a New Road

Perhaps about a wanderer who travelled
Across our land or all over the world   420
And quaffed a horn of large experience
And thereby, somehow, got a final truth
From something he had swallowed to the dregs.

I had begun to wonder if one could
Concoct a major or ultimate truth
Out of our large kaleidoscope of cultures;
And if, moreover, one could become whole
As one took in the multicolored palette
Of that kaleidoscope and wholly owned it.
One truth would form and be so obvious   430
Every soul would know it was the *Truth*
And bow to it and want to own it, too.
Could a lone wanderer produce that truth
And so become a savior of himself
And others as he shared the cup with us?

I thought I would compose one Saturday
As morning sunshine flooded our front room.
I opened up my notebook and prepared
To start a poem about blue and gold,
Something about blue skies and golden gods,   440
But suddenly the radio produced
A melody that stopped me as I wrote:
The *Florida Suite* by Frederick Delius.
Because I was a son of Florida—
Only a son adopted by that state
But still a son, and one who could recall
Her world of ocean and coconut palms,
Of quartz sand beaches and wood fishing piers—
I fell in love with every note of it.
Years later, a grad student, I would order   450
The same recording at the Harvard Coop
And from the record jacket I would learn
That Delius had come to Florida
From England and had managed a plantation;
He fell in love with Florida and found

Book IX

Some images that served his music well,
Memories that allowed his art to blossom.

Sometimes I thought of Florida, and thought
I could return to my old state and work
And buy a sailboat and spend summertime 460
Adrift upon the ocean all alone.
I would pass every hour at home with nature.
Sea food and coconuts would be my fare
Captured by spear gun and my able hand
And I would sail as far as I could go.
Perhaps I would be like my wanderer
Or like the *Wandrer* that Wagner made
Of Wotan, king of all the gods, who journeyed
A large romantic archetype on earth
And sought among mortals whatever knowledge 470
He could not find among his gods and heroes
In fabled Valhalla—an aerial castle
Constructed by a fallen race of giants.

All summer long I thought about Yale College,
A place of gothic towers and battlements
And scholarship buttressed, impregnable
Beyond what I had known or could foretell.

But now the month of August ripened, full
Of summer fruit and bold cicada songs
That told on hottest August afternoons 480
To anyone who understood the music
That summer now must fade, and autumn follow.

One afternoon I journeyed to Cross Keys;
I hoped to see Virginia one more time.
We had to go outside because she was
On duty as a traffic monitor.
We stood and talked on shallow front steps
While students crowded past on their way home;
There was no room for private conversation.
We spoke of college and a hopeful future 490

Cross Keys and a New Road

And poetry, but not a word was spoken
About what I had told her of my love.

She thought I was a promising young student
Who would (perhaps) one day become a poet
And maybe she was flattered by my love;
Her broad education made her mind
Equally broad: she took my adoration
But would not harbor an adulterous thought
Or be untrue to what she had once vowed.

I drove away, was soon on Peachtree Street   500
And home once more where I would pack my books,
Classical records and a small wardrobe
My parents bought toward the summer's end
So when I got to Yale I would not look
Uncouth or out of place among the frosh.

One more day would pass and I would be
On interstate highways and on a journey
Through open countryside and up the coast
To Yale, New Haven, and another world.

Book X

Yale, New Haven and New York

We drove past Phelps Gate on Yale's Old Campus
And looked up at anachronistic houses
Evocative of Oxford and Cambridge
And venerable continental schools,
Structures that looked much older than they were.

How I remember the first strong impression
You made on me as Mom and Dad and I
Walked down your narrow alleyways and saw
Windows ornate with leaden lattices,
Narrow old features, set in Gothic stone   10
That mounted story after story up
To sharply angled roofs with old slate shingles
Gray and somber on a September day.

On Whalley Avenue we took a room
Close to the base of West Rock—a tall cliff
Of black and orange stone that looked forbidding
Against a cold, bleak Connecticut sky.
The clouds above looked distant and like lead,
Long massive slabs of metal in a row,

Book X

Processing somehow slowly across heaven 20
And shutting out any small hope of warmth.

I was enough in touch with nature now
To feel at one with that unwholesome weather
And isolated from all that was good.
I now confronted my environment:
A place that I could hardly call my home,
But one that would become a home for me,
An academic residence of sorts
Portentous as those overhanging clouds.

Those first two days I trod the paths of a freshman: 30
From offices to offices and back
To manage everything from course selections
To room keys, linen pick up, and a mailbox
To call my own at underground Yale Station;
On many future mornings I would go
Down steps into a crowded passageway
And fetch whatever mail had come to me.

Once all was done, my parents and I stopped
At Vanderbilt Hall on the Old Campus.
I would room there with three other men: 40
One from Connecticut, one from Japan
(Born in our country), and one from Chicago.
They were all strange to me, from worlds remote
From what I was familiar with and loved.

Father and Mother hugged me and said good–bye
And as I turned from them and walked toward
Vanderbilt's archway so close and dark
I felt I had just turned my back upon
An old identity, a way of being.
I was a man and would no longer be 50
Under my parents' roof. I was a person
Utterly on my own in a new world:
Someone who was now old enough to vote

Yale, New Haven and New York

And old enough to die in our armed forces
And old enough to be a man at Yale.

I felt a sickness at my stomach's core
(A malady I had not often known)
As I walked off. I only looked back once
To wave good bye to parents who had loved me
And brought me up, and who would always love me; 60
They drove away and waved a final wave
And I walked on alone to my new place.

All freshmen were summoned to Woolsey Hall
That afternoon to file discretely in
And sit in ordered rows before the stage.
Across the stage the president and dean
And other faculty of lesser state
Processed in academic majesty
Clad in long robes of multicolored glory.
They took their places and surveyed the crowd. 70
One after another would take a stand
And help the latest frosh to comprehend
The challenge and importance of our days,
The aura and the magnitude of Yale,
And how our *alma mater* could impact
Our lives for good, and aim us toward a future
Of powerful contribution to our homelands,
Homelands that would lie open to our words.
Woolsey Hall looked grey, old and unpromising
Outside, but once somebody entered in 80
The person saw a creamy, warm interior
Roomy enough to hold a thousand freshmen.
A handsome balcony hung overhead
And coursed around three quarters of the hall.
Cream colored pews stood handsomely in rows
Cushioned in red—almost luxurious
To a newcomer. I could not know then
That only a few days would pass before
I would attend orchestral concerts here.
They would comfort my soul in darkest winter. 90

Book X

Here, too, I would attend one final session
With other classmates at our graduation,
A bookend to the one I sat in now.

Later that afternoon Vanderbilt Hall
Attended a small welcome party hosted
With fluent cocktails by the Dean of Saybrook,
A residential College that would house us
After our freshman year on the Old Campus.
Our Dean's living room was darkly paneled
Like many other rooms in old Yale buildings   100
And two large hunting dogs lay on the floor
Before a blazing fire, evocative
Of kindred scenes in eighteenth century artworks
By English portrait masters. As we stood there
We talked about events and politics
Or just our own backgrounds. I took it in
That I was now at Yale with other frosh
Ambitious, self-important, or unsure,
But all classmates. Only one or two
Would come to matter in my life some day   110
But as we talked in a dark paneled room
What mattered most was that I was now here;
And I thought more about the wood and decor
Of linen table cloth and silver chalice
Of fruity punch the Dean's wife offered us—
The aura and accouterments of culture
Or class—than of the people I was with.

Later that day I posed for a class photo,
Apparently one small *sine qua non*
For all of us who had enrolled at Yale;   120
I thought it was a bother, and the more so
When I was told by the photographer:
No one could have a copy of the yearbook
Unless he paid a price for it that sounded
So far beyond what it could possibly
Be worth, I would have been a fool to pay it;
So I sat up and looked unphotogenic,

Yale, New Haven and New York

As dour and serious as I could manage,
And only after some powerful urging
Produced a smile for that old shutterbug;	130
And I was in fact serious, absorbed
In my own thoughts and attitudes—my soul—
Much more than many classmates, for I had come
With a compulsion I would not abandon:
To grow into a poet and produce
Substantial truth for a corrupted day.

I passed a warm green lawn with sprinklers running
En route to Latin class one sunny morning
By JE College and the autumn sunlight
Created little rainbows in the drops	140
As they rose briefly and fell down again.
The lawn was bordered by an aged wall
Whose stonework was just like that of the college;
Outside the wall a flagstone walkway coursed
Partly in shadow cast by the old wall.
I could take quiet joy in such a scene
So full of peace and order in the sunshine;
And nature in the water and the grass
Encouraged me as I walked toward my class.
She offered beauty in a small vignette,	150
A cameo of herself on my way
In harmony with what men once had built:
Beauty I could not hold, or stay and savor,
But it could send me gladly as I walked
Into a darkly paneled seminar
Where our professor, dull and full of Latin
And almost desiccated with old age,
Would lecture us on Lesbia and Catullus.

I met another student late that Autumn
Who was a sophomore and who wrote poems.	160
Our mutual advisor introduced us.
We met alone for lunch in JE College
And although he seemed courteous enough
I felt no true affinity for him

Book X

Or for whatever aesthetic he had.
During our junior year another classmate
Described this Yalie as somewhat effete,
And decades afterward, as an alumnus,
I happened on a novel by him based
Upon his lifestyle as a homosexual   170
Who had to watch his lover die of aids.
A few years after that as I paged through
An issue of the *Alumni Magazine*
I saw his name enrolled as one deceased.

The fall semester had some happy moments
And humorous ones, too, as I became
Acquainted with our university
And some of the unusual faculty
And hangers-on who made a home of it.
Young Tappy Wilder, who worked in admissions,   180
Took me late one October afternoon
To the Elizabethan Club, a wooden house
Surrounded by a small white picket fence,
Where faculty and students stopped to rest,
Have tea and cookies, and discuss in comfort
Modern or classic literature or what-not.
One fellow I remember wore a vest
That spanned his tubby waist but left some room
For further growth, and while he sat and talked
About the music of Sir Edward Elgar   190
He ate a cookie. As he munched away
The crumbs dropped freely from his mouth to land
On his broad vest. They formed a growing flock.
The golden bits straggled across the waistcoat
Like scattered cattle over hilly land.
They wandered up and down and seemed forsaken
Like the proverbial sheep without a shepherd
Among the unfamiliar hills and valleys.

Although our college was not made for sheep
Old Yale would always have its animals   200
And some may have been students—as one wag

Suggested, who sponsored an open forum
(*Gratis* to all) with an alluring title:
"Are Yale Men Beasts?" Sometimes I thought they were
When I saw how they behaved toward some girls
And toward each other, and among themselves.
Eventually I saw or hoped it was
A process of my own slow maturation
To dwell among such careless liberty
Enjoyed by some, yet live in solitude. 210
Although I went to lectures and became
More acquainted with my class and suite mates
I felt I was alone in all I thought
And was truly alone, because my soul
(Or that strong part of me that longed for joy)
Could not be satisfied by what our school
Offered me from her cornucopia.
I was not understood by those around me,
Or maybe would not be *mis*understood
And so would not expose my truest self. 220

Not all of us were beasts—maybe none were—
But as I walked along one winter night
On my way back from a small laundromat
I saw a beastly form approaching me.
Avoiding icy patches, it stayed close
To where a stone wall met the frozen sidewalk.
It had some urgent business of its own.
We almost ran into each other there
And as we came suddenly face to face
He looked up at me. I looked down at him 230
And then a strong revulsion filled my gut
Because I saw an unusually large rat
Hunched over, with a long and sinuous tail,
As focused on his mission as I was
On mine: rushing along an icy path
To find a warm hole and avoid the cold.

One autumn afternoon I wandered in
And took a seat in a small lecture hall;

Book X

Louis Martz, chair of our English Department,
Gave a brief talk on modern poetry.   240
He quoted from a famous Wordsworth sonnet,
"The world is too much with us," Wordsworth's call
To people who were lost in urban bustle,
One man's forlorn appeal to turn away
From what the mercantile world had to offer.
But after Wordsworth he quoted another,
Someone now forgotten who had just
Produced a book of poems and boldly
Declared, "The world is not with us enough."
The good professor only meant to show   250
How large a turnaround one hundred years
Or so had made in poets' attitudes,
But the one line offended me so much
I thought I had to find some open air;
So I rose up and stood in isolation
Among the hundred people who were there
And turned around and walked out of the hall.
My footsteps echoed loud among the pauses
As the professor carried on his talk.

That old sonnet haunted me as I walked: 260
"The world is too much with us; late and soon,
Getting and spending, we lay waste our powers;
Little we see in Nature that is ours."
His words would trouble me every so often,
But most of all when Christmas holidays
Came on. Then all the force of "late and soon,
Getting and spending" became obvious.
A sizeable multitude laid waste their powers
As they sought some pale shadow of true joy
In forms that were only material   270
And doomed to be forgotten in short order.
I could recall the many Christmases
In Martins Ferry, and then in Florida—
Mornings of snow and clouds, or of cool sun,
But mornings full of joy and not because
Some hoped for gift lay underneath the tree

Yale, New Haven and New York

(However much I could enjoy that, too)
But because I had no doubt Mom and Dad
Loved me with an unconquerable love.

Snowflakes or sunshine on a Christmas Day 280
Summoned me and our family to join
Whatever nature had prepared for us.
She made good on her offer to bestow
Snowy or sunny happiness on those
Who ventured out and left their toys at home.

Not every family member was remote
During those early days at Yale. My uncle
Worked for a year in New York; he would come
On weekends to New Haven. We drove out
Among Connecticut's valleys and hills— 290
Rocks, dens and groves, small bushes, evergreens;
We sampled foliage or bought apple cider
And enjoyed what the country had to offer
To people from the city in the fall.
But it became a bleak experience
As autumn sank towards winter:
The landscape had a cold and stony look,
A face of worn down cliffs, mountains and valleys
Covered with trees denuded of their foliage
'Til every valley, slope and open meadow 300
Was bare of any greenery or life
Except for pine trees interspersed among
Hectares of dry branches ashen grey.
Because of that, after October passed,
I had no further interest in those journeys;
I asked if we could rendezvous instead
In New York City—megalopolis
That I had only looked at from a car.

My first train ride came in mid–November.
I rode the New York and New Haven Railroad 310
To a fabled Big Apple.

Book X

              A coastal town,
New Haven had a harbor but would never
Live up to its potential as a port.

I rode to one of the world's largest harbors,
A town that had embraced from the whole world
So many of its poor and huddled masses.

It was a huge—almost a monstrous—space,
A gargantuan empire of human structures
That groped the clouds and sometimes blotted out
The sun and covered up the far horizon   320
With concrete, glass, aluminum and steel.

I saw those poor and huddled masses now
And what they had become in that great hub:
I saw no trace in any human face
Of contemplative journey or reflection,
Of placid, philosophical detachment
Or inward dreaminess or dormancy
That would become poetry in its day,
Or music that would lift the human soul.
I only saw a hardihood of passage,   330
Of frustrated trajectories and goals
As person after person forged ahead
To be on time somewhere or do some shopping
Or get a place on the next bus or train.
Christmas was not far away, so maybe
Some of them sought a reconciling gift
For one they had offended, or a present
For someone whom they loved—for one could still
Trust that love existed in the city
Just as small trees could be found along streets,   340
Hemmed in by cords and stunted in their growth.

My uncle took me for my only walk
To Wall Street on a quiet Sunday morning.
Although the sky was cloudless and the sun
Cast a memorable splendor on the town

Yale, New Haven and New York

Wall Street had not a person to its name
Except for us. We walked the empty road
Downhill from Trinity Church, St. Paul's Chapel,
At Broadway and Wall. Maybe it was too soon
For anyone to come to Sunday service,   350
Or maybe we had come a bit too late
And everyone was already inside,
But we had not come to go to church
But only to be tourists, in true freedom,
And take advantage of an empty street
On Sunday morning under the sunshine.

My uncle took me to a skyscraper
Not very far from Wall Street, where he worked.
A quiet elevator lifted us
Rapidly upward, and we ambled out   360
Into a large and airy corporate room
With desks and chairs positioned all around:
Cubicles, work stations and office spaces
Arranged on a deeply carpeted floor.
He led me past them to the north window,
A panel of plate glass whose view commanded
The Hudson River, its commercial docks
And colorful visitors: liners and tankers,
Container ships and rusty cargo vessels,
Sporting the banners of all the world's countries   370
And anchored on the New York waterfront.

The ships looked like so many toys set down
By giant parents for a giant boy
To come outdoors and have some fun with them,
Maybe *en route* to church that sunny day.

We overlooked a town of dormant souls,
Enormous under a cloudless sky.
We saw it from a grand, exalted spot
As though we were both gods and stood upon
A heavenly patio, a lofty cloud.   380
I had a brief, illusory sensation

Book X

That all those ships *were* toys, and I the boy
Whose giant parents left them out for him;
Or maybe I was a young god who stood
Plenipotentiary above things human,
One who could handle man-made cargo vessels
And ocean liners and all human works,
And human fates, as though they were just toys
To be turned forward, backward, left or right,
Or up and down just as the fancy took him.   390
Our lofty elevation could encourage
Such thoughts for just a moment. Afterwards
I was myself again and understood
I was no giant boy, and was no god,
And all the altitude I stood upon
Was made by others' labor: former men
Who made a statement of their own ambition
By forcing concrete towers to thrust upward
And loan godlike perspective on the town
That lay so large and somnolent below   400
Under a peaceful sky on Sunday morning.

New York was one gigantic artifact,
An artifact of artifacts in truth,
One huge mosaic compounded of efforts
To build a way to grandeur and to power.

New Haven was a tiny coastal town
That could not hope in any way to rival
Her larger sister lying to the west.
Her harbor was a pale ghost of its promise;
She hardly boasted one authentic stage,   410
Although the Shubert Theater always ran
Productions that would travel on to Broadway;
New Haven had no skyscrapers, no Wall Street,
But in the heart of that small, dreary town
Yale University stood upright, proud,
Founded by Eli Yale's generous present
And very old—more than two centuries old,
So all but ancient by American measure—

With buildings of red brick, colonial style,
And architecture borrowed from the Gothic: 420
Turrets that looked as though they should adorn
Picturesque German castles on the Rhine.

One class I always loved, history of art,
Showed us how art and architecture blossomed
In ancient Egypt, then in Greece and Rome
And through the Middle Ages and Renaissance;
We saw a large succession of great masters,
Baroque, Rococo, English landscape artists,
Turner, Impressionism, and at last
Expressionism, Cubism, and those 430
Abstractions many folks would not call art.
I sat for hours and studied our text,
Helen Gardner's *Art through the Ages*,
And could observe how ancient peoples built
On prior accomplishments—how, for example,
Sculpture evolved from elementary forms
Toward the great heroic shapes of Greece
And the classical realism of Rome;
But in that world of imperial success
A spiritual challenger arose— 440
One we could see in the pale emperor's head,
Enormous eyes and almost vacant stare
Of Constantine, who had become a Christian.
What spiritual metamorphosis
Could make a man look so? and after that
I turned more pages and was puzzled further
By the flat, golden figures of Byzantium,
A form of art inimical to life,
Or so it seemed to me, an abstract palette
That showed humans as they could not have been 450
And could not be, planar and otherworldly
With frozen forms and gold enameling.
Then I remembered William Butler Yeats,
An old man sailing to Byzantium
To find among the singing masters there
Monuments of unageing intellect,

Book X

To call upon the sages so portrayed
To be the last instructors of his soul.

In high school I began to love van Gogh
And French Impressionists and, of course, Dali,   460
And soon I was exposed in two museums
To memorable paintings by those artists.

One Saturday I travelled west once more
To meet my uncle and have lunch with him
At New York's Metropolitan Museum.
We toured her lofty chambers after lunch,
Cream colored halls full of great works of art
And lesser works. We strolled and took them in,
Renaissance statues and canvasses,
Dutch landscape paintings I had come to love   470
For undulating gray-brown coasts and meadows;
Claude Monet and his seasonal haystacks,
And Renoir whose palette was much too florid;
Vincent van Gogh and his crazed vibrancy—
A vision of things as they had not been
And could not be. He made the landscape writhe
And stars too close morph into swirls with tails;
It was as though he longed for the whole world
To assume forms commanded by his soul.

I wandered off alone and found a work   480
So large it took the space of one whole wall,
A *Crucifixion* by Salvador Dali,
Also titled *Corpus Hypercubus*.
I stopped below and stood in awe of it.
I saw Jesus suspended far above me,
Not from a cross but from nine perfect cubes;
He looked away, his flesh and bone surrendered,
And Mary stood beneath him and gazed up
In strong compassion for his final state.
What amazed me most in the whole scene   490
Was the rich chestnut color of her hair,
Portrayed in such detail I almost thought

Yale, New Haven and New York

I could reach out and fondle it and feel
How softly and how supplely it would yield,
Each strand completely open to my touch.
I stood before a master beyond doubt,
A modern artist who could use a brush
And oils to show the substance of his thoughts
So palpable and visible it seemed
Substantial truth and not imagination. 500

What was imagination? What was truth?
Maybe philosophy or literature
Could tell me what, or if not what then how
Or in what sodality to find an answer.

At Yale I was admitted to a program
For forty students called Directed Studies.
We took lectures and seminars together
And spent more hours in the company
Of our professors than the average freshman.
The seminar in world literature 510
Met after supper in the Master's study
Of JE college, just next door to Saybrook;
We talked about Odysseus over sherry
And sat in leather armchairs, comfortably
Ensconced among the volumes of the past
And feeling very civilized no doubt
While somewhere far away the world passed by,
A clamor of sirens or of distant traffic,
Full of its joys and sorrows and its business.

On Tuesday mornings I looked forward to 520
A seminar held in an upper room
Where our philosophy professor taught
Us about Plato and Greek idealism
But also about Aristotle, Locke
And David Hume, a man fated to waken
Immanuel Kant from his dogmatic slumber.
Kant would ponder critically the problems
Of reason and epistemology

Book X

And come to idealistic conclusions;
He grounded all phenomenology   530
In a transcendental unity of apperception
And so he cast his lot not far from Plato—
Almost where the Athenian had begun
Although by a more convoluted route
To which the German syntax was conducive.
But I admired Kant, especially
The clarity of his great argument
That only moral actions could possess
A self-referential consistency.
Toward the end of that same course we studied   540
Nietzsche's colorful book, *Thus Spake Zarathustra*.
It was both powerful and enigmatic
And made me want to understand him better
So I purchased two volumes of his works
At the Yale Coop and brought them home with me
After the school year ended. I would camp
On our back yard patio and read them slowly
Under the shade of thickly planted pines
And let the breezes cool me as I thought.
Nietzsche was a rash philosopher   550
Who called Immanuel Kant a moral cripple
And had a falling out with Richard Wagner
(Although I was still ignorant of that).
He coined a phrase that was unclear to me,
The "will to power." It would prove, one day,
Prophetical of Germany's worst hours.

Not long before we studied Friedrich Nietzsche
(I found his forename, *Rich in Peace*, ironic)
Our longed for Christmas holiday began
And I flew south to see my family   560
And friends. I rode an airport limousine
To JFK Airport (formerly called
New York International Airport).
It was my first trip to a major tarmac
And also my first journey on a jet.
I could feel that I was now a man:

Yale, New Haven and New York

A young man, truly, but an adult male
Who drove in limousines to major airports
And boarded large jet aircraft that would soar
With unaccustomed attitudes of power570
Steeply into the sky I always loved;
At such a moment earthbound human landscapes
Would shrink swiftly to miniature roads
And toy-sized storage tanks and skyscrapers
And then to almost nothing far below.

The holiday was warm and comfortable.
Mother prepared the food I always loved
And I could pass time with a few old friends.
Sadly I had more than enough to do
Because our professors had been generous580
And loaded us with end of term homework.
At Yale an error had just taken root
That would impose on future generations:
The assumption that the volume of our work
Was tantamount to serious education.
It was obvious to me and others after
At Harvard and at Yale that fewer books
Assigned with time to read them thoughtfully
Would prove a better value for us all
Than stacks of books devoured in a hurry590
Under pressure to turn all the pages.

However, no sane man could hurry through
Any book by Immanuel Kant.
Our holiday assignment was to study
His *Fundamentals of the Metaphysics of Morals*,
And as I did it seemed to grasp my soul
Across more than a century and stole
Some precious hours from my holiday.

I got to see Virginia once for lunch.
The two of us were joined by another,600
A young woman who was also a classmate
My senior year at Cross Keys. Agnes, too,

Book X

Was on Christmas vacation from her school.
After lunch she went off on some errand
And I was left alone with Virginia.
We drove away and found another restaurant
And stopped and got some coffee. There we sat
And talked about my freshman year at Yale,
About courses, and about poetry.
On the whole I was just miserable: 610
Virginia knew how much I was in love
But there was nothing to be done about it
And as for her—she loved me in a way
But as a friend; she was gracious but glad
To have the ardent love of a young poet
Who worshipped her and was enrolled at Yale.

Another jet took me north to New York,
Another limousine on to New Haven,
And soon I was once more in snow and ice—
A frozen climate suitable for me 620
Because I felt my soul was frozen, too,
Or locked in bondage to a hopeless love;
But now I had to plunge into my books
And study for my finals, which were hard;
But in the end they comforted me some
And also gave me courage as they showed
How much I had accomplished in one term
And gave me hope of more progress to come.

But my first year at Yale was not all work.
It also had some memorable days, 630
Memorable for fun if nothing more.

One Saturday morning I saw a throng
Around a large and very dusty object:
A giant ball as tall as any man
Colored as though it had been formed of lead.
It was the infamous bladderball, a trophy
With an unusual power to draw Yalies
Of all classes together for a battle

Yale, New Haven and New York

Before our football game with rival Dartmouth.
A boisterous crowd of students rolled the ball   640
Through Phelps Gate and onto the Old Campus
(The freshman quad, overlooked by our room).
A contest for the ages had begun
As young men who had frequented the tap
More often than they ought grunted and shoved
To push the bladderball over the fence
And bounce it onto High Street just beyond.
They rolled it down Yale's gothic alleyways
To Hillhouse Avenue four blocks away
And up against the stately, peaceful mansion   650
Of Kingman Brewster, Yale's new President.
Not many years would pass before the game gods
Pronounced a halt to such youthful presumption:
Once I had moved away to Saybrook College
I never saw the bladderball again.
One day I read the contest had been stopped
Because the students had become too drunk
And too unruly for New Haven police.

As spring began another sort of madness,
A form of outdoor chaos, also blossomed: 660
Late one April evening we looked out
And saw unusual goings on below.
Our yard was full of small, elusive groups
Who darted in and out of dormitories
And shouted messages to one another
Like, "Bluebird comes," or "Shoe is gone," and then
Chased one another all around the Old Campus.
The evening sky had faded now from blue
To darker blue and soon it would be dark
But afterglow lit up the west enough   670
To show our fellow students in the gloom.
Some tossed water balloons that soared aloft
And crashed down on the lawn or on some heads
While others ran and found cover in doorways.
Soon a battle raged around a sofa
Abandoned in the middle of the yard

Book X

And as darkness came down upon us all
The populace below became more manic:
Small tongues of flame rose up, red, orange and yellow
And hungrily began to lick the air   680
Above the sofa—followed by thick smoke.
Soon the furniture roared into flame
And frantic students danced around the blaze;
But then unwanted help came in the form
Of campus police. Some put the fire out;
Others pursued the pyromaniacs,
Cutting the darkness with their baleful torches.
No sooner had they come than students fled
Like wraiths into the evening atmosphere.

Soon all of us would become fugitives   690
And escape New Haven for a long summer.

Our freshman year at Yale had offered wonders:
Enrollees from all cultures and all lands,
Learned professors full of vintage lore,
Abundant knowledge to be had by study
And old traditions, some sartorial,
Like Yale's venerable coat and tie rule.

I had come north out of a naïve state
(Or so it seemed to me) in old Atlanta
And come into a place far loftier   700
And older, too: one with a larger title
To culture, progress, and enlightenment.
Another year would bring more knowledge sure
And good, more growth in language and in art.
I would return a sophomore and study
German taught by true Germans, Russian authors,
Meditative poems, astronomy,
And more sublime than any, John Milton,
One of a handful of enduring poets
Who composed epic poems for the ages.   710

Yale, New Haven and New York

I passed my final night on the Old Campus
Alone and on a bed without a sheet
Because all of our bed linens and towels
Had been returned to the Yale linen service.
I lay silent. I could hear traffic pass
Below our front window; soon I would feel
The growing, gentle chill one often knows
When hours pass and radiant heat departs
On cloudless nights in May or early June.
I had no way to warm or comfort me   720
So I passed quiet hours with my thoughts.
Mostly I thought about the coming day:
How I would haul my luggage down the stairs,
Secure another airport limousine,
A jet, a passage through the stratosphere,
And a welcome reunion with my folks.
The traffic died away at last and silence
Soon overcame my thoughts. Slumber did come
'Til I awoke at sunrise; and because
It was too early to go anywhere   730
I sat on the bedside and read some pages
Of *Egmont* in a new English translation.

I walked across our empty living room
And gazed on the Old Campus. Morning mist
Covered the grass and walkways, and the dawn
Awoke the scene and made it more than natural.
A world of sun and clouds hovered below.
I would not enter it because it was
So serene, unruffled—glorious.
Any mortal passage at that hour   740
Could only mar its cloudy peacefulness
And would have been an act of sacrilege.

Our sunny, hazy yard had just the look
It had on my first morning as a freshman
When I had watched my classmates going forth
In blazers and ties from dormitories

Book X

As they vanished into morning mist
En route to breakfast at the Freshman Commons.

The sunny clouds I saw below me now
Transported me a moment to that hour 750
And formed a visual bookend to my year.

Book XI

Yale and Art

How could Yale be a Fatherland to me?
How could Yale be a homeland for the ones
Who hoped for more than ivy covered walls
Or mock mediaeval buildings could provide?

I had an inarticulate longing
For union with another, for the loss
Of all that kept me bound so I could sink
My soul into that other and be lost
And found in one holy oblivion.

Though that was true, in those days I was just   10
A coconut tossed on a boundless sea.

A number of vague longings filled my soul
But I could hardly put them into words.

My sophomore year was barely underway
Before I grasped one truth that would not alter:
A journey had begun that would not be
As hopeful and naïve as my slow race
Through freshman year. An era was now over,
A faded memory as I encountered

Book XI

New classes, new professors and new students 20
And Saybrook College, a new residence.

For many years I had longed to learn German
Because my father's ancestors came from
Somewhere around Berlin. As a young boy
During the First World War he had been scared
Out of his German by a local postman
Who overheard him using German words
As he was playing with a small toy tank
Made with a match and spool and rubber band.
He warned Dad he would be carted to prison 30
If someone overheard him speaking German;
So what my dad had lost as a young boy
I thought I would recapture now at Yale.

The Yale German department brought on board
Professors and instructors who had journeyed
To New Haven from different German states.
As a result we got to sample voices
Nuanced by the accents of those parts.
Herr Zauchenberger was the program master
And lectured us on grammar every Wednesday. 40
He had three instructors under him
All of whom were women, two of whom
Were beautiful, and most of all Frau Hoskins.
I thought that I could fall in love with her.
I never got to know her, though, because
I was transferred out of her class somehow
Into another one where I learned German
From a much older woman. She, I found,
Enjoyed the Wednesday night Woolsey Hall concerts
And was a good instructor, although not 50
As lovely and distracting as Frau Hoskins.

Woolsey Hall became for me a place
Of refuge and of calm where powerful music
Would fill the hall under the guest batons
Of good conductors and their choice ensembles.

Yale and Art

Even New Haven had a symphony,
Fourth oldest in the country although not
Fourth place in musical ability
But rather lower on the totem pole.
So, I could go and hear great works performed   60
More often than I could have in Atlanta
And many nights I found a solace there
Among the long hours of loneliness,
Hours of study that began to seem
Almost without a goal or rationale.

One Wednesday evening in the dark of winter
We got to hear the Cleveland Orchestra
Conducted by George Szell. He had become
World famous and was making new recordings
Of major works by classical composers: 70
Beethoven's five piano concertos
Performed by Rudolf Serkin, and, by Brahms,
The four colossal symphonies that led
Some to call him Beethoven's one true rival.
On that cold night the conductor opened
With Brahms' *Third Symphony*. His slender wand
Rose up, came down, and as it moved the surge
And crash of those tremendous opening notes,
"F-A-F," resounded through the hall,
Three notes Brahms had endowed with verbal import: 80
Frei aber froh (in English, "Free but happy")
A joyful, robust statement by a man
Whose passionate and powerful symphony
Showed such mature command of the resources
Both intellectual and emotional
That flowed together to create for us
Music that was so novel in his day,
So classical and standard in our own.

An older gentleman sat with his lady
One row ahead of me and when the power   90
Of those first notes came rolling over us
He turned and looked at her with a full smile

Book XI

That emphasized an ample white moustache
And nodded firmly as though he would say,
"Brahms has now come and what he says is true."
I understood his gesture in a moment
From something in the power of the music
Or something in our shared human nature.
I saw at once how such a work as this
Could form a common bond between us two   100
Although we sat apart as total strangers.

We both had souls that understood at once
What had come forth, from Brahms, for all the world.

My soul was full of languages and poems
But as I drank in poetry and drama
I grew impatient with the scholarship
We had to study for our English courses.
The more critics I read the more I thought
Our scholars had created a new sport:
One of them took a work of poetry,   110
A monument of beauty and of truth
Wonderfully constructed by another,
A poet who formed music from his soul.
A scholar took that work and built his own
Ponderous work ingeniously upon it.
He might provide some cultural background,
Or maybe now and then a little nugget
Of understanding born of studious hours
At home or in a college library,
But mostly, when his work was fully ripe,   120
Someone who could not form a work of beauty
Processed the beauty formed by someone else
And made himself a passing reputation.

What Muse or Goddess can portray for me
How melancholy and alone I was
On many days my Sophomore year, or how
Junior year was worse? I enrolled in
Course after course on English literature.

Yale and Art

Our erudite professors were the ones
Who fed and pruned a garden of young students 130
But took the bloom off all discovery.
In every course I read the masterworks
Composed to teach or ennoble a reader
But now I could not read them as a man,
A normal man for whom the works were written;
Rather I was a student with a tool,
An intellectual scalpel to dissect
A chapter or a quatrain and discover
Something I could use for my next paper.

I walked to classes among fallen leaves 140
That swirled around my feet in late November
And the crisp leaves seemed metaphors to me
Of fallen hopes, now withered up and dead.

I trudged to lectures through the winter snow
That crunched beneath my feet as I progressed
And the white snow spoke volumes to my soul
Of hopes frozen to death in deepest winter.

Yale was an academic citadel
Much like a medieval castle, built
To hold herself intact against all foes 150
But also strong to rebuff tenderness
Because she was not formed to nurture men
But only to prepare them for a world
As cold as she could be, only more brutal.

New Haven never was a Paradise
And yet she had a harbor so the ocean
Was never far away. One autumn day
I took a bus to Lighthouse Point Park.
I hoped to see some place that would evoke
The ocean and the sand of Florida 160
But all I found was desolate acres
Of gray and dirty sand and, far away,
A wooden structure, old and long decayed,

Book XI

Once part of an amusement park. I searched
For half an hour up and down the beach
And found a piece of driftwood near the froth,
All silvery and gray with ocean salts.
I admired and took it as a relic
Cast up by ocean, who so generously
Had seasoned and prepared it for the day   170
When I would come along and find it there.

In Florida all nature sang to me.
Her sands covered with multicolored shells,
Her ocean tossing seaweed on the shore
Or some unwanted Portuguese Man o' War
Abandoned on the beach and doomed to fade—
Whatever Florida offered was pristine
And vibrant with her beauty and her truth.
I closed my eyes and travelled back to her.
I saw a scene of palms on a wide beach,   180
A scene I had forgotten long ago.
Sea grapes awoke my long lethargic soul;
Palm fronds caressed my memory that day
As I stood cold with driftwood in my hand
Alone at a Connecticut bus stop.
A wave of melancholy flooded me
And as I caught the bus back to New Haven
And as I rode alone I felt alone.
No one alive loved me except my parents,
And then, my parents would not live forever;   190
I thought our land would not produce a woman
Capable of loving what I was,
Capable of loving what I wrote,
Capable of understanding me
When all I understood about myself
Was that I was a strange bundle of hopes
And talent who aspired to be a poet,
A person who was happiest in Florida,
Who never wanted more than what she offered
Before fate took him out of Paradise.   200

Yale and Art

There were, though, temporary human roads
Out of the melancholy of New Haven.
Sometimes I could escape into a movie,
A world of celluloid that welcomed me
As it had done when I was a young boy.
Yale had a Film Society that showed
Old talking films or silent ones, all classics
Unfamiliar to most people now.
Foremost among them were the German works,
Imaginative efforts built upon   210
Modern fiction—such as *Nosferatu*,
Based on Bram Stoker's novel, *Dracula*—
Or drawn from legends of the Middle Ages
(Such as *Der Golem*, a strange, Jewish story
Of a magician's statue brought to life
To save a ghetto from annihilation).
Strangest of all, maybe, and most disturbing
Was that icon of German Expressionism,
The Cabinet of Doctor Caligari,
Whose characters, unstable and afraid,   220
Groped through scenes or stumbled among landscapes
Angular, bizarre, unnatural;
It was as though one could observe our world
Through insane eyes—or maybe one could now
See our deranged world through normal eyes.

Maybe that was the challenge of the movie:
It dared to say our world could be insane.

Then saw *The Triumph of the Will*,
Leni Riefenstahl's triumphant work.
It brought amazing order to the screen: 230
Row upon row of men in uniform
Lowered their banners in a ritual
Honoring soldiers killed in World War One;
Row upon row of youths in uniform
Who looked almost like Boy Scouts journeyed long
In jubilant march across the hills and vales
Shouldering flags and singing as they walked

Book XI

From every town and hamlet in the land
To congregate in Nuremberg that September
And look up to the one who was Chancellor240
And *Führer* of the *Volk*, Adolf Hitler.

The Chancellor stood on a square rostrum
Bordered on both sides by steps of stone
That could accommodate several hundreds.
A colonnade behind him marched away
Far to his left and right. At either end
A large golden eagle with wings folded
Perched atop a huge block of granite.
They gazed unflinchingly across a campus
Where soldiers stood in columns neatly ordered250
Shoulder to shoulder, helmet next to helmet,
Carbine after carbine firmly strapped,
A multitude of Germany's young men
All happy to be bound in unity
Of blood and soil to save the Fatherland:
To hold the race in noble purity
According to the doctrine of the Führer.
As we watched her movie run its course
I never once imagined that long after
I would stand at Nuremberg alone260
Upon that rostrum. I would look around
From where he gestured before microphones
Across the very field where soldiers stood.
Where he harangued under a blazing sun
I would be silent under a gray sky
And see some relics of the magnitude
One man had forged with a titanic will.

When I was older I would understand
Adolf Hitler was at heart an artist:
Not a youth who painted watercolor270
Postcards for the tourists in Vienna
But one who in the passion of his soul
And in the fury of a thwarted pride

Yale and Art

Produced a state with a colorful palette
Of festivals, parades, and martial music.

He forged his land into a potent tool
Of judgment against all that was impure
And counter to the noble German spirit
He saw in Richard Wagner and his art.

Hitler was a composer whose last *Opus*　　　　　　　　280
Would be the *Götterdämmerung* of old Europe,
A world that would collapse in flame and chaos
Much like Valhalla in Wagner's *Ring* cycle
Because of people who could renounce love
In favor a boundless will to power,
Power symbolized by Wagner in a ring.

I also saw the film, *Olympia*,
Which documented the Berlin Olympics
Of 1936, by Riefenstahl
Who seemed to me a woman far advanced　　　　　　　290
Beyond her day in cinematic art.

Olympic athletes took a practice run
Somewhere outside Berlin. They ran at dawn.
Shafts of morning sun through leafy branches
Made random dew drops sparkle and lit up
A narrow sylvan path they ran along.
The whole scene had a quasi–mythic aura,
A superhuman air as those youths ran
Forested ways of *Wannsee* not so far
From an Olympic stadium that Speer　　　　　　　　　300
Had built austerely grand for the occasion.
Precocious runners looked like Grecian gods
As they prepared for victory in the courses
That lay before them for two weeks in August.

Not far above the mist we also saw
Long brazen horns as pagan trumpeters
Stood in a row atop a solid structure

Book XI

Formed like an altar or a cube of stone.
It had a look of ancient Greece about it
Or ancient Rome. When those strong horns resounded   310
A world responded eager to observe
Olympians who struggled in Berlin—
The *Festivals of Beauty* and *the Nation*—
Olympic acts that would exalt the form
Of man in something like a Grecian grandeur
And woman in an elegance unknown
Before in contests of aquatic beauty.

Only much later did I come to learn
A comment made by Hitler in that day:
After those games all future Olympics   320
Would take place in the German capital.

I sat and watched *Olympia* as it played
And never once imagined that I, too,
Would stand close to that stadium one day
And walk along the *Jesse Owens Allee*
Named after a gold medal winning black man
Whose victory in those Olympic games
Frustrated Hitler and his theories
Of Aryan superiority.
I walked along until I found a bell tower   330
West of the stadium that rose and gave
A panoramic view of all the grounds:
The stadium, the pools, the many fields
That saw such struggles for supremacy,
The amphitheater seats of solid stone
Where sprigs of grass now sprouted in the cracks
And far beyond the stadium Berlin,
Weltstadt without skyscrapers, low and green,
Much as she looked in 1936
Although far different from the giant plan   340
Produced by Speer and Hitler when they built
A model diorama for the future—
The Berlin both men hoped she would become,
Capital not only of the Fatherland

But also of the world, a global hub
Built for the ages in a classical mold.

A hallowed classic from the 1950s
Ran at Yale that year: *War of the Worlds*.
I saw it once when I was only six
At the Victoria Theater in Wheeling.
But that was long ago and now for us
It had the freshness and the sudden drama
Of long forgotten Technicolor footage.

What seemed to be a giant meteor,
A sack of flame that slanted on its way
Across the California sky at dusk,
Crashed on a hill just above a small town.
The unsuspecting populace all hopped
Into their cars and pickup trucks and hurried
To see a visitor from outer space.

What looked as though it was a meteorite,
An oblong, intolerably hot stone,
Lay at the center of an oval crater.
People gawked and walked around and talked
And took a story home; but three brave souls
Stayed to watch the stone just a tad longer.
Silent under summer stars they stood.

Soon they saw a hatch unscrew and then
A flat head on a narrow neck emerge
So like a cobra, powerful and hooded,
It surely could harbor no good for us.
The alien slowly surveyed the landscape.
Now it locked its gaze on those three men.
They quaked and sweated and timidly shuffled
Toward the red invader and then hoisted
A white flag of surrender or good will.
The cobra head pulsed menacingly and
An incandescent ray devoured them.

Book XI

Three forms in ashes on the ground announced
Mute admonition to all who would risk   380
Appeasement in the face of ruthless force.

Soon after a trio of sleek machines
Advanced out of the hospitable pit
And floated on invisible supports.
They scoped the land and saw the road ahead
And scorched armor and howitzers with rays
Disintegrating any who opposed them.
Our soldiers could do nothing more than die
Against a heavenly foe who overmatched us,
Who planned to kill us off and take our world.   390
Soon the Martians had no opposition.
They carried war into our major cities.
But now the creatures we ignore the most—
Bacteria and microbes that compose
An old, familiar part of our small world—
Accomplished what our power and brains could not:
They infected Martians with human diseases
For which our foe had no immunity
And brought a sudden stop to their ambitions.

When I was still a boy in Florida   400
I read the novel by H. G. Wells,
War of the Worlds, on which George Pal had based
His masterwork of 1953.
Although the movie altered in some ways
Wells' composition (to accommodate
Americans)—although it all took place
In California and not in England
And after World War II rather than
At the end of the Victorian Era—
It was a work of art in its own way.   410
Pal honored Wells' original intention
Embodied in a final irony:
We saw aggressive power on the brink
Of global mastery swiftly undone
And brought to ruin by a humble thing.

Yale and Art

Sometimes I wished my only occupation
Were to attend old movies offered weekly
In Dwight Hall by the Film Society.
Those films transported me above our world
And carried me to places far away, 420
Epochs and situations that were formed
Obedient to the rules and wants of art.
As a result they had a rare simplicity,
A clarity, a purity and honor
Seldom found in our unhappy world.

I longed for but could not incorporate
Beauty and truth. I muddled on alone.
I took my classes and I did my work;
As time allowed I found some entertainment
In old films or in music.

                One autumn day 430
I journeyed with two classmates to New York
To attend Richard Strauss' *Salome*
In the world famous Metropolitan Opera.
My German was not adequate to grasp
The dialogue or the musical lines
Performed by Birgit Nilsson with such power.
The opera's basic plot was unfamiliar
So I had to scramble through program notes
Before lights faded and the music started.
I managed to acquire an overview 440
Of a bizarre and unsavory plot.
Although I could not follow every word
The music was a revelation
For now I saw what Strauss had labored toward
As he composed the epochal tone poems,
Don Juan and *Also Sprach Zarathustra*,
Til Eulenspiegel and *Ein Heldenleben*,
Dramatic works that gave the young composer
Musical language for his later operas.

Book XI

The Old Met was a miracle to me,   450
Like an enormous jewel box or casket
Full of an antique red and golden glory.
She was almost ethereal in her splendor.
I understood the audience was human
So every bit as shallow and as vain
As any audience back in Atlanta
Or probably in any concert hall.

As a young man I adored art so much
Because it was lofty and superhuman;
I could not or chose not to guard against   460
A youthful arrogance that isolated
My soul from what was human and much more—
A love that would serve others. Such a love
Surpassed a poem that would outlast bronze.

The Old Met was an artful composition
Constructed in a classic mold to honor
Composers and the works they had created
And would create if the Muses were good.

Soon afterward we learned the noble house
Of many days was booked for demolition   470
And the old opera company would move
To Lincoln Center—a modern venue,
A glass and steel behemoth full of light
But utterly devoid of all the charm
And atmosphere we had enjoyed that night.

Once more the railroad bore me to New Haven,
Back to the melancholy I had fled.

Our sophomore year was one of desperation
Hardly articulate but always growing.
Our studies seldom brought us much contentment   480
Although my German classes were a joy.

Yale and Art

I was afloat among a sea of students
Most of whom were equally adrift;
Yet we were unaware of just how lost
We were, or those who understood could not
Or would not talk about their *ennui*.

Although some of us had grown desperate
We struggled mutely on under a blanket,
A blue Yale blanket woven out of stuff
That formed a college student's normal rounds: 490
Seminars, lectures, papers and exams.

They taught us little of what seemed to matter.

I did not feel the world was all before me.
I could not understand the world around me.

I did not feel I had been with the world
Too much or not enough. I only knew
The blueness I could feel was a Yale blue,
A knowledge that would not resolve a thing.

A slowly growing sense had dawned on some:
All we observed around us was untrue,   500
And in the constant flow of what *was* true
Our venerable old school was a smooth stone
Unmoved among the currents flowing past
Into an ocean of some larger truth.

Book XII

Junior Year and a Titan

The summer in Atlanta flowed along
With nothing to recall: nothing accomplished
(Or nothing I could call memorable).
I must have read a lot (I always did);
I spent long hours at the stereo.

I could enjoy an evening now and then
With an old friend from Cross Keys, but the weekdays
Found me alone with music, books and thoughts
Or sometimes lying thoughtless in the sun.

Richard Wagner was a boon companion   10
On solitary days at home. I studied
Recordings of his masterly output,
Operas he would never have called operas
But, rather, music dramas. They rose up
Out of a turbulent and gifted nature.
He thought to show the German Fatherland
The power of its soul, as Sophocles
Had managed in tragic dramaturgy
To capture Attic nature for the ages.

When my love for his titanic works   20

Book XII

Arose, and how it grew beyond a just
Love of art, I cannot now remember.
It was a metamorphosis so slow
I was another man before I knew it;
But when my junior year began I thought
I had discovered true religion:
Human salvation lay not in the state
Or politics but in pure works of art.
They rose above the ebb and flow of fortunes
(The mere flotsam and jetsam of our days)   30
And stood as monuments of intellect
Or more than intellect, a human soul
Exalted far above the normal lot
Of our humanity: beautiful, true,
And timeless, like a statue of Aphrodite
From ancient Greece. Her form so elegant
And hair trim coiffed and flawless breasts and nipples
Offered far more than man could ever hope,
Although they offered all that man aspired to.

I longed to submerge my soul in music,   40
Profound Wagnerian music, a pure world
More grand and lovely than the world around me,
As coral reefs and parrot fish and porgies
Outdo in loveliness the surface world.

I would have sunk my soul into that ocean
Without a moment's pause, and for all time.

I was a model student my third year,
Attended lectures and composed papers
And took exams but often I stole hours
To study Wagner's music and his thought.   50

I consumed what he wrote on art and culture.
Wagner thought true art could only be
Grounded in no political group
But in the *Volk*, a cultural, racial whole
Such as ancient Athens must have known:

Junior Year and a Titan

A oneness rooted in the very land
And born of blood and soil. On that foundation
A people's soul would gradually grow
Into the form it should; and only from
Such consecrated ground may true art grow.　　　　　　60

A new work came out in the early sixties
That made a large noise in the world of records:
Wagner's *Ring*, conducted by Georg Solti.
Now anyone who could afford the discs
Could play the monumental composition,
Four large music dramas Wagner constructed
Based on the Nordic *Nibelungenlied*.

The *opus* occupied some twenty hours,
Four summer afternoons attended by
Small crowds who made an annual pilgrimage　　　　　　70
To Bayreuth. In that town in Wagner's theater
Funded by Ludwig II of Bavaria
The chosen ones could hear his music float
Across the Mystic Gulf—a sunken space
Between the audience and stage that gave
A dim, portentous light from tiny lamps
Musicians attached to their music stands.
On a royal stage the great Wagnerian
Sopranos and impressive *Heldentenors*
Would show with every tone and studied gesture　　　　　　80
How well they understood those characters
Whom they would help their audience know as well.
The stage was set with colorful scenery.
It showed enough to aid imagination
But not enough to render it unwanted.
The same was true of backdrops that implied
Forests primeval and unfathomable,
Locales where dark or heroic actions
Would find a home. As one act followed another
Wagner ensured that all his media　　　　　　90
Produced a unified result, one that

Book XII

He called the "total art work," also termed
"The artwork of the future" by the man.

I hoped to study Wagner in a program
That granted Yale seniors a rare privilege:
To be a *Scholar of the House* and do
A thesis on a topic one had chosen.
During our Christmas break and through the winter
I wrote a chapter about Wagner's thought;
It formed an introduction to my project. 100
Maybe the program would allow me time
To ponder and to understand myself
As I produced a thesis on the *Ring*.
Although I was frustrated and unsure
What life was all about and what I was
I saw my soul bound up with art somehow.
I found in Wagner's theory and work
A powerful attraction, a picture
Of an exalted ethnic unity
Impossible for us Americans 110
(Our energetic, mongrel generations)
But reminiscent of Old Testament Jews,
A nation who before the birth of Christ
Possessed a purpose and a holy calling
That separated them from other people.

I longed for such an ideal harmony
But could not find it in our native land;
Now I would find it in another world,
The holy world of Wagner and his art.

A young professor offered a new course 120
On Wagner and post–Wagnerian composers.
On Monday, Wednesday and Friday mornings
As winter melted gradually to spring
We twelve sat and devotedly heard portions
From Wagner, Bruckner, Dvorak, Strauss, and others.
I was grateful for those sunny mornings
For now I had classmates who loved good music.

Junior Year and a Titan

Envoys from a noble past resounded
Off the white paneled walls of our old classroom.
One morning our professor played the *Vorspiel*   130
Of *Das Rheingold*: the Rhine weltered upward;
Wave after wave cascaded over us
And produced gasps of astonishment from
Others to whom the overture was new.
Professor Bailey spoke with charm and wit
And helped us understand the music well.

Once the course was over I was sorry
We shared no more mornings of good music
Although by then I had some hoped for news
And more than I had hoped: I had been summoned   140
Into the *Scholar of the House* program
And was also awarded a fellowship
For travel to Germany that summer—
To visit *Wahnfried*, Wagner's house, and to
Conduct research in Bayreuth—as a present
From Jonathan Edwards College and my mentor,
The good professor, who, I understood,
Must have put in a personal word for me
So I obtained the valuable award.

From freshman year I had known four classmates   150
Who roomed together; often I joined them
On dark January nights when all outside
Was frozen cold, a cold that seemed at home
In New England and our small college town.
That winter would have made me feel hopeless
If not for their companionship which though
Not deep and meaningful was yet accepting.
We sat or sprawled on sofas or in armchairs
In a warm, well-lit room and passed the hours,
Students of literature, philosophy,   160
Psychology or maybe economics
Or else astronomy—for as a junior
I took two courses in the sciences
In order to fulfill degree requirements.

Book XII

Yale offered science courses for all those
Who would not major in the sciences:
Oceanography, astronomy,
Geology and paleontology.
Someone in the cavern of the past
Had dubbed them for all ages: waves and stars, 170
Rocks and bones, names to mix and match
According to a person's own selection.
I studied rocks and stars—rocks in the autumn,
Stars in the winter. We did have some fun
Wandering through autumnal salt marshes
Outside New Haven; we mounted and explored
East Rock, a large, ochre basaltic mass
Cousin to West Rock across the crowded valley.
They held New Haven in a stony cradle.
Astronomy was a nostalgic study 180
Because I could recall so much of it
From Florida days when I was young and thought
I would become an astrophysicist;
But now my soul was on another course.
Herr Oster, our astronomy professor,
Had come from Germany to teach at Yale.
He always smiled when I called him "Herr Oster"
Because I was the only one to do it
In our large class, and I would not have done it
Except that I was full of German then. 190
It probably reminded him of home.

After hours of work on snowy nights
A few of us would bundle up and go
Some blocks away to where a pizza place
Stood on a corner, its warm lights ablaze
To welcome hungry passers-by and students.
I usually shared a pepperoni pizza
With one of them. Sometimes we would argue
Without rancor and with a playful spirit
Over pepperonis—whether they belonged 200
On one slice or another—and accuse

Junior Year and a Titan

Each other of *pepperoni imperialism*;
Other times I would order spaghetti
And so avoid the possibility
Of internecine warfare with a brother
Who was after all a Yale man.
A prostitute occasionally wandered in
With a man in tow who bought her food.
I would glance over quickly at them both
Because I was ashamed to stare at them;   210
I wondered how she came to be that way
And how her days would unfold in New Haven,
A town that hardly had a human face,
A frozen sea that did not care (I thought)
About the welfare of its denizens.

My junior year I had to make some cash
Because my parents could not send me much.
I got a student job as an assistant
To a famous professor, Doctor Wimsatt,
Who had become renowned as the father   220
Of an approach to literary study,
Or rather, literary criticism.
Later at Harvard it could look as though
I followed his approach, but that was not
Because I cared about him or his books;
Somehow the same approach to poetry
That he had used and made so justly famous
Had long felt true to me and in some way
I could not understand had grown within me
Separate and independent of his work.   230

One afternoon I had to have some pages
Photocopied for my old professor
At the Beineke Rare Book Library
Out of a *Spectator* from Boswell's London.
Library staff would locate the journal
And carefully produce the photocopies
That he requested. As I walked around
And waited for the copies I looked up

Book XII

And was astounded. The building one saw outside
Was artfully constructed from large plates   240
Of pale marble with wispy, random streaks
Of gray striated through the white panels;
But anyone inside who looked upward
Could watch the plates become a tawny yellow
With striations of ochre or burnt umber
Whenever the sun shone full upon them.
I could imagine that I was no longer
Inside a modern "Rare Book Library";
Rather I was now a young spelunker
Who had suddenly come upon a chamber   250
Luminous with subterranean glory.

By some effect of sunlight on the marble
I could not have explained or understood
I found myself inside a holy place
Of loveliness unfathomable to me.

Laborers' hands and natural sunlight
Collaborated in a work of wonder
And conjured beauty out of lifeless stone.

Our sanctuary had uncommon relics:
One of a few exemplars now extant   260
Of Gutenberg's work, *The Holy Scriptures*,
In all of human history the first volume
Produced by a movable typeface.
After that our world would change forever.
I came upon a Wordsworth manuscript,
Lyrical Ballads, and I was astonished
To see how elegant his penmanship,
How wonderfully formed each letter, was.
A hand like that put my poor one to shame.
I thought I was the product of an age   270
Degenerate and barbaric when compared
With how men were and wrote when Wordsworth walked
Among the rocks and mossy paths of Grasmere.

Junior Year and a Titan

When time allowed I visited a place
Not many students bothered to look at,
The Mellon art museum, the Yale Center
For British Art, founded and funded by
A great philanthropist who both collected
And loved good art. On many afternoons
I wandered there among the careful works 280
Produced by men who had an eye for beauty
And satisfied a longing of my own
For beauty and the happiness that comes
From seeing it and somehow being one,
Or almost one, with something that endures.

I loved the world of Turner, loved the way
In every work of his that I had seen
Sunlight dissolved a scene of ugly matter
And still allowed the ugliness to show
Transformed into a wispy haze that spoke 290
Of loveliness superior to the chaos.
I loved *The Slave Ship*, even though the fish
Who occupied the ocean were unreal
And human limbs were disproportioned,
Because somehow the world of light and waves
Accomplished what a photograph could not.

One small room contained *The Grand Canal
In Venice*. I was taken with the show
Of gondoliers and gondolas and merchants
Who plied the waters of the Grand Canal, 300
A picture of quotidian laborers
Made picturesque by what they floated on
And flanked by architecture purely white,
Almost like marble in its sunny brightness.

Or one could study *Fingal's Cave*, a canvas
Which showed a cavern almost obscured
And swallowed up by light, surrounded by
An amber ocean with one black steamer
Laboring beneath a rack of clouds

Book XII

Almost as dark and ominously so.   310
Some Turneresque cause made those clouds conform
To an enormous headland that was home
To Fingal's famous hollow. Close to me
A lone gull swooped across the canvas,
A pale winged spot over dark water,
And something also floated, a small smudge,
Above the brown sea, something obscure,
Maybe a flying fish or curious sea fowl
Unknowable but native to the place,
A bogey that prompted me to wonder.   320

Apart from art I could also find comfort
In open air. There was a place I walked to
Not far from the Old Campus on spring days
Where I hoped for some peace—a refuge from
The ebb and flow of our quotidian study.
It was an office building, modern, white,
And with a lovely lawn and trees behind.
It was a garden, quiet and secluded,
And full of glory when the sun went down
And cast a golden radiance on the lawn.   330
One could sit there and ponder what one was,
Or if I did not ponder what I was
I had a sense of mellow ambience
One could have at such a place and hour
As good as pondering, or maybe better.

Sometimes I thought of Wotan and the *Ring*.
A god who wrongly sought omnipotence
Came as a man and walked among our people
And would become an epic Wanderer.

Der Wandrer. The very name spoke of   340
Romantic longing and Romantic quest:
A hunger for all knowledge, for all roads,
As though a journey full of mortal tales
Could make a man a god or god a man.

Junior Year and a Titan

At Cross Keys as a poet I once thought
I would compose a sort of epic poem
About a wanderer who saw all things,
Who made his soul a book so full of stories
Our human ways and works, all truth, became
His property and he became a god.   350

I was ignorant of Wordsworth's *Wanderer*,
A humble Guide who took him on the road
From one place to another to explore
What they could fathom about human nature
During post–Revolutionary days
When strong idealism had collapsed
Into a bloody turmoil and a war
That left all Europe scarred, and Russia, too.
Those days were prophetic of days to come
When Germany replaced Napoleon's France   360
As a hotbed of warped idealism
And Hitler out–Napoleoned Napoleon.

The *Wanderer* had spent his younger years
Among a multiplicity of people
At home and on the Continent but mostly
Among the humble and the pastoral,
Farmers who tilled the ground and managed cattle,
Workers whose chief delights were soil and sun,
Raindrops and dewdrops, hill and dale and flowers.
Among such people he could watch and learn   370
The manners and employments and the pastimes,
The passions and emotions that he judged
Essential and eternal in the heart;
They would appear most naturally at home
Among the simple forms of rural life
Where on the faces of the men who owned them
They spoke a language plain for all to see.

But could a person wander among peers
And cultivate a godlike attitude,
Become as much a god as possible,   380

Book XII

Because he spent his hours on the road
And let his soul take in what he observed?
I had no understanding when I thought
Over such things in high school, but I had
A strong Romantic longing, an impulse
I could hardly turn down, to find a road
Or form a road to beauty and to truth.

I could not understand that in our day
Impulse and longing are seldom enough
To help us navigate our troubled world   390
And conduct us toward a nobler place—
A holy land of knowledge and repose,
A quiet garden offering some rest.

My road would be longer before I wrote
A poem of that sort (not yet an epic
But maybe a short epic) as a student
At Yale's arch rival university,
Harvard, where I would study literature
And work toward an English doctorate.
Only two years would pass before the day   400
I went to Harvard—two years after that
Before I took a pencil in my hand
And put a spiral notebook on my lap
And sat alone, and started to compose.

But in the here and now I had some joys
That made my hours at Yale more tolerable.
I passed warm, happy evenings with companions
Content to let the snow and ice have sway—
To let the snow blow any random way
As I sat quiet among them.

                              On my lap   410
Lay a large volume covered by green cloth,
Schirmer's piano version of the opera,
Tristan und Isolde, we would study
For Doctor Bailey's class. And how we labored!

Junior Year and a Titan

I must have felt more pressure than some classmates
Because, although I understood the Master
Or understood his thought, his theories
Better than other students who had not
Explored those theories or who did not care—
Nonetheless I was no music major.   420
We faced our last exam with trepidation.
We had one new performance we could study
Recorded at the Bayreuth *Festspielhaus*
Under a renowned conductor, Karl Böhm.
None of us had yet encountered *Tristan*
And we were overwhelmed by *Liebestod*,
Or "Love–Death," an unnatural concept.
A passionate love that could not be allowed
Took both lovers on a fatal journey
Accompanied by music so unworldly   430
Its rare tonality enchanted us.

May blossomed all around us and the leaves
Of oaks and maples and the smaller trees,
The many shades of green and yellow green,
Plumage of early spring, distracted me
And other students from our chosen work.

Though our exams loomed larger every day
We would soon overmaster any worry
And take our tests at narrow wooden tables.
As for Bailey's class my *Angst* was needless.   440
My love for Wagner and the symphonists
Assured a good result because I was
Accustomed to most of the works we studied.

As exams took their toll another function
Awaited just a few of us that May.
A banquet was thrown for all who had won
A travelling fellowship from JE College.
I went that evening with another winner
From Saybrook College, one who shared my love
For Wagner; we both studied under Bailey.   450

Book XII

Our banquet was a curious mosaic:
We got to talk with students who had journeyed
On fellowships before; we also met
Our cohort who would soon be underway;
And everyone gave courteous attention
As one of the professors labored on
In an elaborate attempt at humor
That did no credit to his doctorate.
He only made me wonder what would come
Of anyone who followed in his footsteps— 460
Of me or any student who would be
A scholar or professor at some college.
Nonetheless the banquet was worthwhile.
It gave our group a strong sense of transition
And new adventures to be had abroad.

Soon I would leave New Haven with my luggage,
Only two bags because I travelled light.
I took a train to somewhere in New York—
Titanic city bathed in summer sunlight
Or almost summer sunlight, early June. 470

I looked upward and once more I saw
Enormous architecture grope the sky.
The Germans dubbed those structures *Wolkenkratzer*,
"Cloud-scratchers," and it was appropriate
But on that afternoon there were no clouds.

Alone and unaccustomed I was ignorant
What road to take or where I should bed down
Or how to pass one evening in a town
Famous for Broadway musicals and theatre
And politics and drugs and gang warfare. 480
I located a cheap hotel and ate
A block away and then took in a movie;
Later because my room was small and hot
I dozed uncomfortably through the night.

Junior Year and a Titan

The "Six Day War" had only now begun
And suddenly all media attention
Focused on Israel and Arab powers
Around her who had one avowed purpose:
To throw her and her race into the sea.
Such matters hardly bothered me back then   490
Because they felt remote and unimportant.
My soul was focused on another topic.
I thought that our salvation lay in art
Just as Wagner thought, although he did
Care about politics and hoped to make
His Fatherland a better place for art
Through politics or even revolution
Or later by a monarch's patronage.

I watched some coverage of the nascent hours
Of the short war and saw immediately   500
How Israel mounted her own *Blitzkrieg*
And won important early victories.
There were no TV satellites back then
So one could not see footage of the war.
I heard enough to grasp the situation
As Israel outfoxed her larger foes.
Historians now had a good example
Of swift preemptive action that had proven
Superior to overweening power.

The morning sun arced over skyscrapers   510
And warmed a cloudless sky as I took breakfast
Among the dark canyons of New York.
I ambled in the shadow of those monsters
Until I could comfortably hail a taxi
And tell the driver where my ship was docked,
At Pier 40, a place I had not seen
And I had some concern I would be late
But all went well and we arrived on time.

Book XII

Soon I was on board the *Aurelia*,
A vessel that would transport me to Europe,   520
First to Southampton and then to Le Havre.

Aurelia, though, was not an ocean liner
In the grand style. She was not *Andrea Doria*,
Olympic or *Titanic*, QE II
Or any ship of world class or renown.
During the last World War she had accomplished
A calling and a purpose in a navy—
The *Kriegsmarine*—as a U-boat tender.
After the war she hauled sides of beef
For an Australian firm, and after that   530
She hauled curious students from our shores
To Europe for a summer holiday.

She was round-bottomed, so with every wave
That struck her side we felt her roll and surge
Uncomfortably as we ate our food
Or groped slowly along her passageways.

On that first, sunny afternoon I stood
Above her stern with fellow passengers
And watched the waves below us churn and foam.
I gazed across the water with some pride   540
As we chugged past the lofty Statue given
By France to mark our chosen liberty.
We watched the giant profile of New York
Grow more remote as we slowly progressed
Toward an Atlantic open, broad and free.

Book XIII

Bavaria and the Alps

America floated far away now,
An obscure stroke of gray on the horizon.
I stood foolishly grand on a surging bow
And saw and smelled the ocean all around,
An ocean that was named after a land,
Fabulous Atlantis, engulfed by waves.
Neptune or Oceanus also swallowed
Ships and flotillas that had been too bold
But on a sunny afternoon in June
I did not care about catastrophes   10
I only felt the wind and saw the sun
And random whitecaps on the frothy deep.
I thought of Germany and my own joy
For I was young and free and on my way
Aboard a ship I paid to carry me
Away from the accustomed and the usual,
From all that was American and rude
To Europe and the Fatherland, the home
Of old traditions and exalted culture.

A journey on the ocean made me see   20
What I had only guessed not long before,
That all my love of Europe and of culture
Produced by Europe in her nobler days

Book XIII

Caused me to doubt the value of our country,
The worth of a culture that was common
And could produce so little of great art
But only what seemed shallow and unable
To stand the test of time. America
And all she stood for in popular culture
Seemed like a hot dog stand beside the road: 30
She offered food that took no time to cook
And had no value for true nourishment
But only several chemicals, and fat
And low grade meat, all camouflaged and seasoned
With flavor that would taste good for a moment
But do more harm than good to those who ate.

I was a young man and I found that I
Could be sarcastic at a moment's notice
When conversation turned to art and culture.
But other matters floated in the air 40
In 1967, and on board
There was debate about another war,
The one in Vietnam that occupied
American attention and concern.

As an American I still assumed
That what America would choose to do
Was for the good of others in the world
And that our military power, too,
Would only be employed to help those people
Who could not help themselves—and so it seemed 50
To me in Vietnam, where Communism,
A brutal faith in nothing but matter,
Threatened to crush a people in the name
Of justice and a humane government.

On board, an academic from some school
Obtained a charter from the shipboard powers
And got a hall and gathered in some students
To open a discussion on the war.
No one who overheard the conversation

Bavaria and the Alps

Could fail to see the antiwar agenda 60
That formed the subject of the many meetings
That he would hold, not only on that voyage,
But also on the voyage that returned;
For he would voyage back and forth that summer
In hope of winning students to his cause;
And if the voice of students ever changed
A course our government would choose to take,
That was the year, and that the summer, too,
Of student action that would cause such change.

Our voyage had some changes of its own 70
As weather soured and enormous waves
Bore down upon us from the North Atlantic.
Clouds became leaden and the wind was strong
And the *Aurelia* rolled with every wave
That struck her broad port side, which was exposed
To each new swell that came as she rolled starboard.
Our stormy weather caused us some amusement:
When we began our supper every soup bowl
Became a tiny ocean whose low waters
Produced enormous tides in a small compass; 80
From coast to coast they slid, forward and back
In harmony with every wave that smacked us
And as those tiny oceans swayed about
One could imagine our own stomach juices
Caromed from side to side in harmony;
And yet, wonder of wonders, I remained
In full control of goings on below
And managed to consume my soup and supper,
Some sort of brains concocted by Rossini
When he retired to Paris to play chef 90
After a lucrative career in opera.
I even had dessert before I stood
And made my way topside to see the ocean
And observe her tumultuous frame of mind.

The storm was memorable, but on the whole
Our days on the *Aurelia* passed away

Book XIII

Without major event, and even more
With a monotony that was quite welcome.
I sat on deck and read a German story
About a battle between two magicians 100
But how it ended I cannot recall;
I do remember I enjoyed the German
And my vocabulary grew a little.

Our days were sunny and as they passed by
My tan grew darker and I felt refreshed;
But I was also ready to debark
And set foot on the soil of mother Europe.
We passed the Scilly Isles under the sun
And saw the Lizard and the southern coast
Of England and Southampton soon enough, 110
And after that, as afternoon advanced,
The coast of France, a distant line of gray
Beyond a deep blue channel—the same water
That stymied Hitler and Napoleon
Although not Caesar in the game of conquest.

Some tugboats, those workhorses of the sea
That look the same in any port or nation,
Helped us approach the quay and soon strong cables
Were looped around the bollards at Le Havre
To hold us snug against the concrete dock. 120
Some hours after that (it seemed forever)
We were on solid ground and made our way
Toward the mandatory customs line.

When we passed customs and I saw *Douanes*,
I could not help but do a metathesis
And conjure "Dounaes" out of the French word.
Dounaes, the creatures of my own invention,
Who populated stories I composed
In Lake Worth Junior High School as a boy,
Arose once more in my imagination 130
And brought a smile as now, a boy no longer,
I stood on the verge of an adventure

Bavaria and the Alps

I had long imagined and dared hope
Would be my lot, to travel on my own
To Germany and see the Fatherland
My grandfather had known and those before him
In older days of European glory.

I took a train to Paris the next morning.
We rolled across a landscape under sunshine
And puffy clouds that augured balmy weather,   140
And so it was, my first full day in France.
Our train slowed down for Paris late that morning
And as we rode along the curving track
One saw low buildings, houses and back gardens
But nothing that was grand or monumental.
I understood that Paris had no skyline
(Unlike the "Big Apple" or even Atlanta)
And many of her buildings were quite old
Because she had not suffered any bombing
During the war that would have cleared the way   150
For modern architecture or skyscrapers.

I took a taxi to the *Gar du Nord*
And passed the Eiffel Tower *en route*,
A monument many had put to scorn
When it was first proposed, but now an icon
Of human ingenuity and daring.

Babel–like it towered among the streets
And boulevards of France's capital.

An old train stood in the *Gar du Nord*
With stenciled signs in German and in French   160
For passengers from France to Germany.

Afternoon sunshine filled the open station
And made the dull grey cars seem glamorous.
I got on board and found a seat; soon after
Our train was underway to Germany.

Book XIII

The day wore on and now the sky grew purple.
We passed the border and I soon observed
My first sign ever in the German tongue
On German soil, and I felt I was home.
We had come to a hallowed Fatherland,   170
Home once to Beethoven and Brahms and Bach,
Dürer as well and Goethe—all artists
Who blessed the world with what had come to them
From the supernal source of all true art.

Our first stop was Bad Aachen in the evening,
A city of hot springs where Charlemagne
Or *Karl der Grosse* as the Germans called him
Constructed an imperial residence.
We never saw the place because our stop
Was brief and we were headed for Cologne.   180
The train was stationary at the platform
And just below the window one could see
A local vendor with a cart of food,
Hot sausages and rolls, and mustard, too,
And because I was famished from our trip
I asked for one and, leaning out the window,
Gave him my German coins and got from him
An evening meal that was in character
With what I thought of Germans and their habits.

I reached Cologne when it was fully dark   190
And found an old hotel close to the *Bahnhof*.
I took a room upstairs and looked outside
And saw not far away through a small dormer
Illuminated spires that towered tall
And broke the darkness with a pale green color
Or rather yellow-green that looked unnatural.
It was the *Kölner Dom*, Cologne Cathedral,
Aspiring up to heaven with a splendor
One could barely imagine, and possessing
An almost revelatory quality.   200

Bavaria and the Alps

It was as though the city welcomed me
To be a part of it—as though the land
Received me as a son who had come home.

The summer sun arose at three o'clock,
An hour when peasants not so long ago
Would have been up and laboring in the fields;
But I woke up much later, fully rested
And ready to explore an ancient town.
I wandered a few miles along the Rhine:
Old Father Rhine, about whom Wagner wrote   210
The *Rheingold* Prelude, full of undulations
That stunned our group at Yale when we first heard it.
There were white boats which cruised along the river
And showed romantic castles to tourists
And I was tempted to embark on one
But I held back and walked along the shore.
I wanted to explore the land close by
And save some money so I could buy food
And sleep with some modicum of comfort.

Cologne Cathedral loomed above the Rhine,   220
Noble, Gothic, soaring architecture
(In 1880 the world's tallest structure),
A work of six long centuries completed
A hundred years before at public cost,
Or largely public cost, and just in time
For Robert Schumann to compose a part,
The fugal movement of his symphony,
The *Rhenish*, which communicated awe
And deep religious passion mixed with joy
Triumphant at the end.

                    It made the work   230
Outstanding among all descriptive music
Composed so far along with Beethoven's
Great *Pastoral*, tone poem of storm and sun.

Book XIII

The tall facade of the romantic structure—
For it was now romantic after Schumann
And the so-called Romantic Century
In which the lofty spires came to a point
And the large sanctuary got a roof
According to the medieval plans
But formed of modern steel, and durable— 240
The old facade was sullied with deposits
Of carbon from coal fires and exhaust.

Another four decades would pass us by
Before the money would be found to wash it
And show the world once more after so long
The creamy stone that was so beautiful
And out of which the artisans of old
Had undertaken a work for the ages.

Through tall front doors I walked alone and now
Was in a place of holy hush, a nave 250
Deep and cool with columns that ran far
Along the sides and could have gone forever
Or so it seemed. I thought one could have stood
Awful for hours without a single word
And without motion. How could I play tourist?

Another world stood all around, a world
Of lofty and attenuated daylight
And gothic arches that invited one
To come out of oneself and contemplate
Or journey into a transcendent state, 260
Not transcendental like the ones produced
By psychedelic drugs and advocated
By Haight-Ashbury gurus, nor the sort
Of meditation practiced by some Hindus,
But a calm and sacred sense—knowledge of One
Whom I could not control, who was among
The soaring arches hammered out of stone
And far above those gothic silences.

Bavaria and the Alps

My soul had a cathedral of its own.
I was a boy who loved a southern sun 270
And adored puffy clouds that floated by
And the warm ocean and her constant song;
I loved the undulating orange orchards
And flat savannahs and tall, waving grasses,
And Everglades whose small sporadic islands
And warm swamp waters harbored alligators.
I loved all nature and her architecture,
Her long familiar ways, flora and fauna
That came and went with favorable seasons.
She would remain unalterably the same 280
With every passing sun and passing wave
Apparently until the stars burned out.

Of course I loved Beethoven, who endured
Passionately and who composed *paeans*
To nature and her summer offerings
As he found her outside a small Vienna
In forest walks under hospitable skies.
He loved all nature irrespective of
His own bare cupboard, or Napoleon's wars.

I left Cologne for Bonn, the capital 290
Of Germany as she was then partitioned,
The birthplace of the Master and the scene
Of his boyhood and youthful compositions.
A statue of him blackened by long decades
Stood all alone in the broad public square,
A solitude appropriate to a person
Preoccupied with music and a Power
That seemed to dominate his soul completely.
One year before a picture of that statue
Was published by the *Journal-Constitution*, 300
Atlanta's one large newspaper. I saw
The photo and perused the article
That stood below it and hoped soon to see
Bonn's open square and statue on my own;

Book XIII

Today, just one year older, I had managed
To do so.

      I could look on and admire
The workmanship but even more the person
Who gave the statue worth beyond well formed bronze,
Beethoven the composer and the man,
Creator of grand music that endured   310
And would endure longer than bronze or tool
Because it would ennoble generations
Who loved it and who understood its worth.
Such music always would deserve our love
And stand above the ebb and flow of hours
For it was grounded in the mind of God.

Another sunny morning I was bound
For Munich, once a royal residence
But now capital of one German state.
My plan had been to phone Professor Bailey   320
At his hotel once he arrived in town
Before I journeyed onward to Bayreuth;
But I arrived in Munich days before him
So I decided to explore the city.

Mostly I walked around the older part
Of an old center. It was founded by
Henry the Lion in the 1100s
And then became a city of the Empire
And afterward capital of Bavaria.
Munich sponsored the first constitution   330
Composed by any German state or kingdom
And as a home of artists and the arts
Was the town where television debuted
To an astounded world in 1930.
Munich was also fêted as the birthplace
And vibrant center of National Socialism.

I paused before the famous *Kriegerdenkmal*,
A monument to those fallen in war.

Sie werden auferstehen ran the motto
Carved into pale stone, "They shall once more   340
Arise." Although the phrase was Christian
And promised one a bodily resurrection
Other thoughts arose within my soul,
Almost themselves like soldiers to exalt
Warfare, its noble goals and attributes.

Then I wondered, had there been an era
When war had been forgotten for so long
As to become unthinkable, outmoded,
Something for days barbaric and long gone?
Back then America was in a war   350
That would not end so well, for it would not
Save the people we had hoped to save.

Could any nation ever be a savior?
Could any country although well endowed
Do more than rescue others from the moment
Only to watch as they descended soon
Back to what they had been or something worse?

That summer I surrendered for long decades
All hope in politics or any trust
In any form of media reportage.   360
They seemed to be purveyors of falsehood
Produced by men who were untrustworthy,
Who chose among a flood of new events
The factoids or bare incomplete details
Compatible with an editor's purpose.
There was no place for poetry or truth
In such a culture as ours had become,
One that had sunk so low it lost itself
In power politics and all they would
Offer in vain to those who hoped in them.   370

Although I loved the sunny days of Munich,
Warm days that saw no clouds or almost none,
Unwholesome thoughts haunted me as I walked

Book XIII

Over an *Isar* that flowed turquoise green
Not far from an old gate, the *Isartor*
(A portal that guarded the eastern road),
Or as I walked along *Kaufingerstrasse*
Or stood before the Richard Strauss fountain,
A small memorial formed of cast bronze
Embossed with scenes from his challenging operas.   380

It was a modest column to commemorate
A son of Munich who was so immodest
He thought he was a hero in his day.

I met with Robert Bailey not long after
And with another student. We all saw
The opera, *Lohengrin*, in a production
At the Bavarian State Opera,
A building with an elegant interior
Whose white balustrades and pilasters
And seat cushions and curtains of red velvet   390
Were orderly and sumptuous at once.
Composed with blue and silver sets the stage
Suited *Lohengrin* in our opinion
And all the singers acted well their parts.
The poetry was luminous, Wagner's best.

Once more I was amazed that in one man
A confluence of talents so prodigious
Could balance and cooperate so well:
Both poetry and music offered us
Immortal drama on a human stage.   400

Munich had now become my *Lieblingsstadt*,
A city I adored above all others
In Germany or any other land.
München, urbane home of *Gemütlichkeit*,
An untranslatable mode of pure joy
And comradeship the southern Germans loved.
The *Hofbräuhaus* embodies it today
As well as any place perhaps, a house

Bavaria and the Alps

Where people quaff and sing and sway together
All hours of the night—at least the hours   410
When ordinary people are asleep.

As I walked along her streets I saw
Loveliness and vitality to spare
Both in her people and her architecture.

At *Königsplatz* I explored two museums.
They stood like Grecian temples with broad lawns;
Grounds which had once been paved for soldiery
And ostentation, for *SA* and *SS*,
Flourished with summer grass and shrubbery.   420

I studied both the grounds and architecture
And had a sense of something monumental,
Of labor surely worthy to endure.
The sun cast favorable light upon
Museums men had thoughtfully constructed
And lawns rolled, mown and watered faithfully.

Human thought and effort had transformed
Soil, grass and stone into a work of art.

I left Munich for Oberammergau
Under the sun and clouds, goodly companions;   430
We passed a broad and undulating landscape,
Farmland I would remember as I hiked
And paused among the foothills of the Alps.
I passed four days in a devoted town
And as I toured her narrow streets observed
Catholic art which decorated houses
And local shops with portraits of the Virgin
And child and paintings of the Crucifixion,
All done with a simplicity and style
That captured my imagination.   440
I took a large number of photographs,
Both of those artworks and of German mottos

Book XIII

That often stood below them and set forth
Something an artist wanted to impart,
Wisdom a thoughtful tourist could take home.

One artist had prepared a fresh cartoon
Of a hunchbacked hag with a warty nose
Who hoped to make a cookie out of Hänsel
And Gretel looked on with a youthful *Angst*.
Below in swarthy Gothic letters rode   450
A tetrameter couplet with a rhyme
That warned us: guard yourself against the hags.

From Oberammergau I took a bus
To *Schloss Linderhof*, one of those castles
That Ludwig II, Wagner's royal patron,
Constructed at outrageous expense.
Outside, a golden fountain spouted water
Majestically into the summer air—
God Neptune and his watery entourage.

Beyond him marble steps cascaded down   460
Symmetrically opposed to one another
From a pavilion of pure white stone
Where nine marble Muses posed for us.

At some locations on the castle grounds
One saw statuettes of Louis XIV
And smaller busts of Marie Antoinette.
Ludwig had long admired the "Sun King"
(Ironically an epithet employed
By Hittite emperors in their days of glory)
And modeled his small *Schloss* upon Versailles.   470
The chambers of the castle were Baroque
Festooned with ornate gold and gold leaf
And airy paintings full of blue and clouds
And gods and goddesses upon the ceilings.

Two things above all won my admiration.
One was a dining room. It had a table

Bavaria and the Alps

That one could lower to a cellar kitchen
And furnish there with dainties for a king
And elevate again, so it rose up
Before the monarch as he sat to dine.   480
Although he ate alone he always had
The table set for four because he thought
He was accompanied by unseen guests:
Louis XIV, Madame de Pompadour,
And Marie Antoinette, whom he admired
Above all others except maybe Wagner.
The other was a grotto he had made
Evocative of fabled *Venusberg*.

A shell boat floated on a small lagoon
As though prepared to transport Tannhäuser   490
Away from Venus and her entourage
To a holy place where he could be saved.

Ludwig constructed other castles, too.
Most famous of them was doubtless *Neuschwanstein*,
A structure that Walt Disney later took
As the prototype of a fairy castle
And emblem for the new show, *Disneyland*.
Much later I would visit *Neuschwanstein*
Astounded how it rose out of the rock
Surrounded on all sides by alpine vistas   500
(Craggy mountains and coniferous vales)
Above the modest village of Schwangau.
Her battlements commanded Forggensee,
A lake that lay unruffled far and wide
Bordered by attractive, grassy shores.
Sailboats travelled untroubled there
Under a monarch's eyrie in the sun.

Soon I would part from Oberammergau
And journey north to Munich, Nuremberg
And then Bayreuth.

Book XIII

                Before that I explored   510
A number of shops that sold wood carvings
Until I found a pair of wooden dwarfs;
One had a pipe, one an accordion.
I got them as a present for my father.

When older I discovered dwarfs in lore
(And also probably in Wagner's operas)
Were figures for the Jew: portrayed as narrow,
Shriveled and cramped, obsessed with yellow gold
And unworthy of trust—a clan apart
And thoroughly unlike Germanic heroes   520
Such as Siegfried—naïve but powerful,
Whose honest blue eyes and long golden locks
Were eloquent of racial purity.
He conquered a foul dragon by his arm
And journeyed down the Rhine in happy triumph:
Siegfried, the hero stabbed in the back
By Hagen, *offspring of a dwarf*—and so
Arose a catch phrase after World War One
That Germany had almost won the war
But was *stabbed in the back* by Jews at home   530
Who did not care about the Fatherland
But only hoped to fill their bags with gold.

Another day and I was bound for Munich
And then for Nuremburg, an ancient town
Where Meistersingers once congregated.

Her cobblers and woodworkers would become
The most exalted songmasters of Europe,
Artists who in their love for poems would
Join verse to verse and cobble rhyme to rhyme
Until something magnificent arose   540
Out of a language common to the people.

I walked around the ramparts of the town
Or what was left of them and to my sorrow
Could see how only a small fraction stood

Bavaria and the Alps

Of ancient houses, shops, turrets and walls
Because most of them had been bombed away
During the war and were now lost to us.
Only, her local artisans and workers
Had lovingly restored a few of them.

One was a corner house where Albrecht Dürer, 550
A northern master of the Renaissance,
Was born; I took a photograph of it
So I could have a picture like the one
That illustrated a biography
Of Dürer we studied in German class.
It was a wonder to me that I stood
Close to a house where such a man was born.
He could portray worthy contemporaries
With masterly precision of detail
Yet also form such visionary woodcuts 560
As his *Four Horsemen of the Apocalypse*,
Avenging angels from above who rode
Roughshod and without mercy over mortals
And carried out God's judgment on our world.

When I was older I would one more time
Journey to Nuremburg and pay a call
On the former *Reichsparteitagsgelände*
Where Hitler summoned an annual congress
And conjured up a vision of one future
Before the enthralled youth of a nation 570
Who stomped and cheered enthusiastically
At every word he uttered and who died
In Poland, Russia or in Africa,
A host on foreign fronts and some at home
As the thousand year Reich came tumbling down
In an ultimate paroxysm.

But Wagner and his art were paramount
That summer in my thought. Soon I would study
At Wagner's house, pore over manuscripts
And watch his dramas on a stage he built. 580

Book XIII

Those halcyon days would be a crowning honor
And end my sojourn in Bavaria

Another morning, one more train and soon
I was *en route* to Bayreuth, a small town
Chosen by Wagner for his *Festspielhaus*,
A concert hall he planned and oversaw
For the performance of his music dramas.

But one more time I had to rendezvous
With Robert Bailey who was my *entrée*
Both to the house and to the theater.   590
Once more I found myself in town some days
Before my mentor so I walked around
And toured local attractions: a tower
Placed on a wooded slope on the outskirts
For sons of Bayreuth who had fallen in
The Franco–Prussian War, and a museum,
The Margrave's Opera House, a monument
To Baroque art with touches of Rococo.

During an evening walk I came upon
Two noble graves in Bayreuth that produced   600
An almost overpowering sense of sorrow:
The plots where Liszt and Wagner now reposed.
Close by Liszt's tombstone stood a marble plaque
Put there by a male chorus from Vienna
And offered up to an immortal master
Who won their ardor and inspired their song.
Although I much admired Liszt I doubted
He would be placed among our best composers
But I loved both of his piano concertos
And some spirited tone poems, like *Les Préludes*,   610
And the gargantuan *Faust Symphony*,
As well as several small piano works.
However good he was as a composer
His grave was modest in a common graveyard
Out of the way and unknown to the crowd.
Wagner's grave was nobly set apart.

Bavaria and the Alps

My Master lay under a slab of stone
In a shady enclosure back of *Wahnfried*,
The home Ludwig had built where he would pass
Out of our world into another state. 620
I stood by the slab under a full moon
And nothing moved around me. Not a motion
Of air and not a footfall from a person
Troubled my soul at that sacred moment.
My thoughts and my emotions were enigmas;
No poetry or music could portray
What I felt then. Only, I was alone,
And thought I must be in a holy place
And almost had communion with the Master.

Soon the hour came when I could enter 630
Wahnfried, a home where Wagner truly found
An end to chaos which had long pursued him.
I was admitted through a small side door
And after introductions was at home
With Robert Bailey in Wagner's library
Among his books and, on one polished table,
Two ornate silver cups Wagner was given
Inscribed and dedicated to the Master
By Katherine, Empress of all the Russias.
Not far away a photo album lay 640
With glossy pictures from the Nazi era
Showing the *Führer* and his entourage
And chosen guests who worshipped at the theater.
Nietzsche was right and Wagner's *Festspielhaus*
Was most of all a temple to his work
For Wagner had produced his own religion.

On dress rehearsal days we were allowed
To go into the theater and watch
Wolfgang Wagner conduct the orchestra.
The music arose magically from 650
The *Mystic Gulf* and flooded the large hall.
Almost, as Nietzsche had observed, one thought
The notes arose in one's imagination

Book XIII

So circumambient were the noble sounds.

Wolfgang Windgassen and Birgit Nillson
Performed in *Götterdämmerung* one day
But they would not perform with their full force:
Some words came out of their wide open mouths
Inaudible to us as Birgit sang
And Wolfgang answered her. Both wanted to   660
Preserve their voices for a true performance
And so they mostly went through singing motions.
We knew it was a privilege for us
Although we almost never caught a word
Just to partake the ambience of a place
Long hallowed by illustrious productions
And full of memories of those performers
Who offered all they had to animate
Wagner's titanic works on his own platform.

A small café on balmy afternoons   670
With tables under umbrellas awaited
Us men and women, young and old, who had
The honor of attending the rehearsals.
Bailey and I and two other classmates,
Both music majors who had fellowships
And hoped to learn more about Wagner's work,
Enjoyed the shade, had beer and sausages
And felt so German on those afternoons,
So full of Wagner and a sense of power
Imparted by his music to us four,   680
We could have stayed in comfort there forever.
We thought it was a counterpoise to what
We drank in Munich at an intermission
For *Lohengrin*. There we had orange juice
Mixed with champagne, a beverage we felt
Was decadent but suited to the moment.

My favorite opera at Bayreuth was *Siegfried*
Maybe because of his heroic stature.
I loved the forest murmurs that arose

Bavaria and the Alps

Out of the "Gulf" and soon surrounded us.   690
One almost felt that one was in the woods.
A young Siegfried stood tall and challenged Fafner
And slaughtered him atop a mound of gold.
Once he discovered he was not a son
Of such an odious dwarf as Alberich
We saw his joy and could exult with him.
Siegfried had found himself among the trees
And rivulets of a musical forest
Among the birds who celebrated him
And as he found himself it was as though   700
Wagner would offer all of us a chance
To look into our souls and there discover
A racial purity that was our own,
A nature that was ours and now unbound.

A cold front passed over Franconia
And drove a ragged vanguard of gray clouds
Whose shadows rushed across the hills and valleys
Close by. Once they had passed the sky seemed bluer
And meadows sharper yellow green toward sunset
As on my final afternoon in Bayreuth   710
I walked along a country path and saw
An old steam powered locomotive chug
Along an elevated way constructed
Of local stone and like an aqueduct
Spanning a valley with Roman arches:
An antique engine, shiny black and green,
Sporting a smokestack shaped much like a funnel
Spouted dark coal-fed smoke into the air
And charged ahead toward a golden sunset,
An apparition from a noble past.   720

I passed my final day in Germany
In Munich. I walked slowly around places
Like *Marienplatz* that had become familiar
And dear to me in only a short time.
I saw the *Neues Rathaus* and its clockwork
Figures who rotated on the hour.

Book XIII

They came out of the shadows when the clock
Summoned them forth to show their finery,
Long medieval cloaks and rich attire,
To an expectant public who stood hopeful   730
Far below to watch or photograph them.
I craned my neck to look up at those figures
Sequestered above me in gothic splendor
Of delicate, meticulous stonework
Produced by thoughtful and devoted workers.
The artisans had brought them into being
And hung in air to put them into place
So people of all ages could enjoy them.

A train took me to Paris and from Paris
Back to Le Havre and *Aurelia*,   740
A small white ship that stood expectantly
To haul another load of students home.

Another seven days and we would pass
Through an unwelcome wall of thick fog;
And once the fog evaporated we
Would be on solid ground at New York harbor.

After just seven days at sea I swayed
As though I had been decades on the ocean.

I found a taxicab and shared the fare
With others who were headed for the airport   750
And then to other parts of our home country.

Book XIV

Final Year at Yale

The Fatherland was now a memory
Of summer sun and splendor in the Alps—
Wagner, Bavaria and noble music
And beer and sausages under the shade
Of trees or umbrellas at small cafés.
By contrast Georgia was a rude descent.
I mostly stayed indoors and read a book
Or wandered in a local pine forest.
I walked and heard the orange needles crunch
As though my footsteps had awakened them.   10
After a month that seemed almost a dream
I was myself. I woke and saw my home.

I could take some solace in the silence
Of summer pine trees under a hot sun
And breathless air. I paused thoughtfully.

Another year at Yale now lay before me:
Another year to offer up to Wagner
And show a few others how I embraced
The Master's point of view, his *Weltanschauung*,
Whatever that would mean for days to come.   20
I had no thought for any other matters.

Book XIV

New Haven had no magic for me now,
No fascination and no unique interest.
I found my room and made myself at home.
I had good work and settled into it
With a focused purpose and a hope
My work would somehow justify my soul.

As a lofty *Scholar of the House*
I took no courses. I could go and play
Or study and compose a senior thesis.   30
Two dozen Scholars of the House would gather
For supper and discussion every month
And compare notes or compare politics.
We also met in smaller monthly groups
Organized according to our topics.
In one of those I met Bart Giamatti.

Bart was a man who appeared to bob
Around our campus without any purpose
But he would soon become Yale's president
And after that Commissioner of Baseball.   40

Fourteen lads were tapped my junior year
For a peculiar Yale sodality
Named "Elihu" after the prosperous merchant,
Elihu Yale, whose generous donation
Of books and money helped to found our school.
During a hundred years and more Yale students
Had formed secret societies for seniors;
"Skull and Bones" was surely the best known
But Elihu was also one and had
A wood, two-story house on Elm Street.   50

Soon I would own a key to the front door.

As part of our admission to that world
All junior inductees had to endure
A ritual prepared by those above us.

Final Year at Yale

One by one members escorted us
Into a cavernous and gloomy hall
And sat us separately at small tables.
Books chosen randomly lay open
Under the wavering glow of tall candles.

Once we had sojourned there a spell   60
They brought us all to separate rooms, to wait
Alone until somebody came for us.
My chamber was a bedroom with a table
Decked with a round doily and some coins.
Odd to say I found I could feel tempted
To pocket four quarters from the change
And see what punishment would come if any
But I would not. Instead I paced around
And practiced mentally a secret vow
I had been told to make that afternoon   70
With fellow juniors who were also chosen
To join the venerable ranks of men
Who had become members of Elihu.

Someone unknown to me entered the room
And stood behind me. He lowered a blindfold
Over my eyes and slowly guided me
To an adjacent chamber of the house.

Now my escort took the cloth away.

I saw four older men, *emeritus* members,
Ensconced behind a long, wooden table   80
In tall, oaken chairs. They looked down on me
With no trace of emotion on their faces.
Upon the table lay an ancient mace
(Crafted of wood and covered with dark knobs)
Far larger than an average man could hold
Or transport comfortably, let alone
Use with authority in mortal combat.
I thought it was a symbol of the order

Book XIV

(A surmise someone soon confirmed to me).
But now the Grand Inquisitor began,   90
The oldest of the four. He asked bluntly
Whether I had the character to stay
The course and grow in brotherhood—for we
Were obligated by our oath to be
Devoted from that moment one to another
In one sodality for all our days.
I cannot now remember what I answered.
I know I made a casual remark
About Camus and Sartre, and at once
A raucous gale of laughter from behind   100
And all around me in the darkened chamber
Startled me and let me know at once
I was surrounded by an unseen host
Of witnesses who watched and overheard
What I had spoken in their hidden world.
However, they were not a hostile crowd
But only hoped to have some fun with us
In all good brotherhood.

                      Once that was done
The chairman stood and asked me to declare
The vow I had so labored on that day   110
And after all of us had pledged our troth
We adjourned downstairs to a dining room
And took our places at a long table
Draped in spotless linen and adorned
With fresh cut flowers and linen napkins
And silverware that was not silver plate
And surely decades old. No grace was said
But supper was served to us by black waiters
Who looked formal in crisp, white jackets.

We could have been in a superb hotel,   120
Say, in the Copley Plaza or the Ritz.

Our banquet was the forerunner of others
We took at Elihu our senior year.

Final Year at Yale

On Thursday evenings we were all obliged
To come at five o'clock for nuts and sherry
And conversation over this or that
Followed by supper in the dining room.
Afterward the company adjourned
And wound its way upstairs to a pale chamber
(The upper room which not so long before   130
Hosted our solemn vows to Elihu).
We took our seats around four long dark tables
Carefully arranged in a rectangle.
On some evenings one or two of us
Would offer a short paper or a skit
But most of those sessions would be devoted
To more important work: someone would share
A short autobiography—his *auto*.

Now I would have an opportunity
To open up my past and love of art.   140
I gladly portrayed my German adventure
And told how I had stood by Wagner's grave
Under a silver moon in solitude.
I told them how profound the moment was,
Almost a holy hour of communion.
One brother looked incredulous and asked
Who cared about old Wagner and the moon
That looked down on his garden in July.
He wondered why a thing should be profound
And all my brothers were in sympathy.   150
It was a shock to me to hear such words
And suddenly I understood that I
Was not only much different from the others
But also more naïve and simple natured.
I wanted truth and beauty hungrily;
I wanted those things as a man might want
A woman who was all the world to him.

Although I was a Scholar of the House
And hoped I would produce a book on Wagner
I also had another book in mind.   160

Book XIV

I dared to hope, now I was twenty-one,
I could compose a work of lasting value.

I composed curious prose, not poetry.
It was poetic prose, full of allusions
And quotes from other poets—not a story
Nor yet a novel, but a rambling trail
Of paraphrases cobbled into meaning
(Or rather into work that looked as though
It had a meaning, but in truth did not).
My Emory professor who had taught   170
Creative writing and whose class I took
The summer after high school graduation
Dubbed it "beautifully written culture."
Once back in Georgia I would carry on
The odd, mellifluous, and pointless work
But give it up after a year of labor
That was both desultory and unhappy.
On two afternoons I wrote a poem
That won my soul once more to poetry,
An ode to Florida, a song of shores   180
Awash with lambent waters in the sun
And scuba divers who gave up their bubbles
Among corals as they explored carefree,
And hammerheads and sting rays and guitarfish
And, on the land, sea grapes and unspoiled shores
And Seminoles and their untutored ways
Before the Spaniards or the Yankees came
(A Florida I never got to see)
And as I wrote about that Florida,
Both old and new, I found again a love   190
That I had long forgotten among books
And chilly libraries and lecture halls.

Now far away another land with palms
And ocean beaches tropical and lovely
And jungles and small villages, and people
Who spoke a language and who formed a world
Alien to ours, was causing trouble,

Final Year at Yale

Or we were causing trouble in their land;
And as the war increased debate also
Became hostile and volatile at home					200
Until America became two camps
Broadly opposed: our government and those
Who favored our involvement in the war
(Who would destroy a nation to rescue it)
And others who opposed "the Establishment,"
Mostly the young, who marched, and sang, and placed
Cut flowers in the barrels of the rifles
Of our reservists who stood nervous guard
To halt unruly action by the crowds
Of demonstrators as they marched and chanted			210
"Make love, not war."

                    Some of those unruled spirits
Sought joy and freedom in another culture,
A psychedelic world of their own forming
Favored by academics who declared
A new adventure for the human mind
Obtainable from chemicals or plants—
Psychotropic mushrooms and some grasses.

Ours was a world of chaos and confusion:
So many ways lay open and we had
So many guides and all of them looked good			220
But none of them would prove worthy of trust.

Our group at Elihu would not be proof
Against debate and, soon, antagonism
Over the war and our whole way of life.
Some argued that our form of government
Should pass away and be replaced by one
That would not cater to those industries
Whose profits soared when our land went to war.
Better, they thought, to have a form of rule
That was, almost, no government—a land			230
Much like the Workers' Paradise imagined
By Marx when he ignored his wife and children

257

Book XIV

And spent his days prophetically composing
Das Kapital in London—capital,
As one wag said, of modern capitalism.

The days of Vietnam would try us all
And undercut the hopes and aspirations
Of many students who would have set sail
In freedom on the vast ocean of life.
All of us, both the ones who fought abroad   240
And those who fought to stay alive at home,
Were altered by those days, and some forever.

Among the snows of winter and the cold
Of our dissatisfaction with our lot
We had a supper guest one Sunday night
At Elihu—Professor Latourette.
One member had invited him to come
And share what he had seen decades before
In China as a Christian missionary.
We found his narrative and company   250
Attractive, for he was a modest man
Who seemed improved by what he had endured
And done in China. There he spread a faith
That none of us could share against great odds.
We could not see the world as he had seen it
But honored him for his integrity
And candor in a day when things appeared
Unsure and complicated all around us.
Before he left I faced him and noticed,
As we stood in a well-lit vestibule   260
And donned our overcoats and gloves to face
The snow and ice and hostile wind outside,
How pure and luminous his face appeared—
Almost transfigured by a vital faith,
A trust that warmed him in the winter cold
Far more than overcoats or gloves could do.

Wagner took all my thought as spring wore on
And I completed a monster tome

Final Year at Yale

Of theory adorned with his *motifs*.
But as I labored hard in warmer weather   270
I lost my way. I found that more and more
The *magnum opus* mattered less and less.
Wagner's music (always *Zaubermusik*)
Continued to enchant my unsure soul.
Siegfried's funeral march could make me weep
As it had done when I first played the record.
I harbored old heroic aspirations
Poetical and personal although
The fervor I had known so long ago
Was gone, or almost gone. I had no love,   280
No hope, no joy, no comfort and no purpose.
I soldiered on from day to day but once
My book was done I took no satisfaction.

A Jewish friend stopped by and we produced
An afternoon of music: we bought beer
And borrowed *Parsifal* from our library
And sat and occupied four sunny hours
Attending Wagner's opera in my room.
It was the second time I heard the work;
It was the first for him and when he saw   290
Old Titurel rose up at the conclusion
Out of his casket by a miracle
He laughed at the absurdity of it
And so did I. The noble music faded;
We toasted our good health in common beer—
A toast we made in German as we both
Had studied German and adored the language.

On May the first I walked around and saw
Red banners floating in a breeze put up
By some who advocated socialism   300
Or outright Marxism. They were no more
Than armchair revolutionaries then
And they were a minority at Yale
But one day some of them would be professors
In academic groves across our land

Book XIV

And they and others of their sort would labor
To transform academia to a nursery
And nurture others to become like them.
But as I ambled through the streets of May
New Haven wore a robe of constant splendor   310
With juvenescent leaves festooning branches
That shimmered as the breezes played with them
And morning sunlight warmed their surfaces
And I could not despair on such a morning,
Nor could I worry much about the future.

Before that May I passed the month of April
At home in Georgia with my Mom and Dad.
I also paid a visit to a man
Who was headmaster of a local school,
Brandon Hall, located on the grounds   320
Of a small mansion built and occupied
Decades ago by an old family
Who made a fortune in oil.

                    The Hall's motto,
Ad renovandum ac florendum, was,
I thought, a good one: to renovate
And flourish. Those were goals I could have set
For my own soul if I had understood
How desperate my need was in those days.
But in my ignorance I chose a way
That offered some security, some income,   330
And most of all, perhaps, some days and months
I could employ to sort my nature out
And understand what I was formed to do.

But after fifteen months of tutoring
Affluent high school students of both genders
I would abandon Brandon Hall and travel
North to New England one more time and Harvard.
En route I stopped at New Haven and there
Among the quiet walkways of Yale College
A strong conviction overpowered me   340

Final Year at Yale

And told me to abandon the Old South
Because New England would become my future.

I had not flourished and was not renewed
But only drove toward my Harvard home
Flooded with strong frustration and confusion,
For now my life was without goal or purpose
Except to have a good degree and job
And so become the master of my days—
Master who did not know what road was good.

Our last week at Yale was occupied 350
By the array of quotidian chores
That dominate one's final hours at school.
We chose what to keep and what to throw,
We tidied up and packed, returned our linens,
Said *au revoir* to those who mattered most
Although it was more probable than not
Our paths would cross no more.

One more time we said good-bye to Yale.
Two close classmates and I ambled at sunset
Across the campus and bade *adieu* 360
To locales we had come to know and love.
At our tour's end we made it to the roof
Of one Old Campus dorm and saw from there
The quad where our adventure as Yalies
Had begun only four years before.

Soon it was the famous twilight hour
Eliot evoked when he composed
The Waste Land. We stood in a cool wind
And looked across the campus westward where
Purple cumulous clouds outlined by gold 370
(Almost bright platinum) before the sun
Stood under a sky otherwise cloudless.

It looked as though Apollo in a hurry
Had whipped his horses to a brilliant froth

Book XIV

So they would rush his chariot underground
To visit those below who had no sun.

On graduation day at Woolsey Hall
Our elect group assembled in good spirits
And sat in ordered rows before the stage.
On the platform our president and dean   380
And other faculty of lesser state
Sat robed in academic majesty.
Each waited for his turn to stand before us
And help the senior class to understand
The history and heritage of Yale,
The magnitude and challenge of our times
And how our *alma mater* had prepared us
To walk away from ivy covered halls
Into a world of opportunity
And contribution to our native lands.   390
Woolsey Hall looked cold and gray outside
But in her creamy, warm interior
Ample to hold our graduating class
I had attended concerts and recitals
That warmed my heart in dark and snowy winters.

Another season, though, had come upon us,
An atmosphere unlike the autumn hours
Four years before in Woolsey Hall when we
Had sat before that august faculty,
Naïve *frosh* on the brink of an adventure.   400

On graduation morning who could know
What lay ahead for me or anyone?
Our days were troubled by another war
And some of us would not live out the year.

We turned and left behind the concert hall
And famous ones who made profound remarks
And Yale with all her power and endowments.

Final Year at Yale

Yale had not been a Fatherland to me
And could not be a Fatherland to me.
She taught me but could never nurture me.   410

Among her gothic buildings and cold days
From class to class with others I had journeyed
Unsure of my own soul—how I would grow
Or ought to grow into a modern poet
I hoped I would become.

                    Her northern cold
Made me more desperate to find a road
Toward a warmer atmosphere, a place
Where sun and palm trees would comfort my soul.

On that day I abandoned a false love
And other empty things I had adored—   420
Vain academia, hollow awards.

Book XV

Australis Redux

Apollonian at Palm Beach Inlet
No more a Sea Hunt boy but now a man
I strode, a German dagger on a calf.
Strewn across the summer sand I saw
Like starfish many-colored in the sea
Lasses blonde, brunette, and full of shape.
Such loveliness could arouse appetite
Even in a young man of no conquests
Such as I was.

              No more a Sea Hunt boy
I waded into water warm and calm   10
And in a shallow spot I sank and slipped
Each foot into a Cressi fin. I washed
A Squalé mask in a swale and spat
Onto its glass and rubbed my spit around
To stop a haze from forming underwater.
A Scubapro tank upon my back announced
My young maturity, a body able
To have a man's adventure far below.

After a year at Harvard I had flown
Back to my home, a rare peninsula   20

Book XV

Of quartz sand, sea shells and sea grapes
Open to my return under the sun.

Not a day had passed before I drove
Once more to a seashore I loved.

A crane stood, rusty and alone,
Above some rocks at Port of Palm Beach.
Arms of rock extended east and west
And braced the land against a deep cut
That was the inlet where pelagian craft—
Cargo boats full of consumer goods, 30
Tankers full of oil or gasoline,
Boston whalers, ordinary speedboats,
Charter boats, sailboats galore
And even rubber rafts—navigated
Toward the Intracoastal Waterway,
Around Peanut Island, and to port.

South of Port of Palm Beach
And oceanward from West Palm Beach
Palm Beach stood aristocratically
Alone in private elegance. 40
A salty Intracoastal Waterway
Separated them—a brown gap.
At low tide umber water flowed between
Those inlet walls and made a dark fan
Into the opalescent green Atlantic—
An awful image of human decay
Because people had made it so
When they dredged up the pure original sand
From its ancient floor for their own use
And left behind a dark and muddy bottom. 50
So now that water was an obstacle:
No scubapro, no matter how accomplished,
Could see his own hand a foot away
When that brown tide surged out,
So I stayed away. Nor when
Green Atlantic waters rushed in

Australis Redux

Was it safe to dive Palm Beach Inlet.
The one who tried was dragged and buffeted
By constant strong currents underneath
And had to grab gorgonians or rocks   60
For anchorage against those unseen streams
That seemed intent on dragging him away.
But neap tide was an ideal time
That gave a man a chance, clear and calm,
To probe old Oceanus' fair demesne,
Investigate his haunts submarine,
And learn archaic lore of animals
Unknown above—sand sharks, or moray eels.

My soul was still naïve enough to love
And long for Florida as I had known her   70
As though a man could be a coconut
Tossed back by waves to a tropical coast.

I swam among enormous rocks, and saw
A sand shark. He floated in a cave
Formed by boulders fallen from above:
Sun and shadow on his dappled back
He hung above the sand, half awake
But ready to consume at any moment
An unwary fish. A scavenger,
He looked for easy prey every day.   80
I hovered close and cautious, and alone.
A long hiss of air as I inhaled
Or exhalation from my regulator
Announced me to an underwater world.
Saucer-shaped bubbles wobbled upward
As I looked around. I was at one
With ocean which in all its panoply
Of beauty was an underwater tomb
Full of dead men's bones, I understood.
But Davy Jones, the keeper of those waters,   90
Was no match for me, a Florida man.

Book XV

I could not understand how anyone
Could have been made for union with the world
I found in Florida or made by whom.

Without much understanding I succumbed
Because her beauty overpowered me.

How could any poet have withstood
Her *voluptas* so generously offered?

A strong wall of Palm Beach Inlet
Composed of concrete four feet thick   100
Arose among a mass of sunken boulders.
Some above the surface, angular,
Unsafe for anyone to walk upon,
Added support against a broad Atlantic
Whose endless and quotidian assault
Commanded human walls to fall apart.
Some fathoms down, I probed along a bottom
Of boulders half submerged in quartz sand
And saw a form, primordial, uncouth,
Hazardous and huge, emerge unasked   110
Out of an arm–sized hole at the base.
It was a moray eel, face to face,
Of convoluted form ambiguous,
That swayed back and forth, unaware
Of any good or bad absolutes,
But all too ready to attack and grab
A hapless finger in its mouth and twist
Until that finger broke away and bled
A plume of crimson blood into the water.
I watched that moray eye dispassionate   120
And able to assume a nasty outcome
I paddled back, and slowly swam away.

I moved along and saw a coral head,
Small and full of green vitality.
It was a brain coral, full of savvy
And oceanic wisdom after ages

Australis Redux

Of parrotfish attacks upon its crust.
A colony of floppy green polyps
Dwelt among those brown folds of brain
And ate plankton just as it came   130
On any local current of good taste.
I was appalled to come upon, below,
A coral of such wisdom, far above
What scholars taught at Harvard or at Yale.
I was a Florida man, full of adventure,
And much enamored of nature love
And much enamored of natural lore.
Because Florida's ocean opened a door
To many intimations from above
I took a brain coral for professor.   140

On a sunny day, careless and free,
Caressed by warm breezes at the beach
Under palm fronds that rustled loosely
For any passing breath, I took a stand.

Come breathe on me, I called,
Land of palms, my immortal beloved.

Oceanic air had called me home.

I found her love in Man 'o War, sea turtles,
Silver barracudas, jack crevalles
And a sea cucumber hard by Key West—   150
An endless waltz of vibrant color
In sunny waters of her many coasts.

I found *amours* in holy forms of nature.

For one autumn term I had become
An assistant professor of English
At Palm Beach Atlantic, a small college
Of Christian liberal arts in West Palm Beach.
One autumn afternoon at Lake Worth
A student and I strolled in shallow waters.

Book XV

She was lovely but would do no wrong 160
And I adored her slender form.
Her hair was long and honey blonde.
We ambled among wavelets in the shallows;
Sun and shade danced around our feet;
Sand and shell fragments, creamy and beige,
A small world of gem stones, also waltzed
Under a play of water and warm sun.

We ambled south of an old wooden pier
On Lake Worth Beach that I had walked upon
When I was a young boy. I got to see 170
Workers construct it with huge cranes and beams;
An act of human will had made it stand
Among a surge of waves that could not stop
Our invasion of their private world.

On our walk we spotted a sea turtle
Stranded upside down close to the water.
His mottled yellow underside was lovely.
His lifeless head hung toward the ground
And from the beak a Man 'o War protruded,
Its purple and half swallowed tentacles 180
As lifeless as he was. Although so young
The turtle was too massive to be moved
By any one soul, but if I could
I would have taken him and carved him out
And made a trophy of his hollowed shell
And set it in my parents' living room,
A hallowed relic of the busy sea.
He was a cautionary tale for me:
A being framed for ocean and for joy
In far pelagian waters, only young 190
And overconfident; he ate too much
Of what was venomous although it was
Provided for him on the open deep.

On any summer day on that long beach
The surface was too hot for me at noon;

Australis Redux

I could not walk across it without pain.
I ran down the slope to where the sand
Was cool because the breakers made it wet
And dark brown, and there I stood and cooled
My tortured soles.

                I donned a mask and fins 200
And paddled casually farther out.
Below me lay pure sand. It undulated
Along the ocean bottom,
Smooth waves that vanished far away
And disappeared in a dark blue haze.
One look toward that unfathomable deep
And sudden panic overcame my soul.
I wanted warm shallows above all
Where sand was rough and shell fragments abounded—
Tiny bits of broken shell all smoothed 210
And rounded off by action of the waves—
Where people stood around and swam and played
On rubber rafts or tossed beach balls in air
Oblivious of the horror of deep water.

On that beach a woman lay alone,
An artist, Mary Otto, and perhaps
She saw among the populated waves
A beauty more arousing than her own.
I sat beside her and began to talk;
She told me of her passion and her art, 220
Her passion for her art, so full of flair
And forms well-placed, wood overlaid on wood
And colored almost as a child would do
In cobalt blue, red, yellow and dark green.
At home I saw her workshop and I met
Her mother, who was blonde like her.
She showed me articles from local papers
About her work. She had displayed her art
Off Royal Poinciana Way, and had
Some temporary renown in Palm Beach. 230

Book XV

I ambled along Cocoanut Row
And window shopped on Worth Avenue.
Shops and small boutiques abounded
For pale tourists colorfully attired
Who wandered out for fun. Art galleries
Sported fresh manufactured canvases
Abstract, neo-impressionist, along
With portraiture and landscapes and much more.
Restaurants such as *Hamburger Heaven*
Or the *Petite Marmite* attracted me   240
And others who could happily afford
A lunch at Palm Beach. Even dogs
Could satisfy their thirst at one small basin
Formed of blue and white ceramic tiles
Located at a storefront on the way.

Palm Beach was a haven of all glory,
From mansions on the waterfront to roads
Ordained for grandeur, such as Royal Palm Way,
An avenue of royal palm trees
That made a stately march to the Atlantic   250
Eastward from the Intracoastal Waterway.
Exotic houses and pink roofed pavilions
Only partly seen by those who walk
Or motor along Ocean Boulevard
Evoked a splendor one saw now and then
In sunlight as one drove along the coast.
I wondered how such beauty could endure
A long assault of elements, or all
Our own development brought in its wake.

A blonde professor at our small college   260
Walked up to me and introduced herself
During our first hour of orientation.
We drove to Palm Beach one day after classes
And lay comfortably on the beach
And talked about small things. We could enjoy
Each other's company under the sun.
I saw her slender form assault the waves

Australis Redux

And we took vigorous plunges in the ocean
And came refreshed and sat down on the sand.
I would gladly have loved her that fall term   270
But she was just someone I hardly knew
Before I left Palm Beach and Florida
And journeyed back to Harvard and the cold.
She had a husband whom I never met
And after my return to Florida
I never saw or heard of her again.

Peninsula of sea grapes and small lizards,
Harbor of ocean and aquatic wonder,
Roll on and capture my confused soul.
With my whole life I would gladly adore   280
Your untold loveliness for its own sake;
I would pour out my soul for you alone.
In boundless passion I would merge with you
Until you had engulfed me totally,
Until I had become what I adore.

Such were the ardent contours of my thought
Or something more unutterable than thought
On days I walked the alleys of Palm Beach.

Only if I could be at one with all
The glory of that subtropical One   290
Would I become a man fully at home.

I snorkeled off the shore of Lake Worth
And sojourned summer hours there as though
I had found a home in lucid water.

Maybe salvation lay in those warm ripples.

Florida had begun to gather me,
But I could also gather some of her.

I found a scotch bonnet, a rare shell
I never saw before, and brought it home

Book XV

And placed it on an old book case 300
Among some other shells: a palm-sized cowry,
Brown and mottled, that I happened on
At Palm Beach Inlet on my first dive there;
Some whorled fragments found off Lake Worth beach;
And one large conch, old and perforated
By sea worms or sea action of some sort,
Dug gently from the sand in Boynton water.

How many years would pass before I saw
Another conch fragment, large and fat,
And then another, hardly less fat 310
At Boston Bay, just up the coast
From a large open pit where black men
Cooked jerk pork over coals and ashes
Of an allspice tree in Jamaica?
As a young man at Lake Worth
I was no prophet and I saw no future
That was not bound to holy forms of nature,
Bound for good to sun and sand and ocean
As I had come to know and love them all
In Florida, goddess who owned me now. 320

That first halcyon summer back home
I tutored English at a private school.
My pupils were two glad little girls,
Third and fourth graders. Their tuition
Enabled me to buy a scuba tank
And plunge at last into her coastal waters
Fully emancipated from the past.
I could dive legally because I had
A round cornered, unlaminated card,
Proof I had taken a scuba course 330
At Yale my junior year—but what a change
From Yale's archaic pool, full of fresh water
And crystal clear, to a tropical Atlantic
Who chose or did not choose to be so lucid
According to her current frame of mind.

Australis Redux

She had a moody depth many admired
But none could master in all Florida.

The ocean was so turbulent sometimes
No one would dare to venture over her
But only stand and watch as she raged on. 340

One afternoon huge breakers slammed the shore.
I paused and looked on under a roof
That covered concrete benches in a row—
A public shelter put up by the town
During the war. A wizened man close by
Stood for over an hour and watched the sea;
It took its color from a leaden sky.
We stood not far apart as the wind blew
Just like fellow sailors on a bow
Aware of the potential of those waves 350
But nonetheless resolved to emerge
Out of the tumult into a good day.
We talked about the ocean off and on
And he recalled moments from World War Two
When merchant ships and tankers plied the deep
Only a couple of miles off our shore.
He told me how a sudden flash and blast
Would sometimes come from one of the large tankers
Followed by acrid smoke that billowed up.
Crowds who gathered under the low roof 360
Would push and shove to get a better view
Through pay binoculars that stood in rows
For public use. What U–boat made the kill
No one would ever know, but as they watched
A distant tanker foundered and was gone
Beneath a silent slipcover of waves
And bore doomed sailors to the bottom.

Sometimes as I walked along the shore
Or waded in the shallows I discovered
A smudge of tar along my foot—a relic 370
Of tanker oil the ocean swallowed up

Book XV

Before regurgitating it ashore
For any wanderer to tread upon.
When I was just a boy I wondered how
Those random wads of tar had come to be.
Only as a man I now discovered
Their fateful and unhappy origin:
I walked upon the cargo of those vessels
That sank and dragged their sailors down with them.
It was almost as though one trod upon   380
The blood and bones of those who had gone under.

The ocean I adored was often calm
And beautiful on July afternoons
Beneath a mild regime of summer breezes
But she was also capable of wrath
And had no concern for our comfort zones.
She tore at waterfronts and in her rush
Could transform landscapes in a single day
And who could rule her moods? A hurricane
Could whip her up into a perfect storm   390
That blasted costly beachfront properties
Until they lay in shards with door frames cracked
And windows broken under open roofs.
After storm water had retraced its path
Generous sunshine poured into the ruins.

I saw her powerful waves come one day
And sweep away those furlongs of quartz sand
That were the boast and joy of all the south,
A place where old and young could soak up sun
On calmer days when ocean was a lake.   400

She gave no warning just how suddenly
Her mood could change, or with what devastation.

Once as a boy I plunged into the surf
And thought I was a match for any wave
Because I had my Squalé mask on tight;
But soon, as I stood up and faced the shore,

Australis Redux

A breaker hit my back and tore the Squalé
Off my head and carried it away.
I panicked. I sank down and dug frantically
Among the roaring waves and churning sand   410
To find the costly mask I loved so much
But strong Atlantic breakers broke me down
And showed me who was mistress and the stronger.
Although I had a claim on youthful vigor
I was no match for her omnipotence.
Ocean was powerful beyond my grasp
And afterward when I became a man
I would succumb and let her have her way.

Late one placid morning at Palm Beach
North of the inlet wall in sheltered water   420
That had a clarity almost like gin
I saw a school of squid, small calamari.
They swayed from left to right as in a dance,
Undulations that could only enchant
Someone unfamiliar with their play.
(Later I observed in supermarkets
Dead calamari laid flat on ice,
Sadly other than what swam before me
In morning water and so full of fun
And unknown purpose in their element).   430
I assumed I could catch one at my whim
For I was large and much more powerful
So I only gave casual chase;
But as I swam I found there was a gap
Of just one foot or so
I could never close now matter how
I drove and thrust with my Cressi fins:
A cloud that always moved in front of me
Up and down and full of permutations
They made a mockery of all my power.   440
One of the slower members almost came
Within my grasp but suddenly he fled
And spurted a small cloud of dark brown ink
To camouflage his tiny tentacles

Book XV

And upper body as he swam away.
I know to my sorrow I caused him harm
Because I saw him jettison
A minor body part as he escaped.
Once I saw the damage I had done
I let the squad return to peaceful waters. 450
Who was I to undercut their fun
And spoil their outing for a silly hunt?
The broad Atlantic challenged them enough.

Across from where the Lido Pools once stood
A calm July ocean covered over
Stumps of wooden pilings abandoned
After men tore down the fishing pier.
I stood my scuba tank on the hot sand
And thought I would go under and explore
The broken stumps. Maybe they had a word, 460
Some narrative or underwater lore,
To share with an unworthy landlubber.
I waded with my tank into the shallows
And squatted down to don it under water.
Around my hips a belt of one pound weights,
The sort a diver always had to wear
To counteract natural buoyancy,
Allowed me to maneuver on the bottom;
I could take my time as I explored
The ruins of the pier. I swam along 470
Toward the deeper water and I saw
Some fragmentary posts of old wood
Upright but waterlogged and covered over
With a coat of soft, brown marine algae.
The wood was eloquent of other days
When Palm Beach Pier had offered anglers hope
Of amberjack and Spanish mackerel,
Tropical fish to hook and carry home,
Cook up and serve on simple rattan tables.

One thought of anglers under the hot sun, 480
Nocturnal anglers under Florida moons

Australis Redux

Or more intrepid ones who even in storms
Caught or did not catch but always had
A love affair with ocean and her moods.

A placid surface told no one today
Any structure had ever been there
Or such a monument to human sport
Had stood awhile among the rolling waves
Until the ocean had her way once more
And swallowed up a work of human hands.   490

I swam among the poles and saw a puffer
Who noticed me and looked on warily.
Surely I looked an odd fish to him,
An outsized monster who could exhale bubbles
And must have come down from another world.
Then I wondered if he wondered at all
Or what he wondered as he looked at me.
He was a tiny one who swam alone
And browsed for lunch among the softened stumps
He often swam among and often saw   500
But never thought about or understood.
How could a puffer know that I was one
Of those who built a pier upon the spot
Or fathom he explored among the ruins
Of a long lost enormous architecture
Constructed for their play by other beings
Who cast cruel fishing hooks into the sea?
I stared at him and he looked back at me
And now I lunged at him and tried to grasp
His spiny body with an open hand.   510
His eyes bulged out, his port and starboard fins
Worked rapidly and with a sudden swell
His body vaulted to enormous size
And bobbed and floated always at a distance
As he observed me with a startled look.
I wondered how he moved around so well,
So suddenly enormous and so agile,
So full of water and at home in water.

Book XV

For one short moment I could envy him
A life that summoned ocean for assistance   520
So that the goddess came and pumped him up
And loaned him ample courage at his need.

For a scuba diver in July
The water off Palm Beach was pellucid
And full of daylight for twelve feet or so
But after that it grew opaque and green,
A warm, sunny, cloudy green, and I
Could only look toward it with discomfort.
How could one be sure what swam beyond?
I probed among the outer pilings and   530
A form emerged out of the sunny haze.
He gave my soul a shock—was he a shark,
A hammerhead, a maco, a man eater?
A long, shiny form appeared at last
Slowly and complacently—composed
And comfortable in his environment:
A barracuda, handsome predator
Who had no one to fear under the waves
But posed no danger to a scuba diver.
He looked me over with a cool eye   540
And told me not a thing of what he thought
But I could well imagine that he thought
Nothing in particular of me.
Of course I was larger than he was
And of a shape he surely had observed:
One of those who often swam above
But seldom dared to venture down to him
And face him in his natural element.
We swam slowly in opposite directions
Fully occupied with other matters   550
Although once I turned to watch him go,
A large form who meandered on his way
Into a turquoise world that was his own.

One day in January (I had come
From Harvard in deep snow to Florida

Australis Redux

And made a truly long Christmas vacation
Out of a desperate resolve to be
Away from snow as much as possible)
I snorkeled in the waters of Palm Beach.
The January ocean was cold   560
But I braved it so I could be a proof
How much warmer the Sunshine State was
Than anything New England had to offer:
The ocean was so moderate that one
Could snorkel comfortably in mid-winter.

I swam far out from shore and saw below
A school of young and slender barracuda
Who formed a large gyre as they swam.
Solar rays glanced off them as they moved
Languidly above the ocean bottom.   570
They were oblivious of me and looked
As though some purpose guided the rotation,
An unknown power that kept them orderly.
For just a moment I could know some *Angst*
As I observed their languid symmetry
In chilly waters that were comfortable
To them although not comfortable to humans.
I had read a book on barracuda
And had a close encounter with just one
But never come upon a school of them.   580
How could one understand what purpose moved them?
All of a sudden I felt suspended
Above them like a morsel in the water,
A scrap some random current brought along
To supplement their diet in the cold.
Because I was unsure of their intent
I backed away and swam toward the shore
Where wintry sunlight beckoned and I could
Grab a towel and wrap me in some comfort
And sit down on the sand above the shallows   590
And watch the ocean that concealed so much
And figure out the meaning of it all
Or try to ponder it.

Book XV

                In West Palm Beach
Close to the Post Office on Olive Avenue
The Norton Art Museum, a local icon,
Stood among palm trees and welcomed me
As I returned from ocean to enjoy
Lofty art from Europe and elsewhere.
The artwork was not like the animals
One could encounter under ocean water   600
Whose forms were so alive and made one wonder
What life was all about and what one was.
I was a rash intruder in their haunts,
Attracted often by their many forms
But sometimes with a heart that palpitated
Because I shuddered at large barracuda
Or sharks or moray eels, or at deep water.
But at the Norton I could walk alone
Without concern for sharks or barracuda
And look upon what man had done for man.   610

Outside in a small courtyard one could see
A bronze statue of a humbled slave
Bent down upon one knee and with an arm
And hand raised upward as though he would plead
With God or with his owner for some mercy
Or freedom from the bondage he was in.
A look of hopelessness and agony
On his strong face (both inarticulate
And fully and artistically composed)
Confronted me in my naïvete.   620
I stopped and looked down on the work of art
Suddenly aware that I also
Had undergone a powerful bondage
Although I stood upright and was a student
At Harvard and could scuba dive and even
Pretend I was a master under water.

Perhaps I loved the ocean and her ways,
Her sandy bottoms and her sunny reefs,

Australis Redux

Her shattered pilings and her sunken ships,
Her submarine locales well populated   630
With fish and sharks, crabs and cephalopods—
An endless dance of life that carried on
With no regard for what tomorrow brought—
Maybe I loved the unfathomable goddess
Because she offered me another world,
A place so obviously other than
The world of human bondage located
Ironically far above the sea
And her large, fair, oblivious populace.

Above that fair and thoughtless populace   640
We human beings moved and had our way.

In June I drove along a concrete wonder
From West Palm Beach down to the Florida Keys
To find a Paradise much farther south:
A place undamaged by development
Where only some would dare to build a home,
Where land was openly embraced by ocean
And no one could escape her warm environs
Unless he chose a road away from her.

My soul longed to be surrounded by ocean   650
And to discover in her holy depths
An underwater home few men could see:
A shallow habitat of coral polyps,
Of parrotfish and grouper and red snappers
Corralled by ocean to a coral hamlet
Populous and full of untold glory
For all who loved the ocean and her ways.
My love for ocean rose in a strong surge
And always overwhelmed any attempt
To have a solid life apart from her,   660
Such as a man from Harvard or from Yale
Should have—one who could conquer his own fate
And rule what came unwanted or unsought.
He mastered those who loved him or who hated

Book XV

And made his life an icon of himself,
A monument to his own words and deeds.

I was no monument and did not want
To make my personhood a work of art
Although some part of me wanted to build
A monumental work of poetry.   670

I was only a young, confused man
Who worshipped exemplars of the good:
Monuments of unageing intellect
Yeats had extolled, or in the body a
Young woman of outstanding loveliness
Who strolled along a beach and sang maybe
(She thought no one was there, only a wind
Romans and Hellenes would have called a god
Who tossed her yellow hair in a caress).

I had become an acolyte of one   680
Who offered grace and power for every footstep
I took along the sand beside the ocean
Or underneath the palm trees at Palm Springs
Or by a brown canal close to our home
Where alligators under lily pads
Admonished with a croak if I approached.
Nature was a source of constant love
Who offered me her beauty every hour
With unhampered abundance and I could
Embrace her every day in Florida   690
With unabashed and naïve openness.

I had become one of those worshippers
Who saw a vital spirit in all clouds
And in the wind that drove the clouds along
And in the palm fronds rattled by the wind
And in the coral snakes that gave me pause
And in the lizards faster than my hand
And in the vacant shells on public shores
Crafted by animals that had passed on,

Australis Redux

Now open for another occupant. 700
By the strong moan and sighing of the sea
And all her creatures that roamed far and free
Nature, my goddess, openly summoned me.

Some people who were much bolder than I
Constructed homes on those tropical islands
And many of them had been elevated
On concrete columns far above the ground,
A ploy of architects and engineers
Who thought they could build houses that would stand 710
Against the flood of waves that tumbled in
When hurricanes awoke a drowsy goddess
And forced her out of a comfortable bed
And escorted her rudely to the shore.
So barbarously handled, she could rage
And run amok among our architecture.
No human construct could arrest her pace
Nor did she care to dally on the land
But flowed across our highways and gardens
And found a natural avenue back home. 720
Devastation came as she passed over
And in her careless wake deposited
A detritus of stranded animals—
Octopus and starfish and small crabs—
Along with shell fragments and scattered seaweed.

I saw so many moods of ocean
I felt almost as though I had encountered
A grand but double personality.

She could behave just like an angry god,
A Triton or Poseidon, well armed 730
With stormy arsenals of waves and tides
He could deploy to break our homes apart
Or sweep away our beaches in his wrath.

On other days ocean would be my goddess
Perpetually virgin and could mother

Book XV

A Venus on a half shell as I saw her
In Botticelli's renowned masterwork.
She lay exposed to me on sunny days
For long hours of tropical surrender.
Soft winds could stroke her from above   740
And provoke sighs of love out of her depths;
They came to me and my complacent ear
Which like an empty conch echoed once more
Music she offered up to comfort me.

I drove along Route 1, our nation's highway,
South of Key Largo beyond Tavernier
On to Plantation and Islamorada
Past Marathon and Big Pine Keys
Through Boca Chica onward to Key West.
I went as far as Mile Marker Zero,   750
The origin and end of Route 1,
And as I stood with others on that spot
I could recall Route 1 as far away
As Maine where it rolled under puffy clouds
Across an open, lush countryside,
Or frozen in December snow and ice
So inhospitable to our race
Although we were the ones who made the road.
I looked across the cloudy turquoise water
And felt a pleasant, humid southern breeze   760
And wondered what could lead someone to chose
A northern climate for his life and work,
A land where months were dark and bitter cold
And life was cramped into a narrow space
(However large the house) insulated
Against a frozen world that seemed opposed
To any opportunity for joy.

By contrast on Key West a Conch Tour Train
Trundled around the island in warm weather
And passengers could see Sloppy Joe's Bar,   770
A favorite spot of Ernest Hemingway
According to Key West historians,

Australis Redux

Or the large, white home of John James Audubon
Who painted whip-poor-wills and belted jays,
Kingfishers, partridges and snowy owls,
Yellow breasted chats and woodpeckers
(A world of aviators he observed)
In colors true to nature. He produced
Watercolors that captured and amazed
Crowds from clammy Liverpool to London, 780
That center of a large imperium
Doomed to fade away after one war.
America's more current empire offered
Sunshine and hope to many not far off
And some of those had desperately voyaged
By night across the Florida Straits
From Cuba. They had fled her dictator
And crowded onto a wooden boat
So small it could hardly hold them all.
The Conch Tour Train pulled slowly to a halt 790
And stopped in breathless sunshine as we looked
In wonderment and awe at the weak craft.
How could a boat so small and unseaworthy
Have born so many people out of bondage
And transported them to another life?
Maybe the boat could teach someone a lesson,
For what looked small and broken and unable
Could translate someone out of hopelessness
Onto another and more open shore.

Sloppy Joe's Bar, a popular spot 800
That Hemingway frequented in Key West,
Stood on a corner and almost had no walls
But large wooden shutters that stood open
On Green and Duval streets all day long.
On a sultry evening, as the sun
Sank beyond Mallory Square, the bar
Routinely welcomed a world of wanderers.
Those who ambled in to have a drink
Entered a spacious, casual ambiance
(An atmosphere that almost offered more 810

Book XV

Than one could understand or put in words).
As day gave way to night in that cosmos
Lanterns cast small halos into space
Like tiny, isolated solar systems.
Sometimes a patron could repose and be
A minor planet at the outer range
Of one such lamp and be all on his own,
A solitary with unbothered thoughts
As ocean breezes wandered through the place
And helped one feel comfortable and at home.   820
One night I sat alone and I recalled
How Edgar Allen Poe had often drunk
Alone and in a melancholy mood
And chose to squander his young, fruitful soul
On substances produced from corn and grain.
Out of that soul came stories eloquent
And horrible that would delight all France
And many generations after him
In our land, and yet secure him nothing
But hollow fame as he lay in the grave.   830

Key West and her sorority of Keys
Formed a small but fecund universe
Founded on broad accretions of dead coral
And covered with palms and other fruit trees:
Grapefruit, cumquats, lemons, oranges
And key limes—whose small and astringent fruit
Was coupled with a singular aroma
And formed the signature ingredient
Of Key Lime Pie, a favorite at restaurants
Not only in the Keys but farther north.   840
It seemed a wonder so much life could flourish
On a base of coral skeletons
And produce exotic southern fruit
Which brought a smile to many peoples' faces
Who would never see the Florida Keys.

Australis Redux

I was happy I could sojourn there
As I sat in a seafood restaurant
And ordered grouper, tea and Key Lime Pie.

The ocean of south Florida and the Keys
Was fruitful beyond measure, a warm womb,   850
And anyone who wanted could obtain
Fruit of the sea at any restaurant
Or fast food place on those small, marly islands.

En route to Key West drivers cross a bridge
Between Key Vaca in the Middle Keys
And Little Duck Key in the Lower Keys.
Henry Flagler oversaw the labor
Which would produce a major railroad bridge
(The only one to span those turquoise waters),
The Florida East Coast Railway extension;   860
And it took passengers to Key West.
Because it covered seven miles of ocean
It got a name: the Overseas Railroad.
Once a hurricane had damaged it
The federal government acquired it
And built a two lane highway over it.
That was Route 1 and soon the local folks
Gave it a name: the Overseas Highway;
So it felt as one drove along it:
An endless passage over narrow concrete   870
With cloudy Gulf waters far below.

The road I motored south on that day
Was a human artwork over water.

Before me I saw large cumulous clouds,
The sort that harbor major thunderstorms
As they mushroom to their full strength
And march slowly across the warm Atlantic.
How many hurricanes, their brawling cousins,
Had lashed the Keys and torn down human structures
Naïvely built to stand against such power?   880

Book XV

Perhaps because the Overseas Highway
Was born of such a storm it would endure
And always carry traffic to the south
Upon its sturdy and compliant back.
So far no hurricane had done it harm
And as I drove across it on my way
I trusted it would also carry me
Toward my southern island of repose
Just as it had carried other souls
Who journeyed to a southern Paradise. 890

But not long afterward as I drove home
I understood no art could transport me
Beyond myself into a Paradise
That was so temporary. Old Key West
May stand, but not forever after all.
It was a destination for a snowbird:
Warmer than West Palm Beach, but just an island
When all was said and done, and unprepared
To transform one into another person.

Although I was in love with Florida 900
And all that spoke of Florida to me—
Those powerful memories out of my youth,
The adolescent paper route, the days
Of sand castles and tanning on the beach
And palms that rustled in an evening breeze
As I stood talking with an old school chum
About our high school science teacher—all
That spoke to me of Florida was good
And had a hallowed place in my young soul.
Nonetheless, after Key West, I knew 910
Her Paradise could never be enough
To heal one who was damaged and confused
As I once hoped.

        So I drove north across
The Overseas Highway, but without joy
Or any sense of good on the horizon

Australis Redux

But only a dull ache. I could not trust
Any goal or power beyond myself.

Ocean had been my lady and my nurse.

No one could be as true and powerful
Or flow into my soul as she alone   920
Had done and make me joyful and forgetful
Of an ineluctable quotidian sorrow
(*Lacrimae rerum* as Vergil once wrote)—
A melancholy mastered in small part:
Sadness unknown to anyone but me.

Your tears and agonies though written large
Upon the sands of your experience—
As though an angry and frustrated child
Had scrawled some wounded feelings into words
Across a sandy shore with a fat stick—   930
Would be eradicated by the ocean
Who washed those scrawls away with gentle waves.
So, anyone who later walked your road
Would never know about the scars you made
Because the sand before him was now smooth.

Who would comfort me beyond all doubt
As ocean often times had come to me
To wash away the anger of my soul
And make it pure as a small infant's soul?

I hoped it would be like an unknown shore   940
Untouched (and so undamaged) by a sole
Of any person who like a mere tourist
Trod on a land he did not care about.

What sort of continent had I become?

Could any surge erase old eidolons
Of love and loss and longing and frustration
For one who bound himself to worship beauty

Book XV

But found her idol hollow after all
And unable to purge away his sorrow?

What room was there for such a thought today   950
Or for confession of it in a poem?

Although our land produced abundant passions
And devoured souls without any reluctance
It was a question I had never posed.

I drove to West Palm Beach in balmy weather
And saw the Intracoastal Waterway
Which looked blue as it would under blue skies
Although under gray skies it was so leaden
One never would have thought it could look blue.
As I drove along I observed   960
Pleasure boats and million dollar yachts
Bound captive to their docks by mooring cables
So they could be available at whim
To those who had the money to afford them.
I watched them with a remote sense of longing.
How could I wear a pair of white ducks
And walk upon those varnished wooden decks
And hold a stainless steel guard rail
And ride the surge and chaos of the waves
And feel the salty spray upon my face   970
And be a man who harbored Paradise
In his own soul as he drove out to sea
And challenged all the ocean brought to him?

I was not one to challenge wave or wind.

Under a cloudy sky as twilight rose
I sat beside the ocean at Lake Worth
And watched the leaden waves roll slowly in.
Sultry summer air surrounded me.
Companionless I wondered how a place
I had enjoyed and loved so very much   980
On days of summer sun and winter sun

Australis Redux

But always welcome sun and sparkling ocean
Could feel so narrow and unsound to me.

I felt the atmosphere must swallow me.

I was a stranger on a foreign shore.

Languid waves rolled among concrete poles
That supported the pier and dully onward
Until they spent themselves on gray sand.

A few teenage girls and young families
With small children toddling not far off990
Made up the populace of the gray beach.

Twilight slowly deepened into night.

One by one or in family groups
Folks left the dark water behind them
Came up the slope and parked their paraphernalia
Beside a public shower on the sidewalk.
One by one they washed their sandy feet,
Located their parked cars and drove away.

I saw a joy beyond my empathy
And only wished I could remove myself1000
From all of my dull anger and frustration
As they had walked away from those dark waves;
I wished I could shower my sorrows off
As they had washed away the grains of sand.

More than four decades would elapse
Before I sat by a sunny bay window
As April snow melted in Massachusetts
And understood my old infatuation
With Florida and her coast *nonpareil*.

When I was young I could not understand1010
How one could be lovesick *and* sick of love.

Book XV

On that obscure and sullen waterfront
I had no oracle, nor could I know
What future days would hold or would withhold;
I only understood I was confused.

I was far from the one I hoped to be
And there was no one good to show a way
Out of the gloom into some holy light.

Sorrow haunted me for youthful days
Squandered in a foolhardy pursuit   1020
Of lovely forms that took me far astray
Because they could only be temporary
And naturally prove untrue to one
Who offered his whole soul upon their altar.

How many days would pass before I sat
By a bay window in a sun soaked room
Far north of Florida the fruitful goddess
And composed verses at the thought of her
Abundant beauty and seductive shores—
As though a man recalled someone he loved   1030
And wrote an ode to her once she was gone
Or he was gone from her warm latitude?

The man composed because he understood
He had to turn away from her for good
Although he loved her now and always would.

Later at Harvard I would read a poem,
"Farewell to Florida," by Wallace Stevens
Who loved her, too, and always was a poet
Although he worked in Hartford and was cold.
The mythic portals of the southern sky   1040
One could imagine on a starry night
Were hardly mythopoeic to a man
Whose soul was open to the balm they brought
And I was still a man who could be soothed

Australis Redux

By those astoundingly large southern stars.

Whatever power lay beyond their beauty
Was powerful to me although I was
So ignorant of what it should be called.

Maybe it was a power I had seen
When I encountered puffer fish and squid   1050
Or sharks and barracuda, moray eels
Or brain coral I thought could tutor me—
Oceanic fauna full of wisdom
Though ignorant of any other world
Beyond the constant surface of the sea.

At home within her waters someone called
With a voice much like the constant sound
Of distant ocean in a sea shell held
Close to the ear by an amazed child.

Among her waves was an unknown someone   1060
Who called to me so unrepentantly
And summoned me with such a rare allure.

Book XVI

Portals of Dawn

A rose colored dawn came up one day,
One old Homer would have loved to see:
Pink shafts of sunshine probed a turquoise sky
Elegant with golden wisps of cloud
As though all heaven were an ornament
To hang about a vast and placid sea—
To hang around the nape of fairest ocean,
To hang around the neck of Amphitrite
Who spawned all fish and shellfish and all dolphins,
A pendant from above just to adorn her.   10

How could I harbor such a pagan thought?
Antiquity. Those Greek and Roman gods
And goddesses were all but long forgotten
Because we know that Jupiter and Saturn,
Venus and Mars and Mercury and Pluto,
Far wanderers of heaven, were no gods
But only planets inhospitable
To human life, or life of any sort.

I walked alone and felt the morning sand
Cool as morning sand alone is cool   20
Beneath my feet and saw the sun come up

Book XVI

A round and golden monarch over water,
A globe of sudden hotness large and looming
About to bring another day upon us.

How could that day hold any good for me?
I walked alone and felt I was alone
And knew I was alone on morning sand
That had no care for me or for my walk
As I left footprints on the hard damp shore,
Footprints the water would soon wash away.   30

I strolled in Palm Beach on a paved path
That paralleled the shoreline under shade
Along the Intracoastal Waterway.
South of Flagler's mansion I walked on
And saw a tree with large upraised roots
That looked like folds and snaked along the ground,
So sinuous they almost looked alive.
Someone had called it a Balboa fig
But I was happy not to know its name
And let it stay mysterious, unknown,   40
So I could stop and stare at it and wonder.

The path was made for cyclists and they pedaled
Several miles of dappled sun and shade
Along the Intracoastal Waterway
Flanked by water and those grand estates
Constructed by the wealthy of our land
Whose large back gardens sported southern flora—
Monkey puzzle trees, ficus and guavas,
Banyan and citrus trees in thick profusion—
The many guarantors of privacy   50
That guarded those estates from any eye
That dared to cast an ordinary glance
Upon those pink and airy palaces,
Upon those stuccoed castles of the south.

Sometimes I wondered how it would have been
If I had grown to manhood in a castle

Portals of Dawn

Stuccoed and roofed with red Spanish tiles
That fronted Ocean Boulevard, perhaps,
Or had a back yard bordered by that path.
Would I have stood in some large, airy room,   60
And pondered metaphysics, or composed
Some music worthy of the grand tradition
That I had come to know in Bach and Brahms,
Or written science fiction in my youth,
And later, when I had become mature,
Composed a poem worthy of the name?
Would I have lived in wealthy solitude
And taken satisfaction in the wind,
And taken satisfaction in the waves
That always echoed from across the road,   70
Or had an artist's pleasure late at night
As I lay on my bed and could recall
A day of poetry that would endure,
A day of truth and beauty that would last,
A day of thought and creativity,
As I lay on my bed and heard the palms
That rustled in the wind and soothed my soul
Until I sank into a welcome slumber,
Until I sank into a well earned sleep?

Henry Flagler built a noble mansion   80
On the Intracoastal Waterway
And called it Whitehall, and it was whitewashed.
It was a vision out of ancient Rome
Adorned with palm trees and large outdoor vases.
Round columns, ranged along the front,
Held a stately architrave aloft
And formed a classic portico below.

On the back lawn stood a railroad car,
A coach Flagler used to call his own,
With brass appointments, leather and dark wood   90
That spoke of moneyed comfort in its day.

Book XVI

I walked along a broad front path
Bordered by royal palms and made my way
Through a doorway with a Roman arch.
The grand hall I observed was opulent
With inlaid marble floors and potted palms,
Oriental carpets and carved chairs,
Each one of them magnificent enough
To be a monarch's throne, while overhead
A cameo of monumental size   100
That housed a painting such as masters painted,
Say, Michelangelo or Leonardo,
Welcomed anyone to stop and gawk.
I toured numerous rooms on two floors
And as I walked along those bedroomed halls
And saw accommodations that evoked
Victorian or Edwardian elegance—
Ornate carved beds and bureaus and boudoirs
For master or for mistress, or for guest—
I wondered how we all had lost our way   110
And wandered down a path so far remote
From human craftsmanship so beautiful
A person could have justly called it art.

I taught at Palm Beach Atlantic one autumn,
A term that would produce good memories.

A student there invited me to take
An old friend's twenty foot cabin cruiser
One sunny afternoon against strong winds
From Port of Palm Beach. We hoped to find
A vessel lost two hundred years before,   120
A small adventurer from Portugal
That sank in shallow water.

                     I was happy
To come aboard with my Scubapro tank
And see a treasure ocean had swallowed:
A hopeless ship destroyed by hurricane

Portals of Dawn

In days gone by when only angry skies
Gave any hint a storm was on its way.

How strong that force of nature was compared
With anything a human could produce.

Our cabin cruiser, jostled by the waves,   130
Rocked to and fro and made me sick
Just as I had been when I was younger
On another voyage from Palm Beach
When mother caught a sailfish and I sat
Beside her sipping Coke to calm my stomach
While the unruly Gulf Stream made sport of us.

Today swells of water tossed our boat
And for a while it looked as though we three
Would not pass through the inlet to the ocean—
Almost as though the goddess laughed at us   140
And mocked the power of our puny boat—
But finally we found the open water.

Our sonar screen glowed uncanny green
As it told our captain how things stood
Just twenty feet below—not very deep
But deep enough to swallow and hold fast
A small and tragic vessel in its grave.
A Portuguese Man 'o War,
A bulbous bladder with long tentacles
Composed of tiny colonies of cells   150
Always at home upon the ocean surface,
Was born to handle the roughest waves;
Not so the ill-starred ship below us.
She was no Portuguese Man 'o War
But just a mortal work of wood and tar
For all the thought put into her unable
To survive a Florida hurricane
That any Portuguese Man 'o War
Could ride out any day and float long after
A troublous hurricane had passed away.   160

Book XVI

Our sonar told us we had found the ship.

I pressed the Squalé mask onto my face
And plunged backward into the ocean;
Water and bubbles rose up all around me
As I sank toward the sandy bottom.
Intake of oxygen and burst of air
Signaled a scuba diver was around.
Both had become familiar sounds to me
And they announced to Davey Jones that I
Was back in my adopted element   170
Where I could move with an accustomed freedom
Among the fauna and flora of the deep.

A student and professor swam along
And saw a modest outline on the floor,
All that ocean left, or almost all
Of what had once sailed happily above,
The outline of a ship that could no longer
Command the sea or transport cargo home.
We saw the wooden surface of a hull
Almost coal black among the sand;   180
Some curved parts also dark and seasoned
By the sea arose out of the wreck—
Fragmentary ribs of a doomed ship.
We swam across the ruin. I imagined
Broken masts and tumult on the deck
As sailors grabbed for rope or random tackle,
Or any sort of help amid the storm,
Before the ship in which they put their hope
Betrayed them to a man and took them down
To a world of hammerheads and macos.   190

I sank toward a rib and took hold.
It was smooth and gentle to the touch.

A softened piece of wood took me to school.
Rough hewn and sturdy before it set sail
Out of its native port in Portugal

Portals of Dawn

It underwent a slow transfiguration
So that someone now could fondle it
And know it would not harm him with a splinter
Because a goddess who had brought it down
Smoothed and softened it and made it gentle.   200

Maybe a current that had led me far
Had also humbled me without my knowledge.

Her potent waves had broken down my will
Until I saw in her immortal nature
An unconquerable power that overcame
And brought me down for good I hardly wanted.

I swam from spot to spot across our wreck
And came upon a little colony
Of unfamiliar globes that huddled close
Together on one side of a short rib.   210
Their surfaces were also black and soft
As though covered with velvet of the sort
One could buy to make a woman's dress.
My student drew a German diver's blade,
Took hold of one small globe, and made a cut;
It showed us both a creamy interior:
A pristine sponge with curious shaped holes
Now open to the ocean and her flow.

I took in far more than I understood,
For not all students understand at once.   220

An unknown diver found me under water,
A surgeon with a well tempered blade
Who cut me open far below the surface
And opened up my soul to the warm sea,
So now her currents flowed through all of me
And I could sample her every mood.

Or else the lesson could be nuanced so:
Unwanted surgery forced my submission

Book XVI

So I could be all openness to her
Or to the surgeon who had operated.   230

Maybe the Gulf Stream had engulfed my soul
And I had lost and found myself in ocean
In order to become what I should be.

Only, the chaos of the powerful water
Was my own chaos and the soul I found
Was an amorphous one composed of currents—
An ebb and flow whose nature mutated
In subtle ways I could not understand.

Oceanic water formed me now;
Another water also tutored me.   240

A dusty red lighthouse stands alone
At Jupiter and has done so for decades
To warn deep water vessels about sandbars.
So it keeps them at a proper distance.
Close by the constant Loxahatchee flows,
A sinuous river with an Indian name,
And on her surface motorboats and rowboats
Add human color to an afternoon
Otherwise owned by gulls and alligators
Or a wild boar snorting among bushes,   250
Hunting for food close to a sandy bank.

Decades later I would stop and share
A picnic lunch with parents and a comrade
At a table just above the river
And watch the sea gulls drop and beg for food.

After lunch we hired a canoe
And launched onto a quiet pool of water.
We paddled from that harbor and soon faced
A powerful and unexpected current.
We found it hard to enter the broad flow   260
So we turned away and hugged the shore

Portals of Dawn

And made our way to a small tributary
Whose surface was calm and easy to paddle.

Just as ocean often challenged me
And made me know the power of her waves
So now the Loxahatchee made me know
Nature had currents we could not oppose,
Powers able to retard our race.

But on that future day I would not be
Unsettled by the Loxahatchee's lore   270
For I had got instruction underwater
When powerful waves pounded down my soul
At Yale and Harvard and then West Palm Beach,
Tsunamis that fell randomly on me
And tore the sandy bottom where I stood
From under me and carried me away
To locales where I had to swim alone
And contend with a harder discipline.

I visited the Loxahatchee often
Because she was unsullied by our progress.   280

One afternoon I paddled from the river
Onto a small, meandering flow
Overshadowed by Australian pines
And other trees with branches almost bare
Except for Spanish moss that hung from them,
A natural ornament above brown water.
I had to paddle slowly to avoid
The shallows that betrayed and as I paused
Unsure of a good way I noticed motion
Along the shore. I also caught a sound   290
Of tiny claws or legs and soon I saw
A crowd of crabs, cadaverously white,
Crawl out of holes along the sloping banks
(The muddy shore was their small hunting ground).
Almost without a sound they scuttled off

Book XVI

Back to their holes when I lifted my oar
For I was large—perhaps beyond their ken.

I stopped in my disgust at our encounter
Ugly and horrific though it was
To see what they would do if I stood there.　　　　　　300
Would they summon courage and come out,
Diminutive monstrosities who loved
The dark and so normally shunned the day?
Would they emerge under a shady branch
And hope to locate insects in the mud
Or other food on a low sandy slope?

Once more they came, once more I raised my oar
And saw them scuttle into their small holes.
Soon tired of the challenge I moved slowly
Along my way and left them to their hunt.　　　　　　310

Nature was not herself that afternoon,
Or my ideal of nature was so false
I was not open to a foreign beauty
Displayed by numerous small crustaceans
And obvious to those who understood:
Nature offered many forms of beauty
Although she nurtured standards of her own
And would not modify them for our whim
But took us to a hard and honest school
Where one was forced to broaden one's aesthetic　　　　　　320
And bow before a generous quality
Proper to her and to her alone
Beyond all human hope of reproduction
Because nobody could encompass it,
Ennoble it or make it glorious
Beyond the glory it already had.

No one could make her wonderful beyond
A form and elegance she had possessed
Before the human race had come to be.

Portals of Dawn

Was all of nature after all a structure, 330
A monument that harbored an idea—
A complex work of architectural prowess?

She was our home but also challenged us
To understand a concept she embodied
Or, better yet, someone who called her home—
Her powerful, ineluctable producer.

Already, though, the Palm Beach area
Showed unwelcome marks of our intrusion,
Inordinate growth that would not be forestalled.

I made one more journey south to escape 340
To balmy islands of the Florida Straits.

The architecture of the Florida Keys
Was a work of understated splendor—
A welcome to a coral centered world
For anyone who chose to drug his soul
In shallow waters of a local reef:
To observe coral polyps in their dance
Or parrotfish who often grazed on them
Or angelfish who came to feed on molluscs
Or fish that swam like butterflies all day 350
And were dubbed butterfly fish for their trouble
Or triggerfish that looked ridiculous
And fed on shellfish all the afternoon.

Off Marathon Key on a sunny day
I was elated to be on a boat
Poised to fall backward into the water
And wander down and explore a small reef
Shallow enough to welcome warm daylight
So various corals and their population
Could show their natural colors unabated 360
By depths that would attenuate the sun.

Book XVI

I swam along and saw a barracuda
Not very far away in shallow water.
He measured over two yards long
And with his magnitude came confidence
No underwater creature could approach him
Or challenge him or offer any harm
Unless he chose to allow some access
Into his dominant vicinity.
I swam toward him with a grown man's caution   370
Because I knew of nothing in my kit
(No flashy ornament or article)
That would reflect the sun and be a lure
Or cause him to mistake me for a fish,
A moving banquet with shiny scales.

I came within a foot or two of him
And as I looked into his watery eye
I wondered what intelligence looked back,
What alien capacity for thought.
Was I a new phenomenon to him   380
Or had he seen a scuba diver once
Or many times before, someone who came
To see what underwater occupants
Owned a home two miles off Marathon?

The colorful attractions of a reef,
Triggerfish and parrotfish and porgies
And many other forms of unknown name,
Formed an underwater gallery
Unnoticed from the surface but exposed
To any scuba diver who would look.   390

The tropical ocean was a vast museum.
I swam toward one hall of that museum,
A coral reef that housed countless portraits
Full of cavorting, vibrant characters
More colorful than any artist's palette.

Portals of Dawn

I left the barracuda far behind me.
He stayed on as a guard of the museum
Who would prowl the borders on his watch
So no unholy person could invade
The shoals, a sanctuary of the sun.

I made my way toward the central reef.

Rocks and shells on a sandy bottom formed
The suburbs of a large brain coral,
Brown and oval, full of shallow fissures
And yellow green polyps that swayed loosely
In currents abundant with plankton,
Miniscule flora and fauna of the ocean.
As I approached the magnanimous brain
I took a generous breath and slowly rose
(My lungs inflated by the oxygen)
And floated over it with room to spare;
Then I exhaled as I passed over it
And floated down along the other side.

Once more the open ocean lay before me.

I wondered what the former of that coral,
A many–fissured similitude of brain
And large intelligence of coral seas,
Would have to say about my curious route—
My elementary scubapro antics.
Outside the world and wiser than us all
Hardly impressed with human acrobatics
Would he sagely, above the ample flow
Of plankton that provided all the food
An ocean full of brain coral could want,
Ignore the small gymnast who floated past
On his slow and unimportant way?

Later, on shore and as the day began
To wane, another opportunity

Book XVI

For exploration posed itself to me,
One I had read about but never known. 430

The underwater world was glorious
On any sunny morn or afternoon;
What would a coral reef full of splendor
In broad daylight offer a scuba diver
Once old Sol had sunk into the sea
And turned the water to a solemn shroud?

It cloaked all of her occupants with darkness
Funereal, obscure and unexplored.

A glorious sunset came and western clouds
Towered pink and orange bordered by gold— 440
Almost spun gold—with filaments aflame
As though scattered from a cauldron tipped
By some careless aetherial alchemist
Into a pool of blue and darker sky.
The western cumuli mounted upward
And looked like lofty scoops of peach ice cream,
A farewell word of glory as we stood
Close to the poop of a long cabin cruiser
Chartered to carry me and others out
Miles from Key Largo so we could observe 450
A reef we had explored at high noon.

The divers sank below the evening waves
And swam toward the bottom in the dark.

Along our way we saw a lemon shark
Arrested by a cone of watery light
Projected from an underwater lamp
That showed our way. In solitude suspended
Much like the barracuda of Marathon
He looked our way with an impassive eye.
A lemon shark is not a man eater 460
But any shark is worthy of respect

Portals of Dawn

So we bestowed a backward glance on him
And more than one as we moved slowly forward.

Two walls of coral towered just before us
And flanked a sandy floor but on the bottom
No sand was visible. The open space
Was taken by intruders—sea urchins
Large and purple, with long poisoned spines.
We understood we had to float above
The lethal flock to keep ourselves from harm.   470

One could import a mythic understanding:
Some Power summoned those dangerous ones
Onto a sandy plane that looked so pure
By day. The floor under the sun had been
Almost vestal and fully welcomed one
But not long after dark it was a home
For interlopers who would have their way.
Perhaps it was a warning from a goddess
To any man who, uninvited, snooped
Around her private chambers after sunset—   480
A small nocturnal warning she dispatched
Subtle or not so subtle to a race
Who violated her at every turn
Although she was numinal and had power.

If ocean was a goddess I was now
Someone she had embraced and swallowed up.

Moreover south Florida had consumed
The soul of one who worshiped her for ages
And bowed to her in spirit and in truth
Though she was not the goddess he had hoped.   490

No sustenance existed on her altar
Although it overflowed with southern fruit—
Cumquats, coconuts and tangerines,
Passion fruit, guavas, grapefruit, key limes,

Book XVI

Lemons and oranges—and a fragrant garland
Of tropical flowers that promised so much.

Maybe all of nature was a temple
And Florida was just an oratory—
A tropical nook of a cosmic shrine.

So I mistook a fraction for the whole. 500

On the south side of old Key West
One afternoon off Smathers Beach
I snorkeled under clouds in warm water.
Over the ocean floor not far below
A world of grass, dull ocean weeds, moved
Slowly back and forth swayed by the flow.
Down among the narrow blades I noticed
An unattractive form ten inches long
And hard to spot among the moving weeds.
A sea cucumber, gray-green and obscure, 510
Undulated modestly along.
I could fancy for one crazy moment
Someone had set it among those low grasses,
A chef who tossed a large marine salad
Marinated in warm salty water.
Day by day a cucumber could manage
Among a host of underwater fauna
But for what purpose would it consume hours
In a small compass? Or what purpose now
Had made a lofty spectator of me 520
Who hovered curiously over it,
A human who could recognize its form
From a book he once saw in a library,
A book no sea cucumber was aware of
Although it spoke of him and his low world?

A *homo sapiens* had apparatus
And had advantages under the ocean
But what could any of that do for me?

Portals of Dawn

One could strap a scuba harness on,
Add a mask and Cressi fins and depth gauge.
One could take a bang stick underwater
In case one met a tiger shark or maco.
One could launch from any dock or beach
And as a master plumb the ocean depths.

What *homo faber* could accomplish now
Was what *I* could accomplish, and I saw
A goddess could no longer rule my soul.

But now I wondered what *could* conquer me.

Who could ravish me as ocean had,
So full of power and seductive moods?

Who would consume my soul as she alone
Had done and make me happy and oblivious
Of sorrows deep within my foolish heart?

Who would overwhelm me as she had
And smooth away the anger of my soul
And make it pure as some small infant's soul
Or level sands no foot had ever trodden?

I could not feel anger or frustration
But only melancholy and despair
For no one could erase those memories
Of love and loss and unconquerable longing
For one who bowed his soul to worship beauty
But found her idol hollow and unable
To lullaby his troubled past away.

She brought me sorrow and she brought me joy
Because I loved her and I always would.

One summer night I walked narrow roads
And alleys of Key West and understood
Whatever joy she brought my *ennui*

Book XVI

(Or any joy that hallowed Florida,   560
Who every day accepted powerful waves
And lay in summer suns that made her warm,
Would give one on a day one asked for it)
For all the languid hours one could obtain
In Florida, goddess of sunny waters,
And although I was one composed of water,
Someone at home in Florida always,
My joy would ultimately be unsound
Because it passed away like summer heat
Or washed away like castles formed of sand   570
Undone by tides under a changing moon.

I walked along a road (was it Duval?)
One evening and encountered a student
Who handed me a small rectangular tract.
The boy was cordial and appeared to be
At peace with the ambience of the Conch Republic
And with himself as he spoke briefly to me.
I pocketed the paper and walked on.
I paid it no attention at that moment
Because I knew it spoke of the old faith   580
The West was founded on.

                        It often seemed
Ironical to me that western culture,
A tower that cast its shadow on the world,
Had become in our day the work of those
Who did not care to walk as Jesus walked—
Jesus, a guru for another day—
Although our very culture had arisen
And through all challenges become mature
Largely on the ground of mother church:
Our drama, music, poetry, all sprung   590
And got their primal impetus from Rome
Under the watchful eye of mitred popes
(Philosophy also as shrewd Descartes
Composed from Holland with an eye toward Rome).

Portals of Dawn

I sat in Sloppy Joe's Bar one more time
As evening dropped a cloak upon the sky,
A darkness uncontested on the ocean
Although punctuated on the island
By lamps above the streets, occasional headlights,
And windows in most houses of the town   600
And by the lamps in Sloppy Joe's Bar.

I was a solitary planetoid
Who hung around one lamp, a minor sun.

How could I justify the space I took?

I wondered in a mutable cosmos
What solar system I should be a part of,
What sun could form the center of my orbit,
What star would capture me and make me move,
As our sun made the solar system move,
By an unseen power of attraction.   610

What sun possessed adequate *gravitas*
To capture and hold on to my small soul
So for all time in constant adoration
I would orbit him and do his will?

Could I tolerate a scrap of paper
A juvenescent boy had handed me?
I was an oak and he was but a sapling.
I was a diver who had seen the ocean
And fathomed the unknowns of coral reefs
And had a brain coral for professor.   620

Aquatic sapience could not carry me
Beyond the ocean to a better place,
Beyond the hackneyed wisdom of our world
Whatever form it took in Rome or elsewhere;
Buddha always seemed a hollow gong
Nietzsche imploded on himself and all
Of Germany's titanic *Kulturkampf*

Book XVI

Had only won global catastrophe,
Not at all what Brahms, Beethoven or Haydn
Imagined in a flow of patriotism   630
Or open handed liberal humanism
Or eighteenth century ratiocination.

Was our whole world confused, or was it I
Who was befuddled on a summer eve
As palm fronds rustled in the breeze, a sound
I loved so much although it comforted
No more, as Florida could soothe no more?

Or, was the world confused as much as I,
So that confusion mastered all of us
For no one had an answer or a way   640
More worthy of attention than a laze
In Florida—a picnic afternoon
Close to Lake Osborne, angling in brown water?

How many days would pass—how many months—
Before one January Sunday morning
When I would hear a word about old Pharaoh
Who sat supreme under a serpent crown
Master of all the world within his ken,
One of a line of Pharaohs from the days
When Cheops built his blocky pyramid   650
To Cleopatra's promiscuity
That would have purchased more Egyptian grandeur
From potent Rome secure across the waters,
Ascendant *urbs* above her *mare nostrum*?
Pharaoh had assurance of his power
Fully aware that he was Amon-Ra,
A god incarnate and invincible,
A match for any god who challenged him,
Especially a god of Hebrew slaves,
A god of mud and straw, a god of shepherds,   660
Who made his people vassals of a Pharaoh
Or else could not prevent their being so.

Portals of Dawn

Superb Pharaoh, who could observe his country
Undone by plague upon disastrous plague,
Would not accept what those plagues demonstrated
To his own land about his human nature.

Was he a god or was he not a god,
And if a god, was he a powerless god
Unable to resist a god of slaves—
Unable to say no to him and triumph?   670

It was a message that came home to me.
Was I a god or was I not a god,
And if a god, what sort of mortal god?

Was I a sun or something much smaller,
A minor, remote chunk of space debris
Afloat in frozen interstellar darkness
Who hoped to be captured by a sun?

Monday morning brought another day
And as I sat and pondered after brunch
What I had heard and thought the day before   680
A sudden thunderstorm rolled down on us:
A tumult of rattled fronds outside
And gusty winds blew curtains left and right,
Dark clouds rolled over the whole neighborhood
And blackened our small world and then it broke:
Titanic power suddenly unbound
Flooded roads and sidewalks as it poured
Calamitously on our graveled roofs.
Then as Florida storms suddenly may
The clouds broke up and floated off, and sun   690
Flooded the empty roads and our small house.

I walked toward one window and I stood
And saw our back yard dripping from the storm
As globes of water like so many gems
Dropped to the grass from cumquat trees and oranges.

Book XVI

Suddenly I had a sense of power
And glory in the droplets and the sun
And in the sunny clouds and holy landscape
Unparalleled by any I had known.

All of the glory that had broken on me   700
Surrounded me and saw me through and through
Although I had no idea how to name
A power that engulfed me totally
And turned my soul onto another road.

April and May would blossom, and August
Would carry her large load of summer fruit,
October leaves would swirl in chilly wind
And snow would fall again in Harvard Yard
Before I understood a gradual change
Someone good had brought about in me.   710
He worked devotedly those days and months
As I walked the streets of Cambridge town
My eyes unseeing on the red brick pavement,
Or on the dogwood blossoms that announced
Winter had died and spring was underway
Now full of hope and unexpected joy.

What spirit labored as I scuba dived
That summer in my old familiar haunts,
Or as I shuffled through the fallen leaves
On Cambridge Common as autumn departed   720
And winter came to whiten all the Common
And cover all of Harvard with a shroud?

One frozen evening, close to Durgin Park,
I stopped and saw a canopy of stars
And understood, with knowledge beyond knowledge,
That somehow, by a storm I had not asked for,
A storm that broke and took me, somehow I
Had come to know the Maker of it all.

Portals of Dawn

How many names could such a God be called?
How many names could qualify the One					730
Who qualified all beings that had been
Or ever would be in the ebb and flow
Of energy and matter we call cosmos—
A name appropriate to our universe,
A masterpiece of architecture formed
To endure through time and space like some large temple
Until the Maker knows the hour has come
To sweep it all into oblivion
Because he wants to build a better home?

All the astounding loveliness of woman					740
All the amazing sanity of Haydn
All of Beethoven's ruled unruly storms
And all the architectonics of Brahms
So noble and so lofty and so grand,
All of Milton's verse so Latinate,
Who justified the ways of God to man,
All of Wordsworth's Lake District, so green
And mountainous and decked with clouds sublime,
All of Shakespeare, all of Turner, all
Of splendor in Big Ben and Parliament,					750
Of fairy elegance in *Neuschwanstein*,
Of raucous laughter in the *Hofbräuhaus*,
Of power and pathos in a Wagner opera,
All that made the Alps magnificent,
All that made a carved dwarf so clever
When he stood with his pipe and looked askance
At English tourists who came by the busload
And thronged the shops of Oberammergau,
All the wisdom of a coral reef
With brain and staghorn coral in abundance,					760
And all the cleverness of parrotfish
Who ate the brain coral and grew so smart,
All the splendor of a Flagler mansion,
All the gothic royalty of Yale,
All the red brick ambience of Harvard,
All the splendor of a dusty fossil

Book XVI

Found in a muddy ditch by a young boy,
All the power of a Brontosaurus
And all the majesty of dinosaurs
Who ambled earth before but now were gone,   770
All the wonder of the galaxies
Innumerable that hung like gauze in space,
All the mystery of the Asteroid Belt,
All the rings of Saturn full of asteroids,
All the majesty of Jupiter,
Monarch of planets over all supreme
So full of jollity as Holst portrayed him
With moons as large as planets in his thrall,
All the double stars that waltzed around,
All the nebulae in outer space,   780
All the supernovas that devoured
Solar systems in a sudden flare—
All the swampy land so close to home
Where tiny frogs astounded with large song
And serenaded people all night long,
All chameleons that scampered off
And found a refuge in hibiscus bushes
When any human footfall came their way,
All the alligators that rose up
On stubby legs and outpaced any prey,   790
All the sea turtles that lost their way
And ended upside down upon the shore,
Mouths full of Man o' War that had undone them
(And all the Portuguese Man o' War
Stranded on the shore and left to bake,
Who popped so loud when someone trod on them),
All in nature that could make one laugh,
All in nature that was so profound
And spoke of more than nature to us mortals,
A symphony of sounds, a mighty fugue   800
Of all phenomena both large and small,
And all of human manufacture too—
Every product of true human art—
All architecture of imagination
That echoed or resembled only dimly

Portals of Dawn

The mind of One who imaged forth all things
And made the world a *cornucopia*
Compounded one grand work and sang one song
To One who made them all and loved their music,
Who saw it all and saw that it was good,   810
Who spoke, and darkness parted from the day,
Who spoke, and water parted from the clouds,
Who spoke, and oceans parted from the land
Who spoke, and sun and moon and stars came out
And star clusters and galaxies galore,
And all the panoply of outer space
Made to adorn and mark off days and seasons,
Who spoke, and laughing dolphins and sand sharks,
All parrotfish and porgies and guitarfish,
Who in their sleep and play would honor him,   820
All giant squid and chambered nautilus,
And all the multitudes that thronged about
Coral reefs or plumbed the darkest chasms,
An avian host that soared gladly above
And penetrated clouds and swooped carefree
(Or penguins who just waddled on the snow),
Came forth and found a home in their environs,
Who spoke, and animals and plants came forth—
All elephants and frogs and alligators,
All oranges, cumquats and passion fruit—   830
And after all was formed as he knew how
Produced a couple to rule and subdue
In true humility and servanthood
Whose noble minds unlike the animals'
Were capable of grandeur and of love:
A man and woman in a garden planted
To be like One who fashioned male and female,
To be like One who planted him and her
To be like One who formed and planted them.

All of nature I had once adored   840
I could embrace and love without adoring—
A newborn freedom, and a simple joy.

Book XVI

The goddess, ocean, owned me no more
Although I loved her and her many moods.

Moreover now I understood dark things,
Poisonous urchins and nocturnal sharks,
Undertow and strong destructive surf,
Were part of one grand *paean* to their Maker
Who made them all and kept them all in order
So they could play a role in a good plan. 850

What Bruckner captured in a symphony
Or Bach in a structured polyphony
I saw displayed in overarching grandeur
In all of nature—all of Florida
From hermit crabs and shallows full of shells
To thunderstorms and purple clouds at dawn.

But I was in a honeymoon of sorts
And a delightful haze, such as a man
And woman know when they are just in love
And nothing else and no one else concerns them 860
Or penetrates their close and warm cocoon.
But other days would come and hours dark
When panic came or existential *Angst*
And I would probe, perhaps as Yeats had done,
What I should be apart from One who made me.
The question was what did I truly want:
Perfection of the life or of the work;
And if it was perfection of the work,
Would I at last forsake a heavenly mansion
And be a poet raging in the dark? 870

To love or not to love—or to obey
Or not obey—that was the only question
I had to face, and anyone must face
Who walks one day or more upon the earth—
Who sojourns in our world one day or less,
Or never grows beyond the age at which
He toddles on under a mother's eye.

Portals of Dawn

And Florida, the lady I adored,
What sort of future would I spend in you?
Hers was a landscape I had slept upon,   880
Whose curvy shores I loved and whose warm breath
Put me at rest when I was turbulent,
Whose coconuts gave milk to slake my thirst—
Who was so constant in her atmosphere
I could rely on her at any hour.

A thousand questions floated in my soul
And could not be resolved at once. I stood
As stout Cortez may once have stood and seen
The broad Pacific with a wild surmise
Silent upon a peak in Darien   890
Or as Lewis and Clarke one day observed
An ocean larger than all human effort
And wondered just how small man truly was
Or should have wondered, if they did not wonder.

As when a storm appears over dark water,
A giant cumulus that towers up
Under the sun like scoops of white ice cream
And sucks all humid air toward itself
And towers more and more over the water
Until it breaks with fury on the shore   900
And pelts the shallows with unbounded power
And afterward departs with sudden speed—
It leaves behind another atmosphere
So anyone who stands upon the shore,
Who saw the rushing grandeur of that storm
And stood and faced the deluge it brought on,
Now has the comfort of a drier air
And stands to breathe a purer atmosphere
Under a sky whose clouds have passed away
While nature seems exalted and restored—   910
So now I stood upon a sunny shore
Under a sky shaken by passing thunder
And on a land washed by a strong downpour.

Book XVI

I also stood upon an unknown coast
And every inhalation was a story,
A novel episode in some new book;
And I was not the author of that book
Although I was a character that moved
From page to page as pen was put to paper
And all I did and thought was written down   920
By one who authored me and kept a record
And told the tale of all my sunny days—
A narrative of all my stormy ways.

I had admired the sanity of Haydn
And longed to have that sanity myself,
And now all of a sudden I imagined
That sanity and clarity could be
My sanity and clarity forever.
Could all the power of a human mind
Be focused on one goal, and could that goal   930
Be truth that always was, and always would be?
Were Haydn's clarity and playful order
A statement of that truth that rose above
The centuries and could be heard today?
And all the hard-won structure I had loved
In symphonies of Beethoven and Brahms,
Where will and mental order would prevail
So passion could be strong and beautiful
And not chaotic—was that also truth?
Beauty is truth, truth beauty, Keats had said,   940
And touched upon a truth beyond his truth,
For what is true is only found in One
Who is the source of beauty and of truth.

Plato had truth, but it was all uncouth
And rumpled by his dark philosophy.
Although he saw himself as one who came
Out of a cave and, on a mountain top,
Saw light and truth that he would carry back
To those who shared the cave with him before,
In fact he had not left the cave at all   950

Portals of Dawn

But fallen asleep in it and had a dream
Of light and truth—attenuated truth
And darkened light—that was philosophy.

I had not met philosophy that day
A storm encountered me with power unknown
And able to transform a random life,
To impart purpose, clarity and truth
To one who lacked them all, who stood alone
As man was never meant to stand alone.

A palm tree at the center of the mind.   960
Was there such a thing, or could there be?
Wallace Stevens wrote such poetry
As would have had a meaning and a purpose
Beyond a final negativity
If only he had loved beyond his love:
He loved the mythic portals of the sky,
The idea of order at Key West,
And yet abandoned it, just as a snake
Sloughed off its skin and left it on the floor.
And yet, beyond that order, and beyond   970
Those mythic portals lay another world,
A world beyond all human myth and order,
As Schiller wrote and Beethoven composed,
Above the starry canopy there was
A Father full of power and of love.

A palm tree at the center of the mind!
Or, coconuts that satisfy one's thirst,
Or cumquats small, and tart, and beautiful,
Whether I saw them in a Christmas basket
Sent by my grandmother from West Palm Beach   980
When I was just a boy in Martins Ferry
Or plucked them from a tree in our backyard
In Lake Park, Florida, as a young man,
Or, any animal that one could name—
A sea cow undulating lazily
In the brown current of Miami's river

Book XVI

Or some young barracuda on the prowl
Among the fishing lines at Lake Worth Pier—
All plants and animals were strong productions
Of one creative mind who saw them all   990
And planned them all, in time and sequence ordered,
Before our universe, before all days
Had come to be, so that each one of them,
Or any other creature one could name,
Could be a symbol or an evidence—
An image at the center of the mind—
That spoke of One who made all images
And made the human race to show again
His nature to each other, and to him.

I had no friend, to wander through the Lakes   1000
And talk about "wild poesy." Such days
And such idealism are long past.
Two hundred years have shown the world at large
What we are made of, and what we devour.
So, as the decades passed, what would I do,
Or what would be my study, and what path
Would lead to works of love, and works of power?

Would I become a scholar, poet, sage,
Philosopher of nature, or a prophet,
Who spoke bold words of love and truth to those,   1010
Many or not, who wanted such tuition?

How many decades would I have—to dream,
To labor and to love, and to discover
The ways of love that One had made for me?

The ways of love are many and are one
For they are grounded in the One who loves
And who is love. The ocean he has formed,
An ocean that enfolds and nourishes,
Shows how he is an ocean, one most vast
Ocean of all—one God, who both sustains   1020
And challenges all those within his scope

Portals of Dawn

To be and grow in him, on those bold terms
Laid down through prophets and poets long gone
Although alive in word and deed among us
Because the Spirit who bore them along
Now makes their words alive for us and does
All they have spoken of and have foretold.

And would I be one of their company?
A lesson I would learn in years to come:
The one who loves him is made one with him;   1030
The one who loves him works as one of those
Who only work as he has done before.

www.ingramcontent.com/pod-product-compliance
Lightning Source LLC
Chambersburg PA
CBHW050617300426
44112CB00012B/1538